D0808886

Face the (GCSE) Spanish Inquisition with CGP!

No doubt about it, you'll be asked some difficult questions in Grade 9-1 GCSE Spanish. Luckily, this CGP Revision Guide is bursting with brilliant notes for every key topic, plus crystal-clear explanations of all the vocab and grammar you'll need.

But that's not all. We've also packed in plenty of exam-style reading, writing, translation, speaking and listening questions — with **free audio files** available from this page:

www.cgpbooks.co.uk/GCSESpanishAudio

How to access your free Online Edition

You can read this entire book on your PC, Mac or tablet, with handy links to all the online audio files. Just go to **cgpbooks.co.uk/extras** and enter this code:

1634 0116 4181 0069

By the way, this code only works for one person. If somebody else has used this book before you, they might have already claimed the Online Edition.

CGP — still the best! ☺

Our sole aim here at CGP is to produce the highest quality books — carefully written, immaculately presented and dangerously close to being funny.

Then we work our socks off to get them out to you
— at the cheapest possible prices.

CONTENTS

CONTENTS

Published by CGP

Editors:
Chloe Anderson
Rose Jones
Matt Topping
Jennifer Underwood

Contributors:
Matthew Parkinson
Jacqui Richards
Clare Swayne

With thanks to Karen Wells for the proofreading.

With thanks to Ana Pungartnik for the copyright research.

Acknowledgements:
Audio produced by Naomi Laredo of Small Print.
Recorded, edited and mastered by Graham Williams of the Speech Recording Studio,
with the assistance of Andy le Vien at RMS Studios.

Voice Artists:
Jessica Gonzalez Campos
David Martel Santana
Ángela Lobato del Castillo

AQA material is reproduced by permission of AQA.
Edexcel material is reproduced by permission of Edexcel.
With thanks to iStock.com for permission to use the images on pages 33, 46 and 60.
Abridged and adapted extract on page 19 from 'Las inquietudes de Shanti Andía' by Pío Baroja.
Abridged and adapted extract on page 36 from 'Pepita Jiménez' by Juan Valera.
Abridged and adapted extract on page 52 from 'Viajes por Europa y América' by Gorgonio Petano y Mazariegos.

ISBN: 978 1 78294 543 7
Printed by Elanders Ltd, Newcastle upon Tyne.
Clipart from Corel®

Based on the classic CGP style created by Richard Parsons.

Numbers

There are some tricky customers among Spanish numbers so make sure you're first in line for top marks.

Uno, dos, tres — *One, two, three*

0	cero		20	veinte
1	uno (un), una		21	veintiuno
2	dos		22	veintidós
3	tres		23	veintitrés
4	cuatro			
5	cinco		30	treinta
6	seis		31	treinta y uno
7	siete		40	cuarenta
8	ocho		50	cincuenta
9	nueve		60	sesenta
10	diez		70	setenta
11	once		80	ochenta
12	doce		90	noventa
13	trece			
14	catorce			
15	quince			
16	dieciséis			
17	diecisiete			
18	dieciocho			
19	diecinueve			

All <u>twenty-something numbers</u> are rolled into one — like 'veintiuno' (*twenty-one*).

<u>After 30</u>, numbers are joined by '<u>y</u>' (*and*), but written <u>separately</u> — like 'treinta y uno' (*thirty-one*).

Grammar — using 'one' with masculine nouns

When you put '<u>one</u>' in front of a <u>masculine</u> word, uno becomes '<u>un</u>'.

veintiún caballos	**21 horses**
treinta y un caballos	**31 horses**

Before a <u>feminine</u> word, the '<u>o</u>' changes to '<u>a</u>':

veintiuna galletas	**21 biscuits**

See p.66 for more on masculine and feminine nouns.

100	cien(to)		700	setecientos/as
101	ciento uno		900	novecientos/as
200	doscientos/as		1000	mil
500	quinientos/as		1 000 000	un millón

'Cien' becomes 'ciento' when used in front of another number (except 'mil').

1826	mil ochocientos veintiséis	2000	dos mil
1984	mil novecientos ochenta y cuatro	2005	dos mil cinco

Primero, segundo, tercero — *First, second, third*

These words always end in '<u>o</u>' for <u>masculine</u> things and '<u>a</u>' for <u>feminine</u> things.

1st	primero/primera (1°/1ª)	6th	sexto/a
2nd	segundo/a (2°/2ª)	7th	séptimo/a
3rd	tercero/a (3°/3ª)	8th	octavo/a
4th	cuarto/a	9th	noveno/a
5th	quinto/a	10th	décimo/a

Grammar — 'primero', 'tercero' + masculine nouns

When '<u>primero</u>' or '<u>tercero</u>' appear in front of a masculine word, they <u>drop</u> the '<u>o</u>'.

el <u>primer</u> baile	*the <u>first</u> dance*
el <u>tercer</u> cantante	*the <u>third</u> singer*

Other useful number phrases

el número = number

una docena	*a dozen*	un par	*a couple / pair*	unos/as	*some / a few / about*

unas diez peras
about ten pears

1ˢᵗ the worst, 2ⁿᵈ the best, 3ʳᵈ the one with the Spanish test...

Lee el texto y contesta a las preguntas en **español**.

'Tener' is a radical-changing verb. See p.84.

Marta tiene veintidós años. Su hermana solo tiene diecisiete años, pero su abuelo tiene ochenta y ocho años. Marta vive muy cerca de aquí — en la segunda calle a la derecha.

e.g. ¿Cuántos años tiene Marta? **Tiene veintidós años.**
1. ¿Cuántos años tiene su hermana? [1]
2. ¿Cuántos años tiene su abuelo? [1]
3. ¿Dónde vive Marta? [1]

2

Times and Dates

Time to learn some really useful phrases which are sure to get you good marks in your Spanish GCSE.

¿Qué hora es? — *What time is it?*

1) You'll need to know how to <u>tell the time</u> for lots of topics. It's bound to come up in your exams...

See p.1 for more numbers.

Es la una.	*It's one o'clock.*
Son las dos.	*It's two o'clock.*
Son las cinco y cuarto.	*It's quarter past five.*
Son las dos menos cuarto.	*It's quarter to two.*
Son las siete y media.	*It's half past seven.*
Son las ocho y cinco.	*It's five past eight.*
Son las tres menos veinte.	*It's twenty to three.*

Grammar — at / it's X o'clock

To say '<u>at X o'clock</u>' , you need '<u>a</u>':
- **a** <u>la una</u>   **at** *one o'clock*
- **a** <u>las ocho</u>   **at** *eight o'clock*

('La' changes to 'las' for anything other than 'one o'clock'.)

To say '<u>it's X o'clock</u>', use '<u>es</u>' or '<u>son</u>':
- <u>es</u> **la una**   *it's one o'clock*
- <u>son</u> **las ocho**   *it's eight o'clock*

('Es changes to 'son' for anything other than 'one o'clock'.)

2) The <u>24-hour clock</u> is also used in many Spanish-speaking countries, so make sure you can tell the time <u>both</u> ways.

The 24-hour clock

(Son) las veintiuna horas treinta minutos.	*(It's) 21.30.*
(Son) las tres horas catorce minutos.	*(It's) 03.14.*
(Son) las diecinueve horas cincuenta y cinco minutos.	*(It's) 19.55.*

Los días de la semana — *The days of the week*

la semana	*the week*
el fin de semana	*(at) the weekend*
lunes	*Monday*
martes	*Tuesday*
miércoles	*Wednesday*
jueves	*Thursday*
viernes	*Friday*
sábado	*Saturday*
domingo	*Sunday*

hoy	*today*
mañana	*tomorrow*
ayer	*yesterday*
anoche	*last night*
pasado mañana	*the day after tomorrow*
anteayer	*the day before yesterday*
el lunes	*on Monday*
los lunes	*on Mondays*
todos los días	*every day*
quince días	*a fortnight*
cada quince días	*every fortnight*
cada tres días	*every three days*

In English, a fortnight is fourteen days, but if you're talking about a fortnight in <u>Spanish</u>, you actually say <u>fifteen days</u>.

Days of the week are always masculine and lower case.

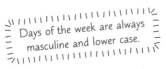

Fui de compras ayer.	*I went shopping yesterday.*
Tengo un examen pasado mañana.	*I have an exam the day after tomorrow.*
Voy al cine los sábados.	*I go to the cinema on Saturdays.*

the day before yesterday — anteayer

tomorrow — mañana

every six days — cada seis días

Times and Dates

Knowing about dates is important — they do tend to crop up every now and then. What's even better is that they can help you sort out your Spanish social life. What's not to love?

More useful time phrases

esta mañana	*this morning*
esta tarde	*this afternoon/evening*
esta noche	*tonight*
mañana por la mañana	*tomorrow morning*
la semana que viene	*next week*
la semana pasada	*last week*

See p.2 for more time phrases.

To say '<u>in</u> the evening', you add '<u>por</u>':

Juego al tenis por la mañana.
I play tennis in the morning.

You don't translate 'at' here — you literally say 'I play tennis the weekend'.

in the afternoon — por la tarde

at the weekend — el fin de semana

Los meses del año — *The months of the year*

Just like the days of the week, the months of the year are all <u>masculine</u> and <u>shouldn't have capital letters</u>.

enero	*January*	julio	*July*	la estación	*season*
febrero	*February*	agosto	*August*	la primavera	*spring*
marzo	*March*	septiembre	*September*	el verano	*summer*
abril	*April*	octubre	*October*	el otoño	*autumn*
mayo	*May*	noviembre	*November*	el invierno	*winter*
junio	*June*	diciembre	*December*		

Voy a la playa todos los años en agosto. *I go to the beach every year in August.*

En invierno, iremos a esquiar. *In winter, we will go skiing.*

¿Qué fecha es? — *What's the date?*

In English, you say '<u>the third</u> of May' or '<u>the twentieth</u> of December'. In Spanish, you can say either '<u>el primero de</u>' or '<u>el uno de</u>' for the <u>first</u> of the month, but for all the other dates, you say '<u>the three</u> of May' or '<u>the twenty</u> of December'...

Bern hoped to impress his date with his alternative choice of transport.

el tres de mayo	*(on) the third of May*
el veinte de diciembre	*(on) the twentieth of December*
Es el uno de / el primero de febrero.	*It's the first of February.*
Es el dos de marzo de dos mil dieciocho.	*It's the second of March 2018.*

You <u>don't</u> translate '<u>on</u>' at the start of dates in Spanish, so <u>both</u> 'the third of May' and 'on the third of May' are written '<u>el tres de mayo</u>'.

Sultanas, raisins, dates — tasty treats for exam revision...

*Listen to what Carlos, Anabel and Julia have to say, and then answer the questions in **English**.*

e.g. How often does Carlos go to the gym? **Every day.**

1. When was Anabel's birthday meal? [1]
2. Where did Anabel go yesterday? [1]
3. When is Julia going to the theatre? [1]

Questions

Knowing about questions will come in handy in your speaking test — you'll have to understand what you're being asked, and in the role-play you'll have to ask your teacher a question or two. Best to be prepared.

Question marks and tone of voice

1) To turn a statement into a question, put an <u>upside down question mark</u> at the <u>beginning</u> and a <u>normal one</u> at the <u>end</u>.

2) When speaking, <u>raise your voice</u> at the <u>end</u> of the sentence to show you're asking a question.

¿Tu sombrero es azul?   *Is your hat blue?*

Literally: *'Your hat is blue?'*

¿Tienes un coche?   *Do you have a car?*

Literally: *'You have a car?'*

"Of course I have a car — why wouldn't a dog have a car?"

¿Qué... — *What...?*

If your question starts with '<u>What...</u>', you normally need to start it with '<u>¿Qué...</u>' in Spanish.

¿Qué comes por la mañana?   *What do you eat in the morning?*

¿Qué quieres hacer el fin de semana?   *What do you want to do at the weekend?*

Go back to p.2-3 for more time phrases.

¿Cuál... — *Which one..? What...?*

1) '<u>¿Cuál...</u>' normally means '<u>Which...</u>' or '<u>Which one...</u>':   ¿Cuál quieres?   *Which (one) do you want?*

2) However, sometimes you might need to use '<u>¿Cuál...</u>' even if you'd use '<u>What...</u>' in English. This is usually when you use the verb '<u>ser</u>' and you're asking for a <u>piece of information</u>, rather than a definition.

¿Cuál es tu problema?   *What is your problem?*

¿Cuál es tu dirección?   *What is your address?*

¿Cuándo? ¿Por qué? ¿Dónde? — *When? Why? Where?*

Question words like this are known as interrogatives. See p.78.

There are <u>loads of other words</u> you can use to <u>begin a question</u> — get them <u>all</u> learnt.

¿Cuándo?	*When?*
¿Por qué?	*Why?*
¿Dónde?	*Where?*
¿Cómo?	*How?*
¿Cuánto/a?	*How much?*
¿Cuántos/as?	*How many?*
¿Quién(es)?	*Who?*
¿Cuál?	*Which?*
¿Es...?	*Is it...?*

Remember that question words need accents.

¿Cuántos/as tienes?	*How many do you have?*
¿Por qué haces eso?	*Why are you doing that?*
¿De dónde eres?	*Where are you from?*
¿Cuál prefieres?	*Which do you prefer?*
¿Es muy difícil?	*Is it very difficult?*

Questions

Now you know how to form questions, you need to get practising them in conversations. If you're asking loads of questions, you might need to be able to say 'please', too — there's more about being polite on p.6.

Tengo una pregunta — *I have a question*

Here are some of the <u>most common ways</u> you can use the <u>question words</u> from p.4.

¿Qué fecha?	*What date?*
¿Qué día?	*What day?*
¿Cuándo es tu cumpleaños?	*When is your birthday?*
¿Cuántos años tienes?	*How old are you?*
¿A qué hora...?	*At what time...?*
¿Qué hora es?	*What time is it?*
¿Por cuánto tiempo?	*For how long?*
¿Cuánto cuesta(n)?	*How much does it / do they cost?*
¿Cuánto vale(n)?	*How much does it / do they cost?*
¿Cuánto es?	*How much is it?*
¿De qué color (es)?	*What colour (is it)?*

Question	Simple Answer	Extended Answer
¿Cuánto cuesta ir al cine?	Cuesta siete euros.	Cuesta siete euros, cincuenta céntimos. Es muy caro.
How much does it cost to go to the cinema?	*It costs seven euros.*	*It costs seven euros, fifty cents. It's very expensive.*

 To learn Spanish or not to learn Spanish, that is the question...

Have a look at the role-play that Carla did with her teacher.

Teacher:	¿A qué hora vas al gimnasio, Carla?
Carla:	Voy al gimnasio a las cuatro de la tarde.
Teacher:	¿Cuánto cuesta ir al gimnasio?
Carla:	Cuesta tres euros cada vez.
Teacher:	¿Vas al gimnasio todos los días?
Carla:	No, solo los fines de semana, pero los jueves, juego al **baloncesto**[1] porque me gusta mucho.
Teacher:	Ah, **vale**[2], muy bien.
Carla:	Y tú, ¿cuándo practicas **deporte**[3]?
Teacher:	Juego al fútbol los sábados.

Grade 8-9

[1] basketball
[2] OK
[3] sport

Tick list:
✓ tenses: present
✓ opinion phrase
✓ correct time phrases e.g. los jueves
✓ correctly formed question

To improve:
+ add a few more complex structures, e.g. cada tres días

Use the instructions on the role-play card to prepare your own role-play. Address your friend as 'tú' and speak for about two minutes. [15 marks]

'!' means you'll need to answer a question you haven't prepared. You can have a good guess at what you might be asked though — here, the question is likely to still be on the topic of tennis as the questions before and after the '!' are about tennis too.

Estás hablando con tu amiga española sobre el deporte.
- *la hora cuando juegas al tenis*
- *la frecuencia con que juegas al tenis*
- *!*
- *el precio de jugar al tenis*
- *? deporte preferido*

When you see '?', you need to ask your teacher a question.

Being Polite

Being polite is an important part of the speaking test — so mind your manners with these tips.

Los saludos — *Greetings*

If you're writing these greetings as exclamations, you need an upside down exclamation mark at the start and a normal one at the end, for example: ¡Hola!

hola	*hello*
buenos días	*good day / good morning*
buenas tardes	*good afternoon / good evening*
buenas noches	*good night*
hasta luego	*see you later*
hasta el lunes	*see you on Monday*
hasta mañana	*see you tomorrow*
hasta pronto	*see you soon*
adiós	*goodbye*

¿Qué tal?	*How are you?*	*(informal)*
¿Cómo estás?	*How are you?*	*(informal)*
¿Cómo está?	*How are you?*	*(formal)*

muy bien	*very well*	great — fenomenal
bien	*well*	so-so — así así
no muy bien	*not very well*	terrible — fatal

Question	Simple Answer	Extended Answer
¿Qué tal?	Bien, gracias.	Estoy fatal. Me duele la cabeza.
How are you?	*Well, thanks.*	*I feel terrible. I've got a headache.*

See p.50 for more illnesses.

Por favor y gracias — *Please and thank you*

You don't want to sound <u>rude</u> in the exam, so learn these <u>charming</u> little words and phrases.

por favor	*please*	Eres muy amable.	*That's very kind of you. (informal)*
gracias	*thank you*	Es muy amable.	*That's very kind of you. (formal)*
muchas gracias	*thank you very much*	De nada.	*You're welcome.*
Lo siento.	*I'm sorry.*	vale	*OK*
Lo siento mucho.	*I'm really sorry.*	¡Claro!	*Of course!*

¡Por favor! / ¡Perdone!	*Excuse me!*	(E.g. for asking someone the way)
¡Con permiso!	*Excuse me!*	(E.g. for wanting to get past someone)

Le presento a ... — *May I introduce ... ?*

If you're <u>male</u>, you say 'encantado', and if you're <u>female</u>, it's 'encantada'.

Use 'Est<u>a</u> es...' for introducing someone <u>female</u>.

Le presento a ...	*May I introduce ... ?*	Encantado/a.	*Pleased to meet you.*
Este es ...	*This is ...*	Mucho gusto.	*Pleased to meet you.*

Here's how a conversation might go if you wanted to <u>introduce someone</u>:

Señora Valls:	Hola Ana, ¿qué tal?	*Hello Ana, how are you?*
Ana:	Muy bien. ¿Cómo está?	*Very well. How are you?*
Señora Valls:	Así así.	*So-so.*
Ana:	Le presento a Arturo.	*May I introduce Arturo?*
Señora Valls:	Encantada.	*Pleased to meet you.*

Ana uses the <u>formal</u> way to ask how Señora Valls is because Señora Valls is <u>older</u> than her. See p.7 for more information.

If you're talking to someone you call '<u>tú</u>', you say '<u>Te</u> presento a...' — it's <u>informal</u>.

Being Polite

And the politeness doesn't end there — here are some more ways to charm the examiner...

Quisiera — *I would like*

1) Don't just say 'I want' — make sure you <u>ask politely</u> for what you would like:

> Quisiera un café. *I would like a coffee.*

2) And this is how to say that you <u>would like to do</u> something:

> Quisiera hablar. *I would like to talk.*
> ¿Puedo sentarme? *May I sit down?*

> go to the toilet — ir al baño
> have a drink — beber algo

'Poder' is a radical-changing verb. See p.84.

Tú y usted — *Informal and Formal 'you'*

Grammar — 'tú' and 'usted'

In Spanish, there are <u>four</u> different ways of saying '<u>you</u>'.

<u>Informal 'you'</u>:

① '<u>Tú</u>' — for <u>one person</u> who's your <u>friend</u>, a <u>family member</u> or of a <u>similar age</u>.

② '<u>Vosotros/as</u>' — for a group of <u>two or more people</u> that you <u>know</u>.
Only use '<u>vosotras</u>' if all the people in the group are <u>female</u>.

<u>Formal 'you'</u>:

③ '<u>Usted</u>' — for <u>one person</u> that is <u>older than you</u> or someone you <u>don't know</u>.

④ '<u>Ustedes</u>' — for a group of <u>two or more people</u> that you <u>don't know</u>.

'Usted' and 'ustedes' <u>don't use the same 'you' part of the verb</u> as 'tú' and 'vosotros'.

- For '<u>usted</u>', use the '<u>he/she/it</u>' part of the verb (see p.83-93).
- For '<u>ustedes</u>', use the '<u>they</u>' part of the verb.

One does not appreciate being called 'tú'.

'Tú', 'vosotros/as', 'usted' and 'ustedes' are all pronouns — see p.76.

So, here are the <u>four</u> different ways of asking where someone is from:

Tú	Vosotros/as	Usted	Ustedes
¿De dónde eres?	¿De dónde sois?	¿De dónde es?	¿De dónde son?

WRITING **Argh, so many 'you's — I'm seeing quadruple...**

Here, Andrés is introducing his two friends Mateo and Lucía to each other.

Andrés:	¡Buenos días, Mateo! ¿Qué tal?
Mateo:	Muy bien, gracias, ¿y tú?
Andrés:	Sí, bien. Esta es mi amiga, Lucía.
Mateo:	¡Hola Lucía! Encantado.
Lucía:	Mucho gusto.
Mateo:	¿Cómo estás, Lucía?
Lucía:	No muy bien, estoy enferma.
Mateo:	Ay, ¡qué lástima![1]
Lucía:	Sí, es una pena[2].
Andrés:	Pues[3], hasta luego, Mateo.
Mateo:	¡Adiós!

Grade 4-5

[1]Oh, what a shame!
[2]a pity
[3]Well

Tick list:
✓ variety of phrases
✓ correct Spanish punctuation
✓ gender agreement

To improve:
+ develop each idea a bit further
+ different tenses (add a past or future)
+ use more varied adjectives, e.g. 'fatal' instead of 'no muy bien'

Now have a go yourself:

*Escribe tu propio diálogo en el que te presentas. Escribe aproximadamente **40** palabras en **español**.*

[8 marks]

Opinions

Having opinions stops you sounding dull — but more importantly, it gets you marks, and lots of them.

¿Qué piensas de...? — *What do you think of...?*

¿Qué piensas?	*What do you think?*
¿Qué piensas de... ?	*What do you think of...?*
¿Qué te parece... ?	*What do you think of...?*
¿Cuál es tu opinión de... ?	*What's your opinion of...?*
¿Le encuentras simpático/a?	*Do you find him/her nice?*
Pienso que / Creo que...	*I think that...*
... me parece...	*I think... is...*
Estoy de acuerdo.	*I agree.*
No estoy de acuerdo.	*I disagree.*
(No) es verdad.	*That's (not) true.*

Urgh. So many questions, so little time.

If you're talking about more than one thing, you need 'me parecen'.

¿Qué piensas de **mi novio**? — What do you think of **my boyfriend**?

Pienso que **es amable**. — I think **he's kind**.

What's your opinion of...? — ¿Cuál es tu opinión de...?

I think — Creo que

See p.14 for more useful describing words.

Las opiniones — *Opinions*

Me gusta... (sing.)	*I like... (singular)*
Me gustan... (pl.)	*I like... (plural)*
Me gusta(n) mucho...	*I really like...*
Me encanta... (sing.)	*I love... (singular)*
Me encantan... (pl.)	*I love... (plural)*
Me interesa(n)...	*I'm interested in...*
Encuentro... fantástico.	*I find... fantastic.*

No me gusta(n)...	*I don't like...*
No me gusta(n)... para nada.	*I don't like... at all.*
... no me interesa(n).	*... doesn't / don't interest me.*
Encuentro... horrible.	*I find... awful.*
Odio...	*I hate...*

Grammar — 'gustar' and 'encantar'

Use '<u>me gusta</u>' and '<u>me encanta</u>' when you want to say you like or love a <u>singular</u> thing.

If you want to say you like or love a <u>plural</u> thing, <u>add</u> an '<u>n</u>' to the end.

Me gusta<u>n</u> las uvas. *I like grapes.*
Me encanta<u>n</u> las películas. *I love films.*

To say you <u>like doing an activity</u>, use an <u>infinitive</u> (see p.83) after the correct form of 'gustar' or 'encantar'.

e.g. **Me gusta <u>bailar</u>.** *I like <u>dancing</u>.*
infinitive

If you <u>don't like</u> something, always try to say what you <u>prefer</u>: Prefiero... *I prefer...*

Grammar — 'preferir' is a radical-changing verb

'Preferir' (*to prefer*) is a <u>radical-changing verb</u> (see p.84 for more). With 'preferir', the second '<u>e</u>' changes to '<u>ie</u>':

prefiero	*I prefer*
prefieres	*you prefer*
prefiere	*he/she/it prefers*
prefieren	*they prefer*

The stem of the 'we' and 'you inf, pl.' forms doesn't change:
'preferimos' = 'we prefer'
'preferís' = 'you (inf, pl.) prefer'

Me gusta el té, pero prefiero el café.
I like tea, but I prefer coffee.

No me gusta cantar — prefiero bailar.
I don't like singing — I prefer dancing.

Opinions

Being able to express your opinion is great — but it's even better if you can justify it. Why? Because it makes you sound great, cool, fabulous, marvellous and definitely not boring...

Porque — *Because*

To start justifying your opinion, you need 'porque' (*because*). Look out, though — 'porque' and '¿por qué?' sound very similar, but they're written differently and mean different things.

¿Por qué te gusta ir al cine?	*Why do you like going to the cinema?*
Me gusta ir al cine porque...	*I like going to the cinema because...*

(No) me gusta porque es... — *I (don't) like it because it's...*

Here's a nice long list of adjectives you can use to justify your opinions and collect some good marks too.

bueno/a	*good*	agradable	*nice, kind*	interesante	*interesting*
estupendo/a	*fantastic*	amable	*friendly*	divertido/a	*amusing, entertaining, fun*
fenomenal	*great*	fabuloso/a	*fabulous*	malo/a	*bad*
genial	*brilliant*	increíble	*incredible*	desagradable	*unpleasant*
guay	*cool*	maravilloso/a	*marvellous*	aburrido/a	*boring*
emocionante	*exciting*	precioso/a	*beautiful*	ridículo/a	*ridiculous*
perfecto/a	*perfect*	bonito/a	*pretty*	decepcionante	*disappointing*
impresionante	*impressive*	entretenido/a	*entertaining*	raro/a	*strange*

These useful little phrases could also help you out:

Me fastidia.	*It annoys me.*
Me aburre.	*It bores me.*
Me hace llorar.	*It makes me cry.*
Me hace reír.	*It makes me laugh.*

> Adjectives change to agree with plural nouns too — see p.68 for more on agreement.

Grammar — nouns and adjectives agree

The ending of the adjective must agree with the noun (p.68).

'el cine' is masculine so 'bueno' must end in 'o'.

El cine es bueno.	*The cinema is good.*
La película es buena.	*The film is good.*

'la película' is feminine so the adjective ends in 'a'.

Adjectives that end with other letters like 'interesante' stay the same for both masculine and feminine nouns.

READING   *I think, therefore I get good marks in Spanish...*

*Luis and Elena are discussing the cinema. Read what they say and answer the questions in **English**.*

Luis: ¿Te gusta ir al cine, Elena?

Elena: Sí, me encanta ir al cine porque es divertido. Me gustan las películas de acción. Y tú, ¿qué piensas del cine?

Luis: No me gusta ir al cine. Prefiero ver las películas en casa. Me encantan las comedias pero odio las películas románticas porque me parecen aburridas. ¿Qué piensas, Elena?

Elena: Sí, estoy de acuerdo. A veces son ridículas.

e.g. Why does Elena like going to the cinema? **Because it's fun.**

1. Does Luis prefer going to the cinema or watching films at home? [1]
2. Does Luis like romantic films? Why / Why not? [2]
3. What does Elena think of romantic films? [1]

Putting it All Together

Now you know all the ingredients that go into giving and justifying opinions, you need to be able to put them all together. This is really useful — you'll have something to say about any of the GCSE topics.

Putting your opinions together

este equipo	*this team*
esta revista	*this magazine*
esta música	*this music*
este grupo	*this band*
esta novela	*this novel*
este actor	*this actor*
esta actriz	*this actress*
esta película	*this film*
este periódico	*this newspaper*
esta canción	*this song*
esta tienda	*this shop*

Grammar — 'este' and 'esta'

'Este' means 'this', but it has to agree with the noun it comes before — see p.70 for more information.

	masculine	feminine
singular	este	esta
plural	estos	estas

¿Qué te parece este grupo? — *What do you think of this band?*

Esta música es fenomenal. — *This music is great.*

¿Qué piensas de estos actores? — *What do you think of these actors?*

Question

¿Cuál es tu opinión de esta revista?
What's your opinion of this magazine?

Simple Answer

Me gusta mucho esta revista.
I really like this magazine.

Extended Answer

Me gusta mucho esta revista porque es muy interesante.
I really like this magazine because it's very interesting.

Remember to always back up your opinions

¿Qué piensas de este grupo? — *What do you think of this band?*

Me encanta este grupo porque me gusta la música rock. — *I love this band because I like rock music.*

¿Estás de acuerdo? — *Do you agree?*

No, odio la música rock — prefiero la música pop. — *No, I hate rock music — I prefer pop music.*

this team — este equipo

their music is brilliant — su música es genial

And you, what do you think? — Y tú, ¿qué piensas?

I find rock music awful — encuentro la música rock horrible

TRACK LISTENING 02 *Don't keep your opinions to yourself — share 'em.*

Listen to Antonio and Carolina talking about what they like doing. Decide whether the statements are true (T) or false (F), and write T or F next to them. The first one has been done for you.

e.g. Carolina likes going to the swimming pool. T

1. Antonio likes listening to music. [1]
2. Antonio thinks the shops in his city are fantastic. [1]
3. Antonio doesn't like reading newspapers. [1]
4. Carolina likes both reading and listening to music. [1]
5. Carolina thinks pop bands are awful. [1]

About Yourself

Being able to talk about yourself is really important — you just can't get by without it.

Preséntate — *Introduce yourself*

el nombre	*name*	el cumpleaños	*birthday*	
el apellido	*surname*	cumplir años	*to have a birthday*	
llamarse	*to be called*	la edad	*age*	
nacer	*to be born*	tener ... años	*to be ... years old*	
el nacimiento	*birth*	la nacionalidad	*nationality*	

Grammar — saying your age

In Spanish, you 'have' an age, so you need the verb 'tener' to say how old you are. 'Tener' is a radical-changing verb — see p.84.

Tengo 16 años. *I'm 16 years old.*

¡Hola! Me llamo Juan.

Hello! I'm called Juan.

My name is Juan. — Mi nombre es Juan.
I'm Juan. — Soy Juan.

Tengo quince años.

I'm 15 years old.

Check p.3 for a reminder of how to say dates.

Mi cumpleaños es el dos de abril.

My birthday is the 2nd of April.

Nací en (el año) dos mil dos.

I was born in (the year) 2002.

English — inglés / inglesa
Scottish — escocés / escocesa
Welsh — galés / galesa
Irish — irlandés / irlandesa

Soy británico/a. Nací en Surrey.

I'm British. I was born in Surrey.

Vivo en Málaga, en el sur de España.

I live in Málaga, in the south of Spain.

See p.51 for more countries and nationalities.

the north — el norte
the east — el este
the west — el oeste

¿Cómo se escribe? — *How do you spell it?*

You might have to spell something out, so learn how to pronounce the letters of the Spanish alphabet.

A — ah	F — effay	K — ka	O — oh	U — ooh
B — bay	G — hay	L — elay	P — pay	V — oohbay
C — thay	H — atchay	M — emay	Q — coo	W — oohbay doblay
D — day	I — ee	N — enay	R — eray	X — ekis
E — ay	J — hota	Ñ — enyay	S — essay	Y — yay
			T — tay	Z — thayta

'h' like 'lo**ch**'   Double 'l' makes a '**y**' sound.

Some Spanish words like 'adiós' have an accent to show which vowel you need to emphasise. Remember to write the accent too.

SPEAKING *It's all about me, me, me...*

Read the question and then look at how Estefanía has answered it.
Háblame un poco de ti.

¡Hola! Me llamo Estefanía y soy de Venezuela.
Vivo en el norte del país, cerca de la ciudad de Caracas.
Mi cumpleaños es el veinticuatro de diciembre. Es un día muy
especial, porque celebramos mi cumpleaños y la Navidad al
mismo tiempo. Nací en el año dos mil.

Grade 6-7

Tick list:
✓ tenses: present, preterite
✓ correctly formed dates and years
✓ justifying opinions with 'porque'

To improve:
+ include an opinion about where you live

Now try to answer the same question. Mention your name, where you're from and your birthday.
Try to speak for about two minutes. [10 marks]

My Family

Learning to talk about who's in your family is an absolute must — examiners seem to love asking about it.

Mi familia — *My family*

los parientes	*relatives*	los hijos	*children*	el abuelo	*grandfather*
el padre	*father*	el marido	*husband*	la abuela	*grandmother*
la madre	*mother*	la mujer	*wife*	los nietos	*grandchildren*
los padres	*parents*	el hermanastro	*stepbrother*	el/la tío/a	*uncle/aunt*
el padrastro	*stepfather*	la hermanastra	*stepsister*	el/la primo/a	*cousin*
la madrastra	*stepmother*	el/la gemelo/a	*twin*	el/la sobrino/a	*nephew/niece*

Háblame de tu familia — *Tell me about your family*

Grammar — saying 'my' and 'your'

Possessive adjectives like 'my' and 'your' have to agree with the noun they come before (see p.70). Remember — 'su(s)' could also mean 'your' if you're being formal — see p.70.

mi **padre**	*my father*	tu **hermana**	*your sister*	su **tía**	*his / her / their aunt*
mis **padres**	*my parents*	tus **hermanas**	*your sisters*	sus **tías**	*his / her / their aunts*

"And don't go asking your father either... The answer is no!"

Tengo una hermana mayor. Ella se llama Ramona.	*I have an older sister. She is called Ramona.*
Hay cinco personas en mi familia — mi madre, mi padrastro, mis dos hermanastros menores y yo. Mis hermanastros se llaman David y Gabriel.	*There are five people in my family — my mother, my stepfather, my two younger stepbrothers and me. My stepbrothers are called David and Gabriel.*
Soy hijo único, pero me gustaría tener hermanos.	*I'm an only child (male), but I would like to have brothers and sisters.*

an older brother — un hermano mayor
a younger sister — una hermana menor
a younger brother — un hermano menor

only child (female) — hija única

I like not having brothers and sisters — me gusta no tener hermanos

Question	**Simple Answer**	**Extended Answer**
¿Cómo es tu familia? *What's your family like?*	Soy hijo único, pero tengo muchos primos. *I'm an only child, but I have a lot of cousins.*	Soy hijo único, pero mi padre tiene cinco hermanos, así que en realidad, tengo muchos parientes. Mis primos viven cerca de aquí y siempre lo pasamos bien juntos. *I'm an only child, but my father has five brothers and sisters, so really, I have lots of relatives. My cousins live near here and we always have a good time together.*

Examiners are fans of families — don't forget to revise them...

Translate this text into **English**. *[9 marks]*

Vivo con mi madre, mi hermana mayor y mis dos hermanas menores. Son gemelas. Para mí, es importante tener hermanos porque siempre tienes alguien con quien puedes salir. Los fines de semana, visito a mi padre, su mujer y mi hermanastro. Nació el año pasado y solo tiene seis meses. Me gustaría pasar más tiempo allí con ellos porque es muy divertido.

Describing People

You'll probably have to describe what people look like at some point in your exam — so carry on reading.

¿Cómo eres? — *What are you like?*

You'll need the verbs 'tener' (*to have*) and 'ser' (*to be*) for this page. They're irregular, so check p.84 and 85 to see how they work.

alto/a	*tall*	joven	*young*	negro	*black*
bajo/a	*short*	viejo/a	*old*	castaño	*chestnut-brown*
de altura mediana	*medium height*	marrón	*brown*	largo	*long*
gordo/a	*fat*	azul	*blue*	corto	*short (hair)*
delgado/a	*slim*	verde	*green*	liso	*straight*
guapo/a	*good-looking*	rubio/a	*blonde*	rizado	*curly*

'Marrón' loses its accent in the plural form.

El aspecto físico — *Physical appearance*

Question

¿Cómo eres?
What are you like?

Grammar — adjectives agree

Adjectives must agree with the noun they describe.

'Los ojos' are masculine plural, so adjectives like 'blue' must be in the masculine plural form — azules.

'El pelo' is masculine singular, so adjectives like 'curly' need to be in the masculine singular form — rizado — even if you're a girl.

Simple Answer

Soy alta. Tengo los ojos azules y tengo el pelo castaño.
I'm tall. I have blue eyes and I have brown hair.

Extended Answer

Soy bastante alta. No soy ni gorda ni delgada. Tengo los ojos azules y llevo gafas. Tengo el pelo corto y rizado, y no tengo pecas.
I'm quite tall. I'm neither fat nor slim. I have blue eyes and I wear glasses. I have short, curly hair, and I don't have freckles.

Soy muy bajo como mis padres. Sin embargo, mi hermano es mucho más alto que yo. Tengo el pelo rubio y tengo los ojos verdes.
I'm very short like my parents. However, my brother is much taller than me. I have blonde hair and I have green eyes.

Soy bajo y delgado. Tengo el pelo negro y tengo los ojos marrones. Tengo una barba también.

I'm short and slim. I have black hair and I have brown eyes. I also have a beard.

dark — moreno

a moustache — un bigote

Es altísima. Lleva gafas y tiene los ojos azules. Tiene el pelo castaño y liso.

She's really tall. She wears glasses and she has blue eyes. She has straight, chestnut-brown hair.

make-up — maquillaje

curly — rizado

Es de altura mediana y bastante gordo. Es pelirrojo y tiene los ojos verdes.

He's medium height and quite fat. He's red-haired and he has green eyes.

He's bald — Es calvo

TRACK LISTENING 03

Describe people well and you'll look like a first-rate student...

María y Jaime describen estas cuatro personas. Empareja cada foto con la descripción de la persona.

 a)

 b)

 c)

 d)

Descripción 1 = foto .....
Descripción 2 = foto .....
Descripción 3 = foto .....
Descripción 4 = foto .....

[4 marks]

Section 2 — Me, My Family and Friends

Personalities

Just saying everyone's nice gets pretty dull pretty quickly, so use these adjectives to spice up your writing.

Mi personalidad — *My personality*

animado/a	*lively*	hablador/a	*chatty / talkative*	egoísta	*selfish*
alegre	*happy*	atrevido/a	*daring / cheeky*	maleducado/a	*rude*
cariñoso/a	*affectionate*	serio/a	*serious*	perezoso/a	*lazy*
comprensivo/a	*understanding*	sensible	*sensitive*	travieso/a	*naughty*
cortés	*polite*	callado/a	*quiet*	torpe	*clumsy*
gracioso/a	*funny*	valiente	*brave*	celoso/a	*jealous*

¿Cómo es ...? — *What's ... like?*

Mi mejor amigo es gracioso y siempre alegre. Es sensible también. Sin embargo, a veces es un poco maleducado porque dice cosas sin pensar.

My best friend is funny and always happy. He's sensitive too. However, sometimes he's a bit rude because he says things without thinking.

My best friend (girl) — Mi mejor amiga

he always arrives late when we go to the cinema — siempre llega tarde cuando vamos al cine

Mis padres son comprensivos y amables. Mi madre es habladora pero mi padre es más callado.

My parents are understanding and kind. My mother is chatty but my father is quieter.

serious — serios

kind — simpáticas

Mis profesoras son amables pero estrictas al mismo tiempo.

My teachers are friendly but strict at the same time.

Grammar — making adjectives agree

Adjectives have to agree with the nouns they describe.
See the normal rules for adjective agreement on p.68.
But some adjectives work differently, like those ending in '-or' or '-ísta/-ista'.

1) 'Hablador' — add an 'a' on the end for the feminine form and then 'es' and 'as' for the masculine and feminine plurals.

2) 'Egoísta' stays the same in the singular and becomes 'egoístas' for both the masculine and feminine plurals.

Mis amigos son habladores.
My friends are chatty.

Mi primo es un poco egoísta.
My cousin is a bit selfish.

WRITING — Me? I'm intelligent, good-looking, wonderful, humble...

Benjamín has written you an email telling you about himself, and his family and friends.

A **decir verdad**[1], mis padres son muy cariñosos, **aunque**[2] pueden ser estrictos, sobre todo **si no arreglo mi dormitorio**[3]. En mi opinión, mis amigos son alegres y atrevidos, pero **según**[4] mis padres, son maleducados. **Cuando era pequeño**[5], era bastante travieso, pero ahora creo que soy comprensivo y gracioso. Me gustaría ser más valiente. Y tú, ¿cómo eres?

Grade 6-7

[1]To tell the truth
[2]although
[3]if I don't tidy my bedroom
[4]according to
[5]When I was little

Tick list:
✓ tenses: present, imperfect, conditional
✓ varied adjectives that agree correctly
✓ conjunctions e.g. aunque, pero

To improve:
+ complex structures, e.g. subjunctive
+ use a wider range of tenses, e.g. future

*Contesta a Benjamín y describe a tu familia. Escribe aproximadamente **90** palabras en **español**.* [16 marks]

Pets

Now's the perfect chance to make sure you don't make a dog's dinner out of your Spanish exams...

¿Tienes mascotas en casa? — *Do you have pets at home?*

el animal doméstico /	
la mascota	*pet*
el hámster	*hamster*
el conejo	*rabbit*
el cobayo /	
el conejillo de Indias	*guinea pig*
el pez tropical	*tropical fish*
el pez de colores	*goldfish*
la tortuga	*tortoise*

Sí, tengo un perro. Lo mejor de las mascotas es que no te juzgan.

No tenemos ningún animal doméstico porque no podríamos pasar mucho tiempo con él, lo que sería cruel.

Yes, I have a dog. The best thing about pets is that they don't judge you.

We don't have a pet because we wouldn't be able to spend much time with it, which would be cruel.

¿Cómo es tu mascota? — *What's your pet like?*

Me gustan los peces tropicales porque es relajante verlos nadar.

I like tropical fish because it's relaxing to watch them swim.

← *but they don't live very long — pero no viven mucho tiempo*

Tengo un gato. Es muy encantador, sobre todo cuando tiene hambre.

I have a cat. He's very charming, especially when he's hungry.

← *adventurous and intelligent — atrevido e inteligente*

Odio el olor de los perros.

I hate the smell of dogs.

snakes because they scare me — las serpientes porque me dan miedo

Grammar — comparing things

Use 'más ... que' to say that something's 'more ... than' something else.
Use 'menos ... que' to say that something's 'less ... than' something else.

Pienso que los gatos son <u>más independientes que</u> los perros.
I think that cats are <u>more independent than</u> dogs.

Los hámsters parecen <u>menos atrevidos que</u> los cobayos.
Hamsters seem <u>less adventurous than</u> guinea pigs.

Jake knew their relationship was coming to an end — after all, they'd been going round in circles for years...

Question	**Simple Answer**	**Extended Answer**
¿Te gustaría tener algún animal doméstico en el futuro?	Sí, quiero un gato porque son muy inteligentes.	Cuando sea mayor, me gustaría tener un perro. Creo que los perros son más fieles que los gatos.
Would you like to have any pets in the future?	*Yes, I want a cat because they're very intelligent.*	*When I'm older, I'd like to have a dog. I think dogs are more loyal than cats.*

My pet mouse just sits on my desk and clicks at things...

Translate this text into **English**. *[9 marks]*

Tengo un pájaro como mascota. Siempre ha sido muy hablador — repite lo que dices y es muy divertido cuando dice cosas ofensivas. Lo bueno de los pájaros es que comen frutas, verduras y cereales, así que su comida no cuesta mucho. Sin embargo, el fin de semana que viene, tengo que llevarlo al veterinario y creo que costará mucho dinero.

Section 2 — Me, My Family and Friends

Style and Fashion

Time to kit yourself out with some handy phrases you can use to talk about style and fashion.

La moda — *Fashion*

estar de moda	*to be in fashion*
pasado de moda	*out of fashion*
de estilo retro	*vintage style*
la marca	*brand*
de rayas / rayado	*striped*
de lunares	*spotty*
el tatuaje	*tattoo*
el maquillaje	*make-up*
el/la famoso/a	*celebrity*

Finally Elena had found a way of taking her tree-hugging passion to the next level...

Grammar — it suits me

To say that something <u>suits you</u>, use the verb '<u>quedar</u>', followed by '<u>bien</u>'. To say something <u>doesn't suit you</u>, use '<u>quedar</u>' followed by '<u>mal</u>'. '<u>Quedar</u>' works like '<u>gustar</u>', so you need to add an <u>indirect object pronoun</u> too (see p.77).

Esta blusa <u>me queda bien</u>.   *This blouse <u>suits me</u>.*

Estas botas <u>me quedan mal</u>.   *These boots <u>don't suit me</u>.*

Question

¿Cómo te vistes normalmente?
How do you dress normally?

Simple Answer

Normalmente llevo vaqueros y una camiseta. Prefiero la ropa cómoda.
I normally wear jeans and a t-shirt. I prefer comfortable clothes.

Extended Answer

Normalmente me visto de negro. No me importa ir vestido/a a la moda. Me gustan los tatuajes, así que cuando tenga dieciocho años, me tatuaré.
I normally dress in black. I'm not bothered about dressing fashionably. I like tattoos, so when I'm 18, I'll get a tattoo.

Gasto mucho dinero en las joyas — tengo cientos de pendientes, anillos y collares.

I spend a lot of money on jewellery — I've got hundreds of earrings, rings and necklaces.

trainers, because it's important to wear certain brands — las zapatillas de deporte, porque es importante llevar ciertas marcas

No me importa estar en la onda. Prefiero vestirme de estilo retro. El fin de semana pasado compré un vestido de lunares de los años cincuenta. Creo que me queda bien.

Being fashionable doesn't matter to me. I prefer to dress in a vintage style. Last weekend I bought a spotty dress from the fifties. I think it suits me.

a velvet jacket — una chaqueta de terciopelo
a straw hat — un sombrero de paja

A mí me gusta vestirme como los famosos que admiro. Su manera de vestirse me inspira mucho.

I like to dress like the celebrities I admire. The way they dress inspires me a lot.

I don't care what celebrities wear. I think many of them are conceited. — Me da igual cómo se visten los famosos. Creo que muchos de ellos son engreídos.

 ## I'm so retro I come to work in a toga sometimes...

Read Akemi's blog post about fashion and then use the text to complete the sentences.

Después de mucha investigación, creo que en los años ochenta había un estilo muy parecido a lo que se puede ver actualmente. Sin embargo, lo que ha cambiado desde entonces es la abundancia de tiendas. En el pasado existía una verdadera falta de tiendas.

Pienso que el Internet ha transformado todo. Puedes elegir algo y si te queda mal, no pasa nada, y lo puedes devolver fácilmente. Otro cambio es que hay más oportunidades para los **diseñadores**[1] jóvenes porque pueden usar la red como una tienda sin pagar los gastos altos de una tienda verdadera.

[1]designers

1. In the 1980s...
   A. fashion was similar to now.
   B. fashion was different to now.
   C. fashion was more important. [1]

2. The internet has...
   A. made things harder for people in the fashion industry.
   B. made people spend more.
   C. made things easier for people in the fashion industry. [1]

Relationships

Saying whether you get on with people is a good way of showing you can use some more complex verbs.

Las relaciones — *Relationships*

aguantar	*to put up with*	conocer	*to know (a person)*
confiar	*to trust*	hacer amigos	*to make friends*
fastidiar	*to annoy*	la amistad	*friendship*
pelearse	*to fight*	llevarse bien / mal (con)	*to get on well / badly (with)*
enamorarse	*to fall in love*	relacionarse (con)	*to be in contact (with)*
la discusión	*argument*	el modelo de conducta	*role model*

You need the personal 'a' with 'conocer' and 'aguantar'. Have a look at p.81 for more information.

Grammar — 'confiar'

'Confiar' is an irregular verb. In the present tense, the 'i' has an accent on it in every form except the 'we' and 'you inf., plural' forms.

Confío en él.   *I trust him.*

To say you trust someone, you need to use 'en'.

Grammar — reflexive verbs

'Llevarse', 'relacionarse' and 'pelearse' are reflexive verbs. Take off the 'se' and add the correct ending to the stem like a normal verb (see p.83). Then choose the right pronoun (see p.92) and put it in front of the verb.

Me llevo bien con mi hermana.   *I get on well with my sister.*
¿Te relacionas con ella?   *Are you in contact with her?*
Nos peleamos mucho.   *We fight a lot.*

Mis padres tienen una buena relación pero yo no me llevo bien con ellos debido a la barrera generacional entre nosotros.

My parents get on very well, but I don't get on well with them due to the generation gap between us.

I get on badly with them — me llevo mal con ellos

Me llevo mejor con mi hermano porque me ayuda mucho. Tiene un buen sentido del humor.

I get on better with my brother because he helps me a lot. He has a good sense of humour.

He's a good role model. — Es un buen modelo de conducta.

Mi hermana y yo nos peleamos mucho porque me fastidia.

My sister and I fight a lot because she annoys me.

I can't stand my sister — No aguanto a mi hermana

Conozco muy bien a mi novio y confío en él. Nos enamoramos hace dos años y no discutimos nunca.

I know my boyfriend really well and I trust him. We fell in love two years ago and we never argue.

'Conozco' (*I know*) is the only irregular bit of the verb 'conocer'.

SPEAKING *Luckily, I get on really well with Spanish revision...*

Read the questions and Víctor's responses below.

¿Qué hay en la foto? ¿Te llevas bien con tu familia?

En esta foto, hay dos chicos — **quizás**[1] son hermanos, pero se llevan bien porque no se pelean.

 Grade 6-7

Generalmente, sí. Confío en mi madre, así que hablo con ella cuando tengo **dificultades**[2] con **amistades**[3], por ejemplo. Mi padre es muy simpático y me conoce bien. No aguanto a mi hermana porque es muy maleducada y estúpida a veces.

[1]perhaps
[2]difficulties
[3]friendships

Tick list:
✓ range of adjectives which agree
✓ complex verbs e.g. 'confiar en'
✓ extended reasons given

To improve:
+ a few more complex structures
+ try to use another tense

*Now answer these questions **in Spanish**. Try to speak for about two minutes. ¿Te llevas bien con tus padres? ¿Tienes una buena relación con tus hermanos / tus primos? ¿Confías en tus amigos? [12 marks]*

Socialising with Friends and Family

Cast your mind back into the past and remember those glorious pre-revision days when you had a social life...

¿Eres un(a) buen(a) amigo/a? — *Are you a good friend?*

pasarlo bien	*to have a good time*	el/la conocido/a	*acquaintance*	optimista	*optimistic*
de buen humor	*in a good mood*	el/la compañero/a	*friend, colleague*	mimado	*spoilt*

Question

Para ti, ¿cómo es un(a) buen(a) amigo/a?
In your opinion, what's a good friend like?

Simple Answer

Un buen amigo es generoso y te escucha.
A good friend is generous and listens to you.

Extended Answer

Para mi la cualidad más importante en un amigo es que te hace reír. Soy una persona optimista y necesito que mis amigos sean alegres también.
For me, the most important quality in a friend is that they make you laugh. I'm an optimistic person and I need my friends to be cheerful too.

En mi tiempo libre... — *In my free time...*

Cuando no estoy en el colegio, me gusta socializar con mis amigos. Para mí es importante mantener las amistades.

When I'm not in school, I like to socialise with my friends. For me it's important to keep up my friendships.

Los domingos comemos en casa de mis abuelos. A veces preferiría estar con mis amigos, pero no quiero causar problemas.

On Sundays we have lunch at my grandparents' house. Sometimes I'd prefer to be with my friends, but I don't want to cause problems.

Cuando era pequeño, me gustaba jugar con mis primos menores, pero ahora me fastidian mucho. Creo que están un poco mimados.

When I was little, I liked playing with my younger cousins, but now they annoy me a lot. I think they're a bit spoilt.

Grammar — When I was little...

Use the <u>imperfect tense</u> (p.87) to say what you <u>used to do</u> when you were little.

Cuando era pequeño/a, <u>me gustaba</u> jugar con mi hermano.

When I was little, <u>I liked</u> playing with my brother.

Remember you'll need to use 'pequeñ<u>o</u>' if you're male and 'pequeñ<u>a</u>' if you're female.

Ahh yes, the time I "lost" my brother in the pumpkin patch...

WRITING

Friendship tip #23: <u>Never</u> forget the doughnuts.

Guillermo ha escrito un blog sobre lo que hace con sus amigos.

Cuando tengo tiempo libre, salgo con mis amigos **en pandilla**[1]. Normalmente somos un grupo de doce o trece jóvenes. Algunos son **mis amigos verdaderos**[2] porque son alegres y comprensivos. Sin embargo, otros son simplemente conocidos. Nos gusta ir al parque o al club de jóvenes en nuestro barrio. Cuando era pequeño, mis padres no me dejaban salir mucho por la tarde, pero ahora me dan más **libertad**[3].

Grade 6-7

[1]in a gang
[2]my true friends
[3]freedom

Tick list:
✓ tenses: present and imperfect.
✓ varied sentence structures

To improve:
+ add a future tense
+ give a few more opinions

Escribe tu propio blog sobre tu familia y tus amigos. Menciona:

- *si te gusta pasar tiempo con tu familia*
- *lo que te gustaba hacer con tu familia en el pasado*
- *si eres un(a) buen(a) amigo/a y por qué (no)*
- *lo que vas a hacer el fin de semana que viene.*

*Escribe aproximadamente **90** palabras en **español**.* *[16 marks]*

Partnership

Thinking about getting married is just round the corner — it might come up in your Spanish GCSE, in fact.

En el futuro... — *In the future...*

estar enamorado/a de	*to be in love with*
comprometerse	*to get engaged*
el casamiento / la boda	*wedding*
el matrimonio	*marriage, married couple*
el anillo	*ring*
el esposo / el marido	*husband*
la esposa / la mujer	*wife*
ser soltero/a	*to be single*
el estado civil	*marital status*

en mi opinión	*in my opinion*
a mi modo de ver	*the way I see it*
desde mi punto de vista	*from my point of view*
debo admitir que...	*I must admit that...*

Grammar — When I'm X years old...

To say '<u>when I'm 30</u>' (or to say 'when' with a future event), use the <u>subjunctive</u>. See p.96.

Cuando <u>tenga</u> 60 años... *When <u>I'm</u> 60 years old...*

Question	Simple Answer	Extended Answer
¿Te gustaría casarte y tener hijos en el futuro? *Would you like to get married and have children in the future?*	No sé si quiero casarme, pero me gustaría tener hijos. *I don't know if I want to get married, but I'd like to have children.*	No sé si me casaré porque no me importa mucho. Me gustaría tener hijos cuando tenga treinta años, pero no sé cuántos hijos quiero tener. *I don't know if I'll get married because it's not very important to me. I'd like to have children when I'm 30, but I don't know how many I want to have.*

¿El matrimonio es importante? — *Is marriage important?*

Quiero casarme porque estoy enamorado de mi novia, y desde mi punto de vista, las bodas son muy románticas.

I want to get married because I'm in love with my girlfriend, and from my point of view, weddings are very romantic.

I want to celebrate with my family — quiero celebrar con mi familia

Debo admitir que preferiría no casarme, porque una boda es bastante cara.

I must admit that I would prefer not to get married, because a wedding is quite expensive.

I never want to get married — no quiero casarme nunca

I'd prefer to buy myself a house — preferiría comprarme una casa

A mi modo de ver, no es necesario casarse antes de tener hijos, pero me gustaría hacerlo de todos modos.

The way I see it, it's not necessary to get married before having children, but I'd like to do it anyway.

marriage is important because it gives you stability — el matrimonio es importante porque te da estabilidad

READING — *Turkey and stuffing — a marriage made in heaven...*

Read this extract from 'Las inquietudes de Shanti Andía' by Pío Baroja, and answer the questions.

Dolorcitas parecía **decidirse por**[1] mí; pero, al mismo tiempo, todo el mundo decía que iba a casarse con el hijo del **marqués**[2] de Vernay, un señor de Jerez, no muy rico, pero de familia aristocrática. Le escribí a Dolorcitas y le hablé varias veces **por la reja**[3].

[1]decide on
[2]marquis
[3]through the window bars

1. *Decide whether these statements are true or false.*
   a) Nobody thought Dolorcitas was going to get married.
   b) The Marquis of Vernay's son didn't have much money.
   c) The narrator never spoke to Dolorcitas.

2. *Use the information in the text to fill in the gap.*
   The Marquis of Vernay's son came from ....

   [4 marks]

Technology

Technology changes really quickly — make sure you keep up to speed by looking carefully at these pages.

La tecnología en la vida diaria — *Technology in everyday life*

el ordenador	*computer*
el portátil	*laptop*
el móvil	*mobile phone*
el mensaje (de texto)	*(text) message*
mandar / enviar	*to send*
recibir	*to receive*
usar / utilizar	*to use*

Grammar — I could / couldn't ...

To imagine what you 'could do' or 'couldn't do', use the conditional tense of 'poder' (see p.91) followed by the infinitive.

Sin mi móvil, no podría hablar con mis amigos.
Without my mobile phone, I couldn't talk to my friends.

No podría hacer mis deberes sin un portátil.
I couldn't do my homework without a laptop.

Question

¿Para qué usas tu móvil?
What do you use your mobile phone for?

Simple Answer

Uso mi móvil para mandar mensajes.
I use my mobile phone to send messages.

Extended Answer

Tener un móvil es muy importante para mí. Sin mi móvil, no podría ni mandar ni recibir mensajes.
Having a mobile phone is very important for me. Without my mobile phone, I couldn't send or receive messages.

Navegando por la red — *Surfing the Internet*

la red	*the Internet*	el usuario	*user*	el videojuego	*video game*
el internauta	*Internet user*	el correo electrónico	*email*	el buscador	*search engine*
el navegador	*browser*	descargar	*to download*	la herramienta	*tool*

Me encanta descargar canciones.

I love downloading songs.

Me gustan los videojuegos porque puedes comunicarte con otros usuarios.

I like video games because you can communicate with other users.

La red es una herramienta muy útil porque puedes usar un buscador para encontrar información.

The Internet is a very useful tool because you can use a search engine to find information.

crucial for modern life — crucial para la vida moderna

Mis padres usan la red para sus cuentas bancarias porque es más fácil que ir al banco.

My parents use the web for their bank accounts because it's easier than going to the bank.

Many Internet users — Muchos internautas

Gracias a la red, es más cómodo hacer las compras. Hace unos días, compré unos regalos por Internet y ya están aquí.

Thanks to the Internet, it's more convenient to do your shopping. A few days ago, I bought some presents online and they're already here.

However, it's difficult to know if you like the product or not because you buy it without seeing it in reality. — Sin embargo, es difícil saber si te gusta el producto o no porque lo compras sin verlo en realidad.

Technology

Singing technology's praises isn't enough — you also need to be able to talk about its disadvantages.

Lo malo de la tecnología... — *The bad thing about technology...*

Grammar — the ... thing is that...

In Spanish, you can say '<u>the good thing</u>' or '<u>the bad thing</u>' by using '<u>lo</u>' followed by '<u>bueno</u>' or '<u>malo</u>'.

<u>**Lo bueno / malo** es que...</u> *The good / bad thing is that...*

You can do this with <u>any adjective</u>:

<u>**Lo mejor / peor** es que...</u> *The best / worst thing is that...*

<u>**Lo peligroso** es que...</u> *The dangerous thing is that...*

To say '<u>the most... thing</u>', just add '<u>más</u>' before the adjective:

<u>**Lo más útil** es que...</u> *The most useful thing is that...*

acceder	*to access*
el archivo	*file*
borrar	*to erase / delete*
el buzón	*inbox, mailbox*
adjuntar	*to attach*
el correo basura	*spam*
la contraseña	*password*
el servidor de seguridad	*firewall*
el disco duro	*hard disk/drive*

Lo peor de los móviles es que la gente puede grabar videos sin informarte.

The worst thing about mobiles is that people can record videos without telling you.

> share your photos with other people you don't know — compartir tus fotos con otra gente a la que no conoces

Es importante tener una contraseña para proteger tu identidad. Si alguien averigua tu contraseña, puede acceder a tus archivos. Por eso no se debe utilizar nunca la red sin un buen servidor de seguridad.

It's important to have a password to protect your identity. If someone finds out your password, they can access your files. Therefore you should never use the Internet without a good firewall.

> ruin your hard disk — estropear tu disco duro

Me molesta cuando recibo correo basura porque tengo que borrar todos los mensajes de mi buzón para encontrar los que me importan.

It annoys me when I receive spam because I have to delete all the messages from my inbox to find the ones that matter to me.

> sometimes it harms your computer and causes you problems — a veces daña tu ordenador y te causa problemas

Question

Dame una desventaja de la tecnología.
Give me one disadvantage of technology.

Simple Answer

Una desventaja es que no puedes escapar de la tecnología.
One disadvantage is that you can't escape from technology.

Extended Answer

Una desventaja es que siempre tienes que estar conectado. Lo más irritante es cuando mis amigos se enfadan cuando no contesto a sus mensajes enseguida.
One disadvantage is that you always have to be connected. The most irritating thing is when my friends get angry when I don't reply to their messages straightaway.

WRITING — *Technically speaking, this page is really, really useful...*

*Translate this text into **Spanish**. [12 marks]*

I couldn't live without technology because it is very useful. I like playing video games online with my brother. We speak to Internet users in other countries. Yesterday, I played with a boy in Chile, but in order to protect my identity, I never use my name. The best thing about mobile phones is that you don't have to be at home to use the Internet. In the future, I think children will have mobile phones when they are 2 or 3 years old.

Social Media

Social media — love it or hate it, it's everywhere. And what's more, it might just come up in your exams.

Las redes sociales — *Social networks*

la red social	*social network*
el sitio web	*website*
la sala de chat	*chat room*
el blog	*blog*
la cuenta	*account*
desactivar	*to deactivate / block*
charlar	*to chat*
colgar	*to post (online)*

Grammar — colgar (*to post*)

'Colgar' (*to post*) is a radical-changing verb (see p.84) that changes in the present tense:

Mis amigos cuelgan fotos en mi muro.
My friends post photos on my wall.

> **Question**
>
> ¿Usas las redes sociales?
> *Do you use social networks?*
>
> **Simple Answer**
>
> Sí, me gusta charlar con mis amigos en las redes sociales.
> *Yes, I like chatting with my friends on social networks.*
>
> **Extended Answer**
>
> Sí, comparto fotos con mis amigos. Mis padres tienen miedo de las redes sociales porque no las entienden.
> *Yes, I share photos with my friends. My parents are scared of social networks because they don't understand them.*

After much posing, Gertrudis was finally happy with her profile picture...

Uso los medios sociales para... — *I use social media to...*

Me encanta usar las redes sociales para hablar con mis amigos que viven lejos de mí.

I love using social networks to talk to my friends who live far away from me.

> my cousins who live in Canada — mis primos que viven en Canadá

Diría que los jóvenes pasan demasiado tiempo en las redes sociales.

I would say that young people spend too much time on social networks.

> should spend more time outside — deberían pasar más tiempo al aire libre

Uso las redes sociales todos los días para charlar con la gente que comparte mis intereses. Me gusta cocinar, así que cuelgo recetas y fotos de la comida en unos sitios web.

I use social networks every day to chat to people who share my interests. I like cooking, so I post recipes and photos of food on some websites.

> I watch videos to learn more about cooking — veo vídeos para aprender más sobre la cocina

Time to make friends with social media...

Lee lo que dice Belén sobre las redes sociales y decide si las frases son verdaderas (V) o falsas (F).

Uso las redes sociales después del colegio. Es relajante charlar sobre cosas estúpidas. Sin embargo, a veces, mis amigos se pelean si alguien ha colgado una foto sin permiso. No podría vivir sin las redes sociales, pero me molesta cuando salgo con mi novio y pasa todo el tiempo viendo cosas ridículas en su móvil en lugar de charlar conmigo.

e.g. Belén sólo usa las redes sociales los sábados. **F**

1. Belén charla sobre cosas no muy serias. [1]

2. Las redes sociales causan problemas entre sus amigos. [1]

3. Según ella, la vida sería mejor sin las redes sociales. [1]

4. El novio de Belén cree que la red es estúpida. [1]

The Problems with Social Media

Being able to talk about the pros and cons of social media is really important for your GCSE.

Las ventajas y desventajas — *Advantages and disadvantages*

la ventaja	*advantage*	por una parte	*on one hand*	debido a	*due to*
la desventaja	*disadvantage*	por otra parte	*on the other hand*	gracias a	*thanks to*

Me encanta que siempre hay alguien con quien puedo charlar en las redes sociales.

I love it that there's always someone I can chat to on social networks.

Por una parte, es muy fácil mantenerte en contacto con los amigos, pero por otra parte, creo que es muy importante salir con los amigos y estar juntos en la vida real.

On the one hand, it's very easy to keep in contact with your friends, but on the other hand, I believe it's very important to go out with your friends and be together in real life.

Debido a las redes sociales, sé lo que está pasando en el mundo.

Due to social networks, I know what's happening in the world.

Chat rooms are useful but they can be dangerous. — Las salas de chat son útiles, pero pueden ser peligrosas.

often, the friends you have on social media aren't real friends — muchas veces, los amigos que tienes en las redes sociales no son amigos de verdad

Looking at pug videos? Me?

I waste time looking at useless things — pierdo tiempo mirando cosas inútiles. '*Pierdo*' comes from '*perder*', which is a radical-changing verb. See p.84.

Question

¿Cuál es tu opinión de las redes sociales?
What's your opinion of social networks?

Simple Answer

Es divertido usar las redes sociales pero pueden ser peligrosas también.
It's fun to use social networks but they can be dangerous too.

Extended Answer

Una ventaja es que no te aburres nunca. Sin embargo, no me gustan las salas de chat porque la gente te puede mentir. Pienso que voy a desactivar mi cuenta.
An advantage is that you never get bored. However, I don't like chat rooms because people can lie to you. I think I'm going to deactivate my account.

SPEAKING — *Update your status to 'revising' and try these questions...*

Have a look at Manuel's answer to this question.

¿Crees que los jóvenes deberían pasar menos tiempo en las redes sociales?

A mi modo de ver, las redes sociales tienen más ventajas que desventajas. Mucha gente dice que pasamos demasiado tiempo charlando con los amigos en el mundo virtual, pero yo no estoy de acuerdo. No puedo salir con mis amigos después del colegio, así que es conveniente usar las redes sociales para comunicarme con ellos. Además, las redes sociales te pueden **enseñar**[1] mucho sobre el mundo y lo que pasa en tu **barrio**[2]. Puede ser más barato navegar por Internet para aprender estas cosas que comprar un periódico.

Grade 8-9

[1]teach
[2]neighbourhood

Tick list:
- ✓ tenses: present
- ✓ comparatives
- ✓ connectives e.g. además
- ✓ opinions

To improve:
- + use more tenses, e.g. future, conditional
- + use intensifiers e.g. muy, bastante

Contesta a estas preguntas en **español** — *intenta hablar durante **5** minutos.*

- *¿Te gusta usar las redes sociales?*
- *¿Cuáles son las desventajas de las redes sociales?*
- *¿Crees que los jóvenes deberían pasar menos tiempo en las redes sociales?*   [30 marks]

Books and Reading

Time to think about your favourite book, whether it's a thriller, a fantasy or your Spanish Revision Guide...

¿Lees mucho? — *Do you read a lot?*

la lectura	*reading*	la revista	*magazine*
leer	*to read*	el periódico	*newspaper*
el libro	*book*	la prensa	*the press*
la novela	*novel*	el libro electrónico	*e-book*
el tebeo	*comic strip*	el lector de libros electrónicos	*e-reader*

Greg soon realised that economic policy wasn't the most entertaining reading material on earth...

Grammar — 'leer' in the preterite tense

The verb '<u>leer</u>' (*to read*) is <u>irregular</u> in the <u>preterite tense</u> (see p.86). In both of the '<u>you</u>' forms and the '<u>we</u>' form, there's an <u>accent</u> on the first '<u>i</u>'. The '<u>he/she/it</u>' and '<u>they</u>' forms have a '<u>y</u>' in them.

<u>Leíste</u> un buen libro ayer.   *<u>You (inf., sing.) read</u> a good book yesterday.*
Ana <u>leyó</u> tres libros.   *Ana <u>read</u> three books.*

A mí me encanta leer las novelas de suspense porque las tramas suelen ser emocionantes.

I love reading thrillers because the plots are usually exciting.

> detective novels — las novelas policíacas

Desafortunadamente, no tengo mucho tiempo para leer novelas largas.

Unfortunately, I don't have much time to read long novels.

> the newspaper every day — el periódico todos los días

Los libros no me interesan mucho. Prefiero ver películas porque no tengo que concentrarme tanto.

Books don't interest me much. I prefer to watch films because I don't have to concentrate as much.

> to read comic strips — leer los tebeos

Question	**Simple Answer**	**Extended Answer**
¿Cuál es tu opinión de los lectores de libros electrónicos? *What's your opinion of e-readers?*	Son una buena idea porque puedes llevar varios libros contigo. *They are a good idea because you can take several books with you.*	Prefiero los libros en papel, pero debo admitir que los libros electrónicos son prácticos, sobre todo cuando vas de vacaciones. *I prefer paper books, but I must admit that e-books are practical, especially when you go on holiday.*

SPEAKING — *Make sure you stay in the examiner's good books...*

Have a look at this example role play. Javier is talking to a librarian.

Librarian: ¿Le gusta leer?

Javier: No leo mucho, pero me gustaría leer más.

Librarian: Hábleme de un libro que le ha gustado.

Javier: El año pasado leí una novela policíaca que se llama 'La noche oscura'. Me gustó mucho. ¿Tiene usted alguna recomendación?

Librarian: Sí, recomendaría 'El jardín misterioso'. ¿Le gustan los libros electrónicos?

Javier: Prefiero los libros electrónicos porque son más ligeros que los libros de papel. ¿Usted tiene un lector de libros electrónicos?

Librarian: Sí, pero no lo utilizo mucho.

Grade 6-7

To improve:
+ Use different opinion phrases to avoid repeating 'gustar'.

Tick list:
✓ tenses: present, preterite, conditional
✓ correct use of 'usted'

*Now prepare your own role-play. Use 'usted' and speak for about **two** minutes. [15 marks]*

Usted está en una biblioteca. Habla con el/la empleado/a.
- leer — frecuencia
- !
- ? género preferido
- los periódicos — opinión
- ? lector de libros electrónicos — precio

Music

Music often comes up in GCSE exams, so learn your stuff and dazzle the examiners.

La música — *Music*

la batería	*drums*
la canción	*song*
el / la cantante	*singer*
cantar	*to sing*
la letra	*song lyrics*
el grupo	*band*
el / la músico/a	*musician*
tocar	*to play (an instrument)*
la grabación	*recording*
en directo	*live*

Grammar — 'tocar' + instrument

Use the verb '<u>tocar</u>' to say you <u>play an instrument</u>.

When you're using the 'yo' form of 'tocar' in the <u>preterite</u> tense (see p.86), the '<u>c</u>' changes to '<u>qu</u>'.

<u>**Toco**</u> el violín.	***I play** the violin.*
<u>**Toqué**</u> el violín ayer.	***I played** the violin yesterday.*
<u>**Tocaba**</u> el violín.	***I used to play** the violin.*

Use the <u>imperfect</u> tense (p.87) to say what you <u>used to do</u>.

Question

¿Tocas algún instrumento?
Do you play an instrument?

Simple Answer

Sí, toco la guitarra y el clarinete.
Yes, I play the guitar and the clarinet.

Extended Answer

Sí, toco la guitarra en un grupo. Cuando era pequeño, tocaba el piano. Me gustaría aprender a tocar la batería, pero mis padres no me dejarán hacerlo.
Yes, I play the guitar in a band. When I was little, I used to play the piano. I would like to learn to play the drums, but my parents won't let me do it.

¿Te gusta escuchar música? — *Do you like listening to music?*

Me encanta escuchar música porque me hace sentir relajado/a. No me gusta la música pop. Diría que mi género de música preferido es el hip-hop.

I love listening to music because it makes me feel relaxed. I don't like pop music. I'd say that my favourite genre of music is hip-hop.

For a reminder of how to express your opinion, see p.8.

rap music — la música rap
rock music — la música rock
classical music — la música clásica

Puedo descargar muchos tipos de música instantáneamente, lo que me parece fenomenal.

I can download many types of music instantly, which seems great to me.

take my music with me and listen to it while I'm jogging or on the train — llevar la música conmigo y escucharla cuando salgo a correr o cuando estoy en el tren

Adoro a DiskoBeetz e intento ir a todos sus conciertos. Sus videos musicales son siempre entretenidos y originales.

I adore DiskoBeetz and I try to go to all their concerts. Their music videos are always entertaining and original.

Their song lyrics are interesting. — La letra de sus canciones es interesante.
I love live music. — Me encanta la música en directo.

TRACK LISTENING 04

It's time to face the music and try this exam style question...

*Marisol is a Spanish singer. Listen to the interview and then answer the questions in **English**.*

e.g. What kind of music is most important to Marisol's sister? **pop music**

1. Which instrument would Marisol like to learn to play? [1]
2. What two advantages of listening to music on the Internet does Marisol mention? [2]
3. Why does Marisol like going to concerts? [1]

Cinema

Make sure you can talk about a film you saw recently — and remember to always back up your opinions.

En el cine — *At the cinema*

la película	*film*	el papel	*role*	la estrella	*star, celebrity*
el actor	*actor*	la trama	*plot*	la banda sonora	*soundtrack*
la actriz	*actress*	el reparto	*cast*	la entrada	*ticket*

HOLLYWOOD

Me encantan las películas policíacas porque son muy emocionantes.

I love detective films because they're very exciting.

◄ science fiction — de ciencia ficción

Prefiero las películas de aventura porque me dan menos miedo que las películas de terror.

I prefer adventure films because they scare me less than horror films.

◄ often the special effects are great — muchas veces los efectos especiales son fenomenales

Romantic films annoy me — Las películas románticas me fastidian

No me gustan las películas de ciencia ficción porque es difícil seguir la trama.

I don't like science fiction films because it's difficult to follow the plot.

◄ you always know what's going to happen — siempre sabes lo que va a pasar

Grammar — I saw...

To say '<u>I saw...</u>' you need the <u>preterite</u> tense.
Check how to form it on p.86.

El viernes, <u>vi</u> una comedia.

On Friday, I saw a comedy.

<u>Unlike</u> most verbs when they're in the '<u>yo</u>' form of the <u>preterite</u> tense, '<u>vi</u>' <u>doesn't</u> have an <u>accent</u>.

La última película que vi... — *The last film I saw...*

Question

Describe la última película que viste.
Describe the last film you saw.

Simple Answer

El sábado, vi una película de acción. Me gustó mucho.
On Saturday, I saw an action film. I really liked it.

Extended Answer

El fin de semana pasado, vi una película de acción. Se trataba de dos familias que luchaban durante cientos de años. Tengo ganas de ver la nueva película de Geoff Frank porque me gusta el reparto.
Last weekend, I saw an action film. It was about two families who were fighting for hundreds of years. I'm looking forward to seeing the new film by Geoff Frank because I like the cast.

Grammar — 'se trata de'

Use '<u>se trata de</u>' to say what a film is about:

<u>Se trata de</u> **unos jóvenes muy ricos.**
<u>It's about</u> **some very rich young people.**

And you can use it in the <u>imperfect</u> to say what a film <u>was</u> about:

<u>Se trataba del</u> **amor.**   ***It was about* love.**

Remember — 'de' + 'el' = 'del' (p.80).

Don't let your Spanish GCSE become a horror film...

Translate this text into **Spanish**. *[12 marks]*

I love films. In my opinion, detective films are the best. They are the most entertaining films because you have to think about the plot. Last week, I saw a really funny film. I like seeing films with my friends at the weekend. In the future, I would love to be an actress.

Make sure you're always using the right tense.

TV

Here's the page where you get to chat about all the TV programmes you watch — hurrah.

¿Qué hay en la tele? — *What's on TV?*

el programa	*programme*	las noticias	*the news*	los dibujos animados	*cartoons*
la cadena	*channel*	el documental	*documentary*	la telenovela	*soap opera*
el anuncio	*advert*	el concurso	*game show, contest*	el reality show	*reality show*

Question

¿Te gusta ver la tele?
Do you like watching TV?

Simple Answer

Sí, me gusta ver la tele los fines de semana.
Yes, I like watching TV at the weekend.

Extended Answer

Sí, me gusta ver la tele los fines de semana. Mi cadena preferida es BBC1 porque no hay anuncios.
Yes, I like watching TV at the weekend. My favourite channel is BBC1 because there aren't any adverts.

¿Qué te gusta ver? — *What do you like watching?*

The race for the remote control was always a hard-fought contest...

Grammar — 'la gente' is singular

In English, 'people' is a plural noun. In Spanish, 'la gente' is singular, so you need the 'he/she/it' bit of the verb and the feminine singular form of 'many'.

Mucha gente **cree** que... *Many* people *believe* that...

A mí me gusta ver las telenovelas. Mucha gente dice que son aburridas y ridículas pero me ayudan a relajarme. No me gusta ver las noticias, especialmente cuando hablan sobre política.

I like watching soap operas. Many people say that they're boring and ridiculous but they help me relax. I don't like watching the news, especially when they're talking about politics.

Some people think that — Alguna gente piensa que

I don't understand why people complain — no entiendo por qué la gente se queja

See p.31 for how to use the verb 'soler'.

Suelo ver varios tipos de programas. Hoy en día hay tanta diversidad. Sin embargo, quisiera ver más documentales y menos dibujos animados.

I usually watch several types of programmes. These days there is so much diversity. However, I would like to see more documentaries and fewer cartoons.

there's so much rubbish — hay tanta basura

Now there's something for everyone. — Ahora hay algo para todo el mundo.

Mi abuelo pasa todos los días viendo la tele porque no puede salir. A él le encantan los concursos porque puede participar desde el sofá.

My grandad spends every day watching TV because he can't go out. He loves game shows because he can join in from the sofa.

TV is very important for him. — La televisión es muy importante para él.

Don't let revising TV give you square eyes...

Read Eli's email about TV, then decide whether the statements are true or false.

¡Hola Melissa! ¡Lo pasé fenomenal durante el intercambio contigo! Lo que me sorprendió fue la cantidad de telenovelas en la televisión británica. Sin embargo, no había tantos anuncios como en España. En España preferimos los dramas, sobre todo los que se tratan de figuras históricas. Creo que son muy emocionantes y han tenido mucho éxito recientemente.

e.g. Eli enjoyed the exchange. **True.**

1. The number of soap operas didn't surprise Eli. [1]
2. British TV had more adverts than Spanish TV. [1]
3. Historical dramas are popular in Spain. [1]
4. Eli thinks historical dramas are exciting. [1]

Food

This page is guaranteed to get your taste buds tingling — and it'll come in handy for your exam, too.

Los alimentos — *Foods*

la manzana	*apple*	las legumbres	*vegetables, pulses*	la zanahoria	*carrot*
el melocotón	*peach*	las verduras	*vegetables*	la col	*cabbage*
la fresa	*strawberry*	las judías verdes	*string beans*	la patata	*potato*
la naranja	*orange*	los champiñones	*mushrooms*	la cebolla	*onion*
el plátano	*banana*	los guisantes	*peas*	la lechuga	*lettuce*
la pera	*pear*				
las uvas	*grapes*				
la piña	*pineapple*				

		el aceite	*oil*	el arroz	*rice*
		el ajo	*garlic*	una barra de pan	*a loaf of bread*
		el huevo	*egg*	la tostada	*toast*
la carne	*meat*	la pimienta	*ground pepper*		
la carne de vaca	*beef*	la sal	*salt*		
la carne de cordero	*lamb*	el azúcar	*sugar*	el café	*coffee*
la carne de cerdo	*pork*	la nata	*cream*	el té	*tea*
la carne de ternera	*veal*	el queso	*cheese*	el zumo	*juice*
el filete	*steak*	la mantequilla	*butter*	la leche	*milk*
el jamón	*ham*			el vino	*wine*
el pollo	*chicken*			la cerveza	*beer*
la salchicha	*sausage*	los calamares	*squid*		
el pescado	*fish*	el chorizo	*Spanish sausage*	el caramelo	*boiled sweet*
el atún	*tuna*	el gazpacho	*cold soup*	la mermelada	*jam*
las gambas	*prawns*	la tortilla	*omelette*	la galleta	*biscuit*
los mariscos	*seafood*	las tapas	*nibbles, bar snacks*	el pastel	*cake, pie*
		los churros	*long doughnuts*	el helado	*ice cream*

¿Qué te gusta comer? — *What do you like to eat?*

Grammar — meal times

These are the <u>nouns</u> for Spanish meals:

el desayuno	*breakfast*
el almuerzo	*lunch* — You can also say 'la comida'.
la merienda	*afternoon snack*
la cena	*dinner*

These nouns can be made into <u>verbs</u>:

desayunar	***to have breakfast***
almorzar	***to have lunch*** — You can say 'comer' too.
merendar	***to have an afternoon snack***
cenar	***to have dinner***

Almuerzo a la una. Suelo comer un bocadillo. — *I have lunch at one o'clock. I usually eat a sandwich.*

'Almorzar' (*to have lunch*) is a <u>radical-changing verb</u> ('o' to 'ue'). See p.84.

Mis padres trabajan mucho, así que comemos mucha comida basura. Mi plato preferido es pollo al curry. — *My parents work a lot, so we eat a lot of junk food. My favourite meal is chicken curry.*

I love Chinese / Mediterranean food. — Me encanta la comida china / mediterránea.

Whenever I seafood, I eat it...

TRACK LISTENING 05

Listen to three people's opinions about food. Tick the statements that are true. [3 marks]

e.g. When he was younger, Joaquín ate lots of sweets. ✓

1. Joaquín likes eating junk food.
2. Alejandra doesn't think she eats enough fruit.
3. Raquel thinks it's difficult to find things she can eat in restaurants.

Eating Out

Restaurants often come up in the role-play section of the exam — so get learning your stuff.

¡Vamos al restaurante! — *Let's go to the restaurant!*

pedir	*to order, ask for*	el plato (combinado)	*(set) dish*	
traer	*to bring*	el primer plato	*starter*	
el camarero	*waiter*	el segundo plato	*main course*	
la camarera	*waitress*	el postre	*dessert*	
la carta	*the menu*	la bebida	*drink*	
el tenedor	*fork*	la cuenta	*bill*	
el cuchillo	*knife*	la propina	*tip*	
la cuchara	*spoon*	a la plancha	*grilled*	
el vaso	*glass*	tener hambre	*to be hungry*	
incluido	*included*	tener sed	*to be thirsty*	

Grammar — ordering politely

Use 'quisiera' to order what you'd like politely. 'Quisiera' comes from the imperfect subjunctive of 'querer' (*to want*). See p.91 and 97.

Quisiera un filete.
I'd like a steak.

You can also say 'me apetece', which means 'I fancy'.

Me apetece un café.
I fancy a coffee.

Question	Simple Answer	Extended Answer
¿Qué le gustaría tomar?	Quiero la sopa, por favor.	De primer plato, quisiera la sopa, y de segundo plato, el atún.
What would you like?	*I want the soup, please.*	*For the starter, I'd like the soup, and for main course, the tuna.*

Me encanta ir a restaurantes pero normalmente no puedo comer mucho. Sin embargo, siempre pido un postre porque me gustan las cosas dulces.

Comemos en restaurantes a menudo, especialmente cuando tenemos hambre y no tenemos tiempo para cocinar.

Una vez probé unas gambas a la plancha — estaban muy saladas.

I love going to restaurants but normally I can't eat much. However, I always order a dessert because I like sweet things.

We often eat in restaurants, especially when we're hungry and we don't have time to cook.

Once I tried some grilled prawns — they were very salty.

but sometimes it's hard to choose what you want to eat — pero a veces es difícil elegir lo que quieres comer

To say you're hungry or thirsty, you need to use the verb 'tener' (to have). I'm thirsty — tengo sed

fried — fritas

spicy — picantes

Hopefully this page has given you some food for thought...

Here's an example of a role-play — Pedro is eating in a restaurant.

Pedro está hablando con un camarero en un restaurante.   Grade 8-9

Camarero: Buenas tardes. **¿En qué puedo servirle?**[1]

Pedro: Quisiera gambas a la plancha con verduras y arroz.

Camarero: De acuerdo.

Pedro: ¿Usted tiene algo para mi amigo? No le gustan los mariscos.

Camarero: Sí, le recomendaría una pizza margarita con ensalada.

Pedro: ¡Muy bien! Y, de postre, me apetece un helado grande con dos cucharas.

Camarero: Sí, muy bien.

[1]How can I help you?

Tick list:
✓ tenses: present, imperfect subjunctive, conditional
✓ correct use of 'usted'

To improve:
+ use more varied conjunctions

Estás hablando con un camarero.
• lo que quieres comer
• lo que no te gusta comer
• !
• ? comida vegetariana
• lo que comiste durante tu última visita al restaurante

Prepare the role-play on the right. Address the waiter as 'usted', and try to speak in **Spanish** for about **two** minutes. [15 marks]

Sport

It doesn't matter if you're not the sportiest person on earth — you still need to learn the vocab on this page so you can recognise the names of sports and say which ones you like or don't like doing.

¿Practicas algún deporte? — *Do you play any sports?*

el fútbol	*football*	el baloncesto	*basketball*	la pesca	*fishing*
el rugby	*rugby*	la equitación	*horse riding*	el atletismo	*athletics*
el tenis	*tennis*	la natación	*swimming*	el alpinismo	*mountain climbing*
el hockey	*hockey*	la vela	*sailing*	el patinaje	*skating*
el bádminton	*badminton*	el piragüismo	*canoeing*	los deportes de riesgo	*adventure sports*

jugar al fútbol / tenis	*to play football / tennis*	correr	*to run*	el polideportivo	*sports centre*
montar a caballo	*to ride a horse*	bailar	*to dance*	la piscina	*swimming pool*
montar en bici	*to ride a bike*	nadar	*to swim*	el estadio	*stadium*
ir en monopatín	*to go by skateboard*	patinar	*to skate*	la pista	*track, court, slope*
ser aficionado/a a...	*to be fond / a fan of...*	pescar	*to fish*	la pista de hielo	*ice rink*

Question

¿Te gusta practicar deporte?
Do you like doing sport?

Simple Answer

Me gusta montar en bici porque es divertido.
I like riding my bike because it's fun.

Extended Answer

Me gusta montar en bici después del colegio porque es divertido estar con mis amigos al aire libre.
I like riding my bike after school because it's fun to be with my friends in the fresh air.

Grammar — 'jugar' + 'a' + sport

Use 'jugar a' to say what sports you play. In Spanish, you can't say 'Juego a el fútbol'. So if the sport is a masculine noun (like 'el fútbol'), the 'a' and the article 'el' combine to form 'al' (see p.80).

Juego al hockey.   *I play hockey.*
Juegas al tenis.   *You play tennis.*

'jugar' is a radical-changing verb — its stem changes from 'u' to 'ue' in the present tense. See p.84.

Mi deporte preferido es... — *My favourite sport is...*

Me encanta montar a caballo varias veces por semana. Para mí, es crucial hacer deporte.

I love going horse riding a few times per week. For me, it's crucial to do sport.

I like going to the ice rink — Me gusta ir a la pista de hielo

Juego al rugby los lunes. Me gusta porque puedo divertirme con mis amigos y hacer deporte al mismo tiempo.

I play rugby on Mondays. I like it because I can have a good time with my friends and do sport at the same time.

the sports centre where we practise is near my house — el polideportivo donde practicamos está cerca de mi casa

See p.14 for how to make the adjective 'deportista' agree.

No soy exactamente deportista, pero el deporte es bastante importante para mí — voy al colegio en monopatín y los fines de semana, pesco con mi padre.

I'm not exactly sporty, but sport is quite important to me — I go to school on my skateboard and at the weekend, I fish with my father.

and sport isn't very important to me — y el deporte no es muy importante para mí

but in my spare time, I prefer to cook or read — pero en mi tiempo libre, prefiero cocinar o leer

Sport

A double sport session — aren't you lucky? It's really important that you can talk about sports in an interesting way, showing off your Spanish as you go, so — on your marks, get set, go!

El deporte en la tele — *Sport on TV*

el partido	*match*	marcar un gol	*to score a goal*		
la carrera	*race*	el campeón	*champion*		
ganar	*to win*	el campeonato	*championship*		
perder	*to lose*	el torneo	*tournament*		
el equipo	*team*	la copa	*trophy, cup*		
el jugador	*player*	los Juegos Olímpicos	*the Olympic Games*		

Grammar — 'usually' + infinitive

Use the verb 'soler' plus the infinitive to say what you usually do. It's a radical-changing verb — its stem changes from 'o' to 'ue'. See p.84.

Suelo ver el tenis los viernes.
I usually watch tennis on Fridays.

Prefiero jugar al hockey que verlo en la tele. En vez de pasar mucho tiempo viendo la tele, los jóvenes deberían practicar deporte.

I prefer playing hockey to watching it on TV. Instead of spending a lot of time watching TV, young people should do sport.

Suelo ver el fútbol en la tele los fines de semana. Me encantaría visitar un estadio. Me imagino que sería muy emocionante estar allí si tu equipo marca muchos goles y gana el partido.

I usually watch football on TV at the weekend. I would love to visit a stadium. I imagine that it would be very exciting to be there if your team scores a lot of goals and wins the match.

Me encanta ver los Juegos Olímpicos porque es interesante ver los deportes menos populares como el piragüismo. Sueles aprender algo sobre ellos y son emocionantes también.

I love watching the Olympic Games because it's interesting to watch the less popular sports like canoeing. You usually learn something about them and they're exciting too.

I'm a fan of basketball. — Soy aficionado/a al baloncesto.

At primary school, I usually played football during break time. — En la escuela primaria, solía jugar al fútbol en el recreo.
'Solía' is the imperfect tense of 'soler'.

The verb 'imaginarse' means 'to imagine / suppose'.

the championship — el campeonato
the tournament — el torneo

it's exciting when someone from your country wins a medal — es emocionante cuando alguien de tu país gana una medalla

Be a good sport and try out this practice writing question...

Julia has written a blog about the sporting opportunities her school provides.

Mi colegio se llama Westwater College. Quisiera compartir unos **datos**[1] con vosotros **para que sepáis**[2] por qué es un colegio excepcional. **En cuanto a**[3] la educación física, se puede elegir entre varios deportes, entre ellos el tenis, el baloncesto y el hockey. **Tenemos mucha suerte**[4] porque nuestro profesor de hockey participó en los Juegos Olímpicos. Además, tenemos una piscina enorme. Después del colegio, se puede practicar deportes de riesgo, **incluso**[5] el piragüismo.

Grade 8-9

[1] information, facts
[2] so that you know
[3] With regard to
[4] We're very lucky
[5] even

To improve:
+ use another tense e.g. future

Tick list:
✓ tenses: present, preterite, present and imperfect subjunctives
✓ connectives e.g. 'además'
✓ idiomatic phrases e.g. 'tenemos mucha suerte'
✓ complex sentences including opinions

Escribe tu propio blog sobre el deporte en tu colegio. Menciona:

* *tu opinión sobre las oportunidades deportivas en tu colegio*
* *una actividad deportiva reciente en el colegio*

*Escribe aproximadamente **150** palabras en **español**.*
Responde a los dos aspectos de la pregunta. [32 marks]

Customs and Festivals

Spanish-speaking countries have lots of different festivals that they celebrate throughout the year.
In this section you'll find out about some of the most famous ones — life could be worse...

¡Celebremos! — *Let's celebrate!*

la fiesta	*festival, party*	¡Feliz cumpleaños!	*Happy Birthday!*	
festejar	*to celebrate*	¡Felicitaciones!	*Congratulations!*	
el día festivo	*public holiday*	¡Feliz año nuevo!	*Happy New Year!*	
el santo	*saint's day*	Nochevieja	*New Year's Eve*	
la fecha patria	*national independence day*	el Año Nuevo	*New Year*	
		tener suerte	*to be lucky*	

Grammar — Let's...

To say 'let's...', use the 'we' form of the present subjunctive (see p.96).

Hablemos de las fiestas. *Let's talk about festivals.*

'La Tomatina' es una fiesta que tiene lugar en agosto en Buñol, Valencia. Los participantes se lanzan tomates los unos a los otros. Atrae a miles de turistas cada año.

En Nochevieja en España, es tradicional comer 12 uvas para traer buena suerte.

'La Tomatina' is a festival that takes place in August in Buñol, Valencia. Participants throw tomatoes at each other. It attracts thousands of tourists each year.

On New Year's Eve in Spain, it's traditional to eat 12 grapes to bring good luck.

San Fermín — *The running of the bulls*

One festival in Spain that causes some controversy is <u>San Fermín</u>, which takes place in <u>Pamplona</u> each July.

el toro	*bull*	la plaza de toros	*bullring*	polémico	*controversial*
la corrida	*bullfight*	el torero	*bullfighter*	la tradición	*tradition*

Muchas personas corren por las calles estrechas con los toros peligrosos hasta la plaza de toros.

Durante la fiesta, los habitantes y los turistas llevan ropa blanca y pañuelos rojos.

La corrida de toros es una tradición común en España, pero es polémica porque alguna gente piensa que es cruel. Sin embargo, otros creen que es un arte.

Many people run through the narrow streets with the dangerous bulls to the bullring.

During the festival, locals and tourists wear white clothes and red scarves.

Bullfighting is a common tradition in Spain, but it's controversial because some people think that it's cruel. However, others believe it's an art.

Fest-iv-al, a reading question...

Read the text on the right, and then decide whether the sentences below are true (T) or false (F).

1. The festival started because of an argument between a local man and a tourist.	
2. The argument was settled calmly.	
3. The streets are full of people.	
4. 'La Tomatina' takes place in Valencia.	
5. They grow the tomatoes in Extremadura.	

[5 marks]

La fiesta que se llama 'La Tomatina' comenzó en 1945 a causa de una disputa entre los habitantes. La disputa se convirtió en una pelea con verduras. Hoy en día, mucha gente viaja a Buñol para participar en la fiesta. **Toneladas**[1] de tomates vuelan por el aire y las calles están llenas de gente. La fiesta tiene lugar en Valencia, pero los tomates se cultivan en Extremadura.

[1]Tonnes

Customs and Festivals

Next up it's All Souls' Day and a day that's a bit like April Fools' Day. But, spoiler alert — it's not in April in the Spanish-speaking world. And that's not me just trying to fool you...

El Día de los Muertos — *All Souls' Day*

El <u>Día de los Muertos</u> is a Mexican, Central American and Filipino tradition. According to <u>folklore</u>, heaven's gates open at midnight on <u>1st November</u> and the spirits of the dead <u>reunite</u> with their families for <u>24 hours</u>.

la Catrina	*popular female skeleton icon*	morir	*to die*
la calavera de azúcar	*skull made of sugar*	el muerto	*dead (person)*
el maquillaje	*make-up*	el mariachi	*Mexican musician*

'Muerto' is an irregular past participle — see p.89 for more.

En la tradición mexicana, la muerte no es espantosa.

In Mexican tradition, death isn't frightening.

← the lives of the dead are celebrated — se celebran las vidas de los muertos

El Día de los Muertos, las familias limpian y arreglan las tumbas de sus parientes y celebran fiestas.

On All Souls' Day, families clean and tidy the graves of their relatives and throw parties.

← friends — amigos

← share stories — comparten historias

Alguna gente se disfraza de 'la Catrina'. Honran a los muertos y lo demuestran con calaveras de azúcar, flores y música del mariachi.

Some people dress up as 'la Catrina'. They respect the dead and show it with sugar skulls, flowers and Mexican music.

← wear make-up like — lleva maquillaje como

An example of how some people dress to celebrate All Souls' Day.

El Día de los Inocentes — *28th December*

El Día de los Inocentes is like <u>April Fools' Day</u>, but it takes place in December in the Spanish-speaking world.

la broma	*joke, trick*
los medios de comunicación	*the media*

Salt

Es tradicional gastar una broma a alguien, por ejemplo sustituir el azúcar con la sal.

It's traditional to play a joke on someone, for example substitute sugar with salt.

Los medios de comunicación presentan noticias falsas como broma.

The media feature false news stories as a joke.

SPEAKING *My tea tastes salty — what's the date today?*

Laura has answered the following questions.

1. **¿Qué hiciste el año pasado para festejar tu cumpleaños?**
2. **¿Cuál es tu opinión de las fiestas en los países donde se habla español?**
3. **¿Cómo celebrarás la Nochevieja?**

Tick list:
✓ tenses: preterite, present, future
✓ good use of reflexive verbs

1. El año pasado fui a patinar sobre hielo para celebrar mi cumpleaños. Me lo pasé bien pero el único problema fue que me hice daño en el hielo.

Grade 6-7

2. Me fascinan las fiestas del mundo hispanohablante. Por ejemplo, las tradiciones y las costumbres del Día de los Muertos me interesan mucho.

To improve:
+ more detailed answers
+ more adjectives

3. No estoy segura, ¡pero quizás comeré uvas como se hace en España!

Now answer the same questions. Speak for about 3 minutes. [15 marks]

Customs and Festivals

Last year, I asked Father Christmas for a third page of festival-based fun — and he didn't disappoint.

Semana Santa — *Easter week*

The Catholic festival <u>Semana Santa</u> is the biggest religious celebration in Spanish-speaking countries.

la Pascua	*Easter*	la iglesia	*church*
el paso	*statue paraded at Easter*	la costumbre	*custom, way*

La Pascua es un evento sombrío. Hay procesiones con música. Se llevan pasos por las calles y los participantes llevan ropa que esconde sus identidades.

Easter is a sombre event. There are processions with music. Statues are carried around the streets and the participants wear clothes that hide their identities.

Grammar — impersonal verbs

To say that something is done <u>without</u> saying <u>who</u> does it, use '<u>se</u>' and the <u>3rd person</u> part of the verb (p.95).

Se ven las procesiones.
The processions <u>are watched</u>.

¡Feliz Navidad! — *Merry Christmas!*

Nochebuena	*Christmas Eve*	el Día de Reyes	*Epiphany, 6th January*	Papá Noel	*Father Christmas*
Navidad	*Christmas*	el villancico	*Christmas carol*	el turrón	*Spanish nougat*

Muchas comunidades participan en la lotería el 22 de diciembre.

Many communities participate in the lottery draw on 22nd December.

→ because they want to win 'El Gordo', the big prize — porque quieren ganar 'El Gordo', el gran premio

Muchos españoles celebran el Día de Reyes. Los Reyes Magos traen regalos a los niños o, si no se han comportado bien, un trozo de carbón.

Many Spaniards celebrate Epiphany. The Three Kings bring the children presents or, if they haven't behaved well, a piece of coal.

I love to sing Christmas carols — me encanta cantar villancicos

we usually eat turkey — solemos comer pavo

En Navidad, me gusta comer turrón. *At Christmas, I like to eat nougat.* ←

Otras fiestas religiosas — *Other religious festivals*

El Eid al-Fitr es una fiesta musulmana que marca el fin del mes de Ramadán.

Eid al-Fitr is a Muslim festival that marks the end of the month of Ramadan.

Muchos judíos celebran Hanukkah. Se encienden velas y se comen alimentos fritos.

Many Jews celebrate Hanukkah. Candles are lit and fried food is eaten.

No coal for you, just this lovely present...

TRACK LISTENING 06

Listen to these people talking about Christmas celebrations and complete the sentences below.

1. **The winning lottery number is...**
   A) ...80673.
   B) ...13773.
   C) ...80636. *[1]*

2. **Ana's going to...**
   A) ...travel the world using her winnings.
   B) ...buy a new car and an island.
   C) ...buy a luxury flat and go on holiday. *[1]*

3. **Carla's favourite food at Christmas was...**
   A) ...seafood.
   B) ...turkey.
   C) ...chocolate nougat. *[1]*

4. **For Christmas, Diego's brother got...**
   A) ...some toys.
   B) ...a bike.
   C) ...a mobile. *[1]*

Talking About Where You Live

For your Spanish GCSE, you'll need to be able to describe where you live, even if it's not remotely exciting...

En mi barrio... — *In my neighbourhood...*

el pueblo	*town*	el mercado	*market*	Correos	*Post Office*
el centro	*centre*	el parque	*park*	la comisaría	*police station*
las afueras	*outskirts*	la mezquita	*mosque*	la peluquería	*hairdresser's*
el edificio	*building*	la biblioteca	*library*	la carnicería	*butcher's*
el ayuntamiento	*town hall*	el museo	*museum*	el estanco	*tobacconist's*
el aparcamiento	*parking*	la fábrica	*factory*	el puerto	*port / harbour*

'Correos' doesn't have an article.

Question	**Simple Answer**	**Extended Answer**
¿Dónde vives?	Vivo en un pueblo en Cumbria.	Vivo en un pueblo pequeñito en el campo. Preferiría vivir más cerca de Londres porque hay más que hacer. Aquí no hay ni una tienda de ropa, lo que me fastidia mucho.
Where do you live?	*I live in a town in Cumbria.*	*I live in a really small town in the countryside. I'd prefer to live closer to London because there's more to do. Here there's not a single clothes shop, which annoys me a lot.*

Grammar — adding 'ito'

In Spanish, you can <u>add bits</u> onto the ends of <u>nouns</u> and <u>adjectives</u> to <u>change</u> their <u>meanings</u>. Adding '<u>ito/a/os/as</u>' makes the word <u>smaller</u> or <u>cuter</u>. Find out more on p.75.

Háblame de tu pueblo — *Talk to me about your town*

En mi barrio, hay mucho que hacer. Por ejemplo, el viernes fui al teatro. Sería casi perfecto si tuviera una bolera.

In my neighbourhood, there's a lot to do. For example, on Friday I went to the theatre. It would be almost perfect if it had a bowling alley.

if it had a pedestrian zone — si tuviera una zona peatonal
'<u>Tuviera</u>' is the <u>imperfect subjunctive</u> of '<u>tener</u>' — see p.97.

Mi ciudad tiene varios edificios impresionantes. También hay una carnicería y una librería.

My city has various impressive buildings. There's also a butcher's and a bookshop.

pretty — bonitos
modern — modernos

a pastry shop — una pastelería
a fishmonger's — una pescadería
a bakery — una panadería
a stationery shop — una papelería

Creo que es mejor vivir en el campo que en la ciudad. En un mundo ideal, viviría más lejos de las fábricas porque hacen mucho ruido.

I think it's better to live in the countryside than in the city. In an ideal world, I'd live further away from the factories because they make a lot of noise.

from the shopping centre because there are so many people — del centro comercial porque hay tanta gente

---

Go to town on your Spanish revision...

Tu amigo español te ha escrito para describir su pueblo.

¡Hola George! Voy a contarte todo sobre el pueblo que visitarás el mes que viene. En el centro, hay el ayuntamiento y varios edificios oficiales. Además, se puede visitar el museo del pueblo y hay **un montón de**[1] tiendas. Según mi padre, van a construir un polideportivo, lo que sería fenomenal, porque ahora hay poco que hacer por la tarde después del colegio y los jóvenes **acaban**[2] en la calle, molestando a la gente.

Grade 8-9

[1]loads of
[2]end up

To improve:
+ use a past tense
+ use a comparative

Tick list:
✓ tenses: present, future, conditional
✓ connectives
✓ use of 'se puede'
✓ well-explained opinion

Ahora describe tu barrio, y menciona:

- *cómo es tu pueblo;*
- *cómo cambiarías tu pueblo.*

*Escribe aproximadamente **150** palabras en **español**. Responde a los dos aspectos de la pregunta.*

[32 marks]

The Home

Home is where the heart is — and where the marks are — so you need to be able to describe it.

Mi casa — *My house*

mudarse (de casa)	*to move house*	el salón	*lounge*
la casa (adosada)	*(semi-detached) house*	la cocina	*kitchen*
el piso	*flat*	el comedor	*dining room*
la planta baja	*ground floor*	la escalera	*stairs*
la segunda planta	*second floor*	el dormitorio	*bedroom*
la habitación	*room*	los muebles	*furniture*
el cuarto de baño	*bathroom*	la estantería	*shelves*
el aseo	*toilet*	la pared	*wall*
la ducha	*shower*	el sótano	*basement*

Grammar — there is / are

To say what <u>there is</u> in your house, use '<u>hay</u>'. It <u>stays the same</u> regardless of whether the thing you're talking about is <u>singular</u> or <u>plural</u>.

En mi casa, <u>hay</u> un salón.
In my house, <u>there is</u> a lounge.

<u>Hay</u> siete habitaciones.
<u>There are</u> seven rooms.

Vivo en una casa adosada.
En mi dormitorio, hay una cama, un armario, una alfombra en el suelo, una mesita, y un espejo.

I live in a semi-detached house. In my bedroom, there's a bed, a wardrobe, a carpet on the floor, a little table, and a mirror.

In the kitchen, there's a sink, a fridge and an oven. — En la cocina, hay un fregadero, una nevera y un horno.

Vivimos en un piso pequeño.
La habitación que más me gusta es el salón porque es cómodo.

We live in a small flat. The room I like best is the lounge because it's comfortable.

there are armchairs — hay sillones

Me gustaría mudarme a una casa más grande.

I'd like to move to a bigger house.

to have more electrical appliances — tener más electrodomésticos

Question

¿Cómo sería tu casa ideal?
What would your ideal house be like?

Simple Answer

Mi casa ideal tendría muchas habitaciones y un jardín grande.
My ideal house would have a lot of rooms and a big garden.

Extended Answer

La casa de mis sueños tendría un jardín enorme y una piscina de lujo. Además, sería mejor si no tuviera que compartir mi habitación.
The house of my dreams would have an enormous garden and a luxury pool. It would also be better if I didn't have to share my room.

Make yourself at home and try this question for size...

Read this passage from 'Pepita Jiménez' by Juan Valera.

Tiene la casa limpísima y todo en un orden perfecto. Los muebles no son artísticos ni elegantes; pero tampoco **se advierte**[1] en ellos nada pretencioso y de mal gusto. **Para poetizar su estancia**[2], tanto en el patio como en las salas y galerías, hay multitud de flores y plantas. No tiene, en verdad, ninguna planta rara ni ninguna flor exótica; pero sus plantas y sus flores, de lo más común que hay por aquí, están cuidadas con extraordinario **mimo**[3].

[1]is observed
[2]To make her surroundings more poetic
[3]care

Decide whether the following statements are true or false.

e.g. The house is very clean. **True**

1. The furniture is elegant.
2. The flowers are only in the kitchen.
3. There are many flowers and plants.
4. The flowers are mostly exotic.
5. The flowers are well looked after.

[5 marks]

What You Do at Home

Doing chores might be a bit of a drag, but at least talking about them in Spanish is more fun... probably.

Un día típico — *A typical day*

despertarse	*to wake up*
levantarse	*to get up*
ducharse	*to have a shower*
lavarse la cara	*to wash your face*
vestirse	*to get dressed*
acostarse	*to go to bed*
dormirse	*to go to sleep*

Grammar — reflexive verbs

All of these verbs are <u>reflexive</u> — they help you say what you do <u>to yourself</u>. To use them, <u>remove</u> the <u>reflexive pronoun</u>, <u>conjugate the verb</u> as normal, and put the <u>reflexive pronoun</u> back <u>in front of the verb</u> in its <u>correct form</u> (see p.92).

<u>Me despierto</u> a las siete.   *<u>I wake up</u> at seven o'clock.*

¿A qué hora <u>te levantas</u>?   *What time <u>do you get up</u>?*

<u>Se acuestan</u> temprano.   *<u>They go to bed</u> early.*

Some of these verbs are radical-changing too. See p.84.

Question	Simple Answer	Extended Answer
¿Qué haces por la mañana? *What do you do in the morning?*	Me despierto a las siete y luego me ducho. *I wake up at seven o'clock and then I have a shower.*	Me despierto a las siete, pero no me levanto hasta las siete y media. Luego me ducho y me visto rápidamente. *I wake up at seven o'clock, but I don't get up until half past seven. Then I have a shower and get dressed quickly.*

Las tareas domésticas — *Chores*

arreglar	*to tidy*	hacer la cama	*to make the bed*	pasar la aspiradora	*to do the vacuuming*
ayudar	*to help*	pasear al perro	*to walk the dog*	hacer las compras	*to do the shopping*
limpiar	*to clean*	cortar el césped	*to mow the lawn*	sacar la basura	*to take out the rubbish*

Hago mi cama y arreglo mi dormitorio antes de salir de casa. Es importante que todos ayuden en casa.

I make my bed and I tidy my bedroom before leaving the house. It's important that everyone helps at home.

'Es importante que' needs to be followed by the subjunctive form of 'ayudar' — 'ayuden'. See p.96-97.

Después de la cena, pongo todo en el lavaplatos y paseo al perro.

After dinner, I put everything in the dishwasher and I walk the dog.

I clear the table — quito la mesa
I take out the rubbish — saco la basura

En verano, corto el césped, pero mis padres no me dejan hacer las compras porque siempre compro cosas que no les gustan.

In the summer, I mow the lawn, but my parents don't let me do the shopping because I always buy things they don't like.

lay the table because I break the glasses — poner la mesa porque rompo los vasos

---

READING

Hopefully your Spanish is now squeaky clean...

Translate this text into **English**. *[9 marks]*

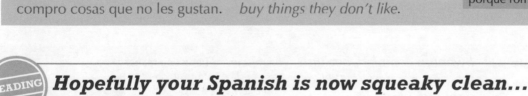

Creo que es importante ayudar en casa, pero no pienso que sea justo si yo hago mucho y mi hermano menor hace muy poco. Me encanta pasear al perro. Mi padre me da dinero si corto el césped, así que lo haré el domingo que viene. La semana pasada tuve que limpiar el cuarto de baño. ¡Qué asco!

Shopping

Time to indulge in some retail therapy and pick some marks up along the way.

¡Vamos al centro comercial! — *Let's go to the shopping centre!*

los grandes almacenes	*department store*
el/la dependiente/a	*sales assistant*
la talla / el número	*clothes size / shoe size*
el descuento	*discount*
las rebajas	*the sales*
el recibo	*receipt*
cambiar	*to change*
pagar	*to pay*
devolver	*to return (an item)*
reembolsar	*to refund*
quejarse	*to complain*
en efectivo	*(in) cash*
la tarjeta de crédito	*credit card*

Question

¿Te gusta ir de compras?
Do you like going shopping?

Simple Answer

Sí, me gusta ir de compras, sobre todo cuando hay rebajas.
Yes, I like going shopping, especially when there are sales.

Extended Answer

Sí, me gusta ir de compras pero a veces es estresante si no tienen la talla correcta o si tienes que cambiar algo.
Yes, I like going shopping but sometimes it's stressful if they don't have the right size or if you have to change something.

¿Me puede ayudar? — *Can you help me?*

You might have to pretend you're in a shop in the role-play. Make sure you know how to ask a shop assistant for different items.

Grammar — I would like...

To say what you'd like, you can use 'quisiera' as well as 'me gustaría'.
'Quisiera' is the imperfect subjunctive form of the verb 'querer'. See p.97.

   Quisiera un descuento, por favor.   *I'd like a discount, please.*

If you're telling someone what you'd like them to do, you need the present subjunctive form of the verb. See p.96.

   Quisiera que me reembolse, por favor.   *I'd like you (form., sing.) to give me a refund, please.*

Me encanta esta rebeca pero me queda grande. ¿Hay otra talla?

I love this cardigan, but it's too big for me. Is there another size?

Use 'quedar' with 'grande' or 'pequeño' to say that something is too big or small for you.

Estoy buscando un bolso de cuero que no sea muy caro.

I'm looking for a leather bag which is not too expensive.

When you're imagining something that may or may not exist, you need the present subjunctive. 'Sea' is the present subjunctive form of 'ser'. See p.96.

Quisiera un collar pero no quiero gastar demasiado.

I'd like a necklace, but I don't want to spend too much.

some earrings — unos pendientes
a tie — una corbata
a dress — un vestido

Quiero quejarme porque la falda tiene un agujero. Quisiera un reembolso, por favor.

I want to complain because the skirt has a hole. I'd like a refund, please.

has a stain — tiene una mancha
is ripped — está rasgada
is broken — está rota

Hoy hay muchas rebajas. Compré este chándal a mitad de precio.

There are a lot of sales today. I bought this tracksuit half-price.

I had to queue for ages. — Tuve que hacer cola durante mucho tiempo.
'Tener' is irregular in the preterite tense. See p.86.

The queue for the fancy hats stretched right down the road...

Shopping

Going hungry in Spain wouldn't be fun — make sure you can ask for a box of biscuits or a slice of cake.

En la tienda de comestibles — *In the grocery shop*

la cantidad	*quantity*	una ración	*a portion*
una caja	*a box*	una bolsa	*a bag*
un cartón	*a carton*	lleno/a	*full*
una lata	*a tin*	vacío/a	*empty*
un pedazo	*a piece*	pesar	*to weigh*
un trozo	*a slice, piece*	un kilo	*a kilogram*
un tarro	*a jar*	un gramo	*a gram*
un paquete	*a packet*	varios/as	*several*

Grammar — agreement with weights

When you're talking in <u>hundreds</u> in Spanish, the <u>number</u> has to <u>agree</u> with the <u>weight</u>.

Doscien<u>tos</u> gram<u>os</u> de uvas, por favor.
Two hundred grams of grapes, please.

In Spanish, when you say '<u>half a kilo</u>', you <u>don't need</u> the '<u>a</u>' like in English.

Medio kilo de fresas, por favor.
Half <u>a</u> kilo of strawberries, please.

Quisiera un trozo de tarta, por favor. ¿Cuánto cuesta?
I would like a slice of cake, please. How much does it cost?

a portion of Manchego cheese — una ración de queso manchego

Deme dos kilos de naranjas, por favor.
Give me two kilos of oranges, please.

Although this sounds a bit rude, it's <u>normal</u> to use the <u>imperative</u> 'give me' in Spanish when you're at a market. See p.98 for more imperatives.

¿Puede usted pesar estas peras, por favor?
Could you weigh these pears, please?

We need — Nos hacen falta
Use '<u>hace</u>' instead of '<u>hacen</u>' to say you need a <u>singular</u> item.

Necesitamos unos tomates.
We need some tomatoes.

Hacer las compras en la red — *Shopping online*

Question

¿Te gusta hacer las compras en la red?
Do you like shopping online?

Simple Answer

Sí, me gusta hacer las compras en la red porque es fácil.
Yes, I like shopping online because it's easy.

Extended Answer

Sí, me gusta hacer las compras en la red porque resulta más barato. Además, no tienes que salir de casa porque hay un servicio de reparto a domicilio.
Yes, I like shopping online because it turns out cheaper. Besides, you don't have to leave the house because there's a home delivery service.

Grammar — before / after doing something

To say '<u>before doing something</u>', use '<u>antes de</u>' and the <u>infinitive</u>. To say '<u>after doing something</u>', use '<u>después de</u>' followed by the <u>infinitive</u>.

<u>Después de hacer</u> las compras, tomo un café.
<u>After doing</u> the shopping, I have a coffee.

Prefiero ir de compras en un centro comercial porque para mí, es mejor ver las cosas antes de comprarlas.
I prefer to go shopping in a shopping centre because, for me, it's better to see things before buying them.

TRACK LISTENING 07

Don't shop 'til you drop — have a rest and do some practice...

Montse is in a grocery shop. Listen to the dialogue and answer the questions in **English***.*

e.g. What is Montse making a tortilla for?   **a birthday party**

1. What quantity of onions does she need? [1]
2. Which ingredient doesn't she need to buy? [1]
3. Why doesn't the shopkeeper have any olive oil? [1]
4. How much does the shopping cost in total? [1]

All that onion-chopping resulted in a lot of tor-tears...

Giving and Asking for Directions

If you're feeling a bit lost, this is the page for you — you'll be on the straight and narrow in no time.

¿Dónde está? — *Where is it?*

cruzar	*to cross*
tomar	*to take (a road)*
seguir	*to continue*
a la izquierda	*on the left*
a la derecha	*on the right*
al lado de	*next to*
detrás de	*behind*
delante de	*in front of*
entre	*between*
enfrente de	*opposite*
en la esquina	*on the corner*
al final de	*at the end of*

For more prepositions, see p.80.

Question

¿Dónde está la peluquería?
Where's the hairdresser's?

Simple Answer

La peluquería está al final de la calle.
The hairdresser's is at the end of the street.

Extended Answer

La peluquería está justo al lado de la piscina, enfrente del cine. Es muy fácil encontrarla.
The hairdresser's is right next to the swimming pool, opposite the cinema. It's very easy to find it.

Grammar — 'estar' for locations

In Spanish, there are <u>two verbs</u> for '<u>to be</u>' — '<u>ser</u>' and '<u>estar</u>'. To describe <u>where things are</u>, you need to use '<u>estar</u>' — see p.85. You can also use '<u>estar situado</u>' to say <u>where something is situated</u>.

Wilbur was feeling really very lost...

La estación está enfrente de Correos, en el norte de la ciudad.	*The station is opposite the post office, in the north of the city.*	See p.11 for the other compass points.
El banco está situado detrás de la iglesia.	*The bank is situated behind the church.*	is on the right of — está a la derecha de
Los servicios están en la esquina.	*The toilets are on the corner.*	on the left — a la izquierda

¿Cómo se llega a...? — *How do you get to...?*

Siga todo recto y el museo está entre la catedral y la biblioteca.	*Continue straight on and the museum is between the cathedral and the library.*	behind — detrás de
El parque está detrás del colegio. Tome esa calle y verá un semáforo. Luego gire a la izquierda.	*The park is behind the school. Take that road and you'll see some traffic lights. Then turn left.*	the police station — la comisaría

Grammar — giving instructions

To give <u>instructions</u>, use the <u>imperative</u>. See how to form it on p.98. You probably <u>won't know</u> the person who's asked for directions, so you should use the '<u>usted</u>' form.

<u>Siga</u> **todo recto y** <u>cruce</u> **la calle.**
<u>Continue</u> straight on and <u>cross</u> the street.

<u>Tome</u> **la segunda calle a la derecha.**
<u>Take</u> the second street on the right.

TRACK LISTENING 08

Stay on the right track with your Spanish revision...

Escucha a Iker describir su barrio y escribe verdadero (V) o falso (F) para cada frase.

e.g. Es un barrio muy viejo. **V**

1. El teatro está al lado del supermercado. *[1]*
2. Hay tres supermercados. *[1]*
3. Hay un supermercado enfrente de la comisaría. *[1]*
4. Para llegar a la iglesia, hay que seguir la calle San Felipe y tomar una calle a la izquierda. *[1]*

Weather

Come rain or shine, moaning about the weather is a favourite British pastime — enjoy.

Hace buen / mal tiempo — *It's good / bad weather*

Está...	It's...			Hace...	It's...		Hay...	There is / there are...
despejado	*clear*	caluroso	*hot*	sol	*sunny*		niebla	*fog*
nublado	*cloudy*	fresco	*fresh*	viento	*windy*		hielo	*ice*
lloviendo	*raining*	húmedo	*humid*	calor	*hot*		tormenta	*a storm*
nevando	*snowing*	tormentoso	*stormy*	frío	*cold*		chubascos	*showers*
		seco	*dry*					

el clima   *climate*   el pronóstico   *weather forecast*   el cielo   *sky*

Question

¿Qué tiempo hace?
What's the weather like?

Simple Answer

Hace buen tiempo hoy.
It's good weather today.

The British summer was going swimmingly...

Extended Answer

Hoy hace mucho sol en el sur, pero mañana cambiará: habrá truenos y relámpagos.
Today it's really sunny in the south, but tomorrow it will change: there will be thunder and lightning.

Grammar — weather verbs

To describe the weather in English, you often use '<u>to be</u>', e.g. '<u>it's rainy</u>'. You can do this in Spanish with some types of weather:

<u>Está</u> despejado / nublado / nevando / lloviendo.
***It's** clear / cloudy / snowing / raining.*

But sometimes, you have to use the verb '<u>hacer</u>' instead:

Hace sol / viento / frío.   ***It's** sunny / windy / cold.*

And sometimes, you need the verb '<u>haber</u>':

<u>Hay</u> niebla / hielo.   ***There's** fog / ice.*

It sounds complicated, but just learn which types of weather go with which verb. Remember you can put the verbs into <u>different tenses</u> too.

¿Qué tiempo habrá? — *What will the weather be like?*

Estará tormentoso por todas partes.	*It will be stormy everywhere.*	dry — seco
Nevará en Inglaterra este invierno.	*It will snow in England this winter.*	It will rain — Lloverá
Hará mucho calor en el sur de Europa este verano. Sería mejor si no hiciera tanto calor porque prefiero las temperaturas más bajas.	*It will be very hot in the south of Europe this summer. It would be better if it weren't so hot because I prefer lower temperatures.*	

See p.3 for the seasons.

It would be perfect if it were just as hot all the time. — Sería perfecto si hiciera tanto calor todo el tiempo.

 READING

Don't let revision rain on your parade...

*Read this weather forecast, and then answer the questions in **English**.*

Hoy en el norte de España, habrá niebla, mientras que en el sur, estará despejado. En el oeste, cerca de Portugal, hará frío, con la posibilidad de lluvia. Para el fin de semana, hará buen tiempo por toda España, pero para la semana que viene, podemos esperar que las temperaturas bajen, con un riesgo de tormentas.

e.g. What will the weather be like in the north of Spain today? **It will be foggy.**

1. Which part of Spain will have clear weather?   [1]
2. Where will it be cold?   [1]
3. What will it be like at the weekend?   [1]
4. What'll happen to the temperatures next week?   [1]
5. What else might happen next week?   [1]

Environmental Problems

Time to think green and start talking about the things that affect the environment.

El medio ambiente — *The environment*

el cambio climático	*climate change*	el combustible	*fuel*	agotar	*to use up*
el calentamiento global	*global warming*	la lluvia ácida	*acid rain*	la escasez	*shortage*
el efecto invernadero	*greenhouse effect*	nocivo	*harmful*	la inundación	*flood*
la capa de ozono	*ozone layer*	la marea negra	*oil spill*	la sequía	*drought*
los productos químicos	*chemicals*	el vertedero	*rubbish tip*	echar la culpa	*to blame*
los gases de escape	*exhaust fumes*	dañar	*to damage*	preocuparse	*to worry*

Question	**Simple Answer**	**Extended Answer**
¿El medio ambiente es importante para ti? *Is the environment important to you?*	Sí, creo que es muy importante proteger el medio ambiente. *Yes, I think it's very important to protect the environment.*	Es importantísimo proteger el medio ambiente. Si no actuamos ahora, las selvas y los bosques desaparecerán. *It's really important to protect the environment. If we don't act now, the jungles and forests will disappear.*

El cambio climático — *Climate change*

El cambio climático es un problema que me preocupa bastante. El uso de ciertos combustibles contamina el aire y causa el calentamiento global.

Climate change is a problem that worries me quite a lot. The use of certain fuels pollutes the air and causes global warming.

Debido al efecto invernadero, las temperaturas suben, lo que amenaza la supervivencia de unos animales, por ejemplo los pingüinos.

Due to the greenhouse effect, temperatures rise, which threatens the survival of some animals, for example penguins.

Exhaust fumes can be harmful and they damage the ozone layer. — Los gases de escape pueden ser nocivos y dañan la capa de ozono.

causes a shortage of water in some regions of the world — causa una escasez de agua en algunas regiones del mundo

El desperdicio de agua — *Water wastage*

El agua es necesaria para todo el mundo. Sin agua, los cultivos no pueden sobrevivir.

Water is necessary for everyone. Without water, crops can't survive.

Debemos usar menos agua en nuestra vida diaria.

We should use less water in our daily lives.

It's an important resource that we shouldn't use up. — Es un recurso importante que no deberíamos agotar.

use — utilizar
waste — malgastar

La deforestación — *Deforestation*

Los bosques son importantes porque reducen la cantidad de dióxido de carbono en la atmósfera.

Forests are important because they reduce the amount of carbon dioxide in the atmosphere.

Hoy en día cortamos muchos árboles para producir combustibles. Esto contribuye a la destrucción de los bosques, y al cambio climático.

Nowadays we cut down lots of trees to produce fuel. This contributes to the destruction of forests, and to climate change.

Environmental Problems

Raise your nature-loving credentials and impress the examiners by spicing up your opinions.

La contaminación — *Pollution*

Las mareas negras ensucian el mar y las playas. Luego, los peces y los pájaros sufren mucho y muchas veces mueren.

Oil spills make the sea and the beaches dirty. Then, the fish and birds suffer a lot and often they die.

Oil is harmful for the creatures that live in the sea. — El petróleo es nocivo para las criaturas que viven en el mar.

Aquí, tenemos un problema con la cantidad de basura. Es muy fácil olvidarse de la basura cuando está en un vertedero y no en la calle, pero sí existe.

Here, we have a problem with the amount of rubbish. It's very easy to forget about rubbish when it's in a tip and not in the street, but it does exist.

I don't understand it, because it's very easy to recycle cardboard and plastic packaging. — No lo entiendo, porque es muy fácil reciclar cartón y envases de plástico.

Algunos problemas graves — *Some serious problems*

Grammar — using the subjunctive

Use the subjunctive to give your opinion and say what you want to happen. Check how to form it on p.96-97.

You need it after 'no pienso que...' (*I don't think that...*).

No pienso que sea justo echar toda la culpa a las fábricas.
I don't think that it's fair to put all the blame on factories.

It can also be used to express an emotion about something.

Es terrible que haya tanta basura en la calle.
It's terrible that there is so much rubbish in the street.

And when you're saying what you want someone else to do, use 'quiero que' followed by the subjunctive.

Quiero que el gobierno haga más por la naturaleza.
I want the government to do more for nature.

Grammar — the future

To talk about what things might be like in the future, you can use the immediate future tense (ir + a + infinitive) or the proper future tense (iré — *I will go*, tendré — *I will have*, etc.). See p.90.

Es esencial que protejamos la naturaleza porque sin ella, no podremos vivir.

It's essential that we protect nature because we won't be able to live without it.

we combat the effects of climate change, because if not, we're going to suffer — combatamos los efectos del cambio climático porque si no, vamos a sufrir

Quiero que todos hagan más para reducir la cantidad de basura que producimos. Si no, los vertederos estarán llenos pronto.

I want everyone to do more to reduce the amount of rubbish that we produce. If not, the rubbish tips will be full soon.

think more about the environment and not waste so many things — piensen más en el medio ambiente y no gasten tantas cosas

Es terrible que no pensemos más en el futuro de la Tierra.

It's terrible that we don't think more about the Earth's future.

future generations — las generaciones del futuro

 Learn Spanish and the world's your (polluted) oyster... nice.

Translate this text into **Spanish**. [12 marks]

Climate change worries me a lot. Factories and cars contribute to the greenhouse effect. For me, the worst thing is that people in some poor countries suffer due to floods and droughts. It isn't fair. I think we should work together to reduce the effects of climate change, but it will be very difficult.

Problems in Society

Time for another cheerful topic to make your day happy and joyful — it's social problems.

Los problemas sociales — *Social problems*

el gobierno	*government*	la desigualdad	*inequality*
la libertad	*freedom*	el prejuicio	*prejudice*
el peligro	*danger*	la guerra	*war*
la pobreza	*poverty*	los "sin techo"	*homeless people*
la violencia	*violence*	el desempleo	*unemployment*
la igualdad	*equality*	estar en paro	*to be unemployed*

Although Dexter was grateful for his job, a stint as Santa wasn't quite what he'd had in mind...

Los efectos de la guerra — *The effects of war*

Grammar — 'me parece'

Use '<u>me parece</u>' to say how something '<u>seems</u>' to you. You can use it to <u>vary</u> the way you give <u>opinions</u>.

<u>Me parece</u> inquietante que...
<u>It seems</u> worrying <u>to me</u> that...

<u>Me parece</u> interesante que...
<u>It seems</u> interesting <u>to me</u> that...

Debido a la guerra, muchas personas tienen que emigrar a otro país y empezar la vida de nuevo.

Due to war, many people have to emigrate to another country and start their lives all over again.

No me parece justo que la libertad que tienes dependa tanto del país en que naciste.

It seems unfair to me that the freedom you have depends so much on the country in which you were born.

La igualdad social — *Social equality*

Sería agradable creer que todos somos iguales en nuestro país, pero no es así.

It would be nice to believe that we're all equal in our country, but that's not the case.

A veces, la desigualdad provoca violencia entre los ricos y los pobres.

Sometimes, inequality causes violence between the rich and the poor.

Me encantaría vivir en un mundo más justo.

I would love to live in a fairer world.

inequality doesn't exist — la desigualdad no existe

discrimination against immigrants — discriminación contra los inmigrantes

Here we are lucky because our country is quite fair. — Aquí tenemos suerte porque nuestro país es bastante justo.

La violencia juvenil — *Youth violence*

Question	Simple Answer	Extended Answer
¿Crees que la violencia es un problema grave hoy en día? *Do you think that violence is a serious problem nowadays?*	Sí, en mi barrio, hay un grupo de jóvenes violentos que nos dan miedo. *Yes, in my neighbourhood, there's a group of violent youths who scare us.*	Sí, hay grupos de gamberros que salen por la noche. Son muy violentos e intimidan a la gente mayor, lo que me enfada mucho. *Yes, there are groups of troublemakers who go out at night. They are very violent and they intimidate the older people, which makes me really angry.*

Problems in Society

And the social problems don't end there — you still have poverty and unemployment to get through.

La pobreza — *Poverty*

Question

¿Crees que hay mucha pobreza en este país?
Do you believe there is a lot of poverty in this country?

Grammar — 'deber'

To say what someone should do, use '<u>deber</u>' followed by the <u>infinitive</u>.

<u>Deberíamos luchar</u> contra la pobreza.
<u>We should fight</u> against poverty.

Simple Answer

Creo que hay más pobreza que hace diez años. El gobierno debería apoyar a los "sin techo".
I think there's more poverty than ten years ago. The government should support homeless people.

Extended Answer

Creo que hay demasiada pobreza en nuestra sociedad. Vivo en un país rico, pero todavía hay mucha gente sin comida y sin hogar. Deberíamos ayudar a los más necesitados porque es fácil acabar en la pobreza si pierdes tu trabajo. La pobreza puede afectar a cualquier persona.
I think there's too much poverty in our society. I live in a rich country, but there are still lots of people without food and without a home. We should help the most needy people because it's easy to end up in poverty if you lose your job. Poverty can affect anyone.

El desempleo — *Unemployment*

This could be the examiner's <u>favourite topic</u> in the <u>speaking</u> exam, so learn how to talk about it.

Hay mucha gente en paro en mi ciudad.

There are lots of unemployed people in my city.

Casi todos los estudiantes por aquí se preocupan por el desempleo. Si pudiera cambiar algo, crearía más trabajos.

Nearly all the students around here worry about unemployment.
If I could change anything, I'd create more jobs.

El desempleo es un problema muy grave porque los que están en paro se encuentran en un círculo vicioso. Los expertos dicen que si estás en paro, es más difícil encontrar otro trabajo.

Unemployment is a very serious problem because those who are unemployed find themselves in a vicious circle. Experts say that if you're unemployed, it's harder to find another job.

Nobody has a problem finding work — Nadie tiene problemas para encontrar trabajo

It is a big problem that we must solve. — Es un gran problema que debemos solucionar.

the worst affected are young people — los más afectados son los jóvenes

Well, that was a bit bleak — and unfortunately, there's more...

TRACK LISTENING 09

A charity for the homeless is talking about the situation in Spain. Listen, and then fill the gaps.

e.g. ..Thousands.. of people are homeless in Spain.

1. Many people have lost their jobs and homes due to .... [1]
2. Homeless people often have a .... life. [1]
3. Homeless people are often the victims of .... [1]
4. According to the report, many people think homeless people are .... [1]
5. To change the situation for homeless people, we should .... [1]

Contributing to Society

So now you've battled through all the problems, it's time to get creative and find some solutions.

¿Qué podemos hacer? —*What can we do?*

la basura	*rubbish*	renovable	*renewable*
los desechos / los residuos	*rubbish*	salvar el planeta	*to save the planet*
el reciclaje	*recycling*	la organización benéfica	*charitable organisation*
reciclar	*to recycle*	la tienda solidaria	*charity shop*

Question	Simple Answer	Extended Answer
¿Qué haces para proteger el medio ambiente? *What do you do to protect the environment?*	Apago las luces para ahorrar energía. *I turn the lights off to save energy.*	Cuando voy de compras, siempre reutilizo las bolsas en vez de comprar nuevas. *When I go shopping, I always reuse the bags instead of buying new ones.*
¿Qué haces para ayudar a otras personas? *What do you do to help other people?*	Los domingos trabajo en una tienda solidaria. *On Sundays I work in a charity shop.*	Ayudo con el club de jóvenes en mi pueblo. Es esencial que hagamos algo para los demás. *I help with the youth club in my town. It's essential that we do something for others.*

¿Cómo podemos ayudar? — *How can we help?*

Me gustaría ayudar a los refugiados que vienen a vivir en nuestro país.

I would like to help the refugees who come to live in our country.

→ *the victims of natural disasters like hurricanes and fires* — las víctimas de desastres naturales como huracanes e incendios

Es importante que apoyemos a las organizaciones benéficas.

It's important that we support charitable organisations.

'Acabar de' + infinitive means 'to have just done something'. See p.93.

Acabo de participar en una protesta en contra del uso de los combustibles fósiles.

I have just participated in a protest against the use of fossil fuels.

a campaign — una campaña

SPEAKING ***I rode there and back... that's enough recycling, right?***

Look at the answers to these questions — then it's time for a photo question.

¿Recicláis mucho en casa?
¿Qué haremos en el futuro para proteger el medio ambiente?

Sí, intentamos reciclar muchas cosas. Reciclamos envases de plástico, botellas y cartón. Si no podemos reciclar algo, intentamos reutilizarlo **para que no acabe**[1] en un vertedero.

Grade 8-9

Creo que tendremos coches eléctricos. También reduciremos la cantidad de basura que producimos y reutilizaremos las cosas más antes de tirarlas.

Tick list:
✓ tenses: present, future present subjunctive
✓ topical vocab, e.g. cartón, vertedero

To improve:
+ explain opinions more
+ more complex connectives e.g. sin embargo

*Answer these questions in **Spanish**. Talk for **2** minutes.*

- ¿Qué hay en la foto?
- ¿Podríamos hacer más para salvar el planeta?

[1]so that it doesn't end up

- ¿Crees que es importante reciclar?   *[10 marks]*

Global Events

Covering everything from music festivals to hard-hitting campaigns, global events is a pretty wide topic. Use this page to make sure you're well prepared for anything that might come up in the exam.

Los eventos internacionales — *International events*

asistir a	*to attend*
el evento	*event*
la campaña	*campaign*
recaudar dinero	*to raise money*
a beneficio de	*in aid of*
la organización caritativa	*charitable organisation*
el festival (de música)	*(music) festival*
los Juegos Olímpicos	*Olympic Games*
el Mundial	*World Cup (football)*

Grammar — capital letters

Just as in English, there are some nouns which have <u>capital letters</u> in Spanish, <u>wherever in the sentence</u> they come, like the <u>Olympic Games</u> and the <u>World Cup</u> — 'los <u>Juegos Olímpicos</u>' and 'el <u>Mundial</u>'.

Sometimes you might see '<u>mundial</u>' with a lower case '<u>m</u>' — in this case, it's an adjective meaning '<u>worldwide</u>' or '<u>global</u>'.

Question

¿Has asistido a algún evento internacional?
Have you attended any international events?

Simple Answer

No, pero me gustaría asistir a los Juegos Olímpicos.
No, but I would like to attend the Olympic Games.

Sí, fui a un festival de música rock en Escocia.
Yes, I went to a rock music festival in Scotland.

Extended Answer

El año pasado fui a Benicàssim para un festival internacional de música. Atrae a gente de muchos países.
Last year I went to Benicàssim for an international music festival. It attracts people from all around the world.

No, pero planeamos ir al próximo Mundial. Habrá un ambiente fenomenal.
No, but we're planning to go to the next World Cup. There will be a great atmosphere.

Las campañas mundiales — *Global campaigns*

Las campañas mundiales nos enseñan sobre los problemas del mundo.

Global campaigns teach us about the world's problems. ← *the importance of working together* — la importancia de trabajar juntos

Lo malo de las campañas es que cuando terminan, mucha gente se olvide de ellas rápidamente. Es difícil cambiar el mundo para siempre.

The bad thing about campaigns is that when they finish, many people forget about them quickly. It's difficult to change the world permanently. ← *people's behaviour* — el comportamiento de la gente

Dedicar días especiales a las campañas mundiales es una buena manera de recaudar dinero y cambiar el mundo.

Dedicating special days to global campaigns is a good way of raising money and changing the world. ← *attracting people's attention* — llamar la atención de la gente

---

 What do we want? More revision! When do we want it? Now!

*Translate this text into **Spanish**. [12 marks]*

> This year, we have worked with a charity which helps disadvantaged children in Asia. We organised a concert and we wrote to some singers to ask them if they would support us. Three of them came and everyone had a good time. In the future, I would love to go to the World Cup. I think it would be really fun.

Section 8 — Lifestyle

Healthy Living

Time for a whole page about eating well, keeping fit and staying healthy. Pass the biscuits, then.

¿Te mantienes en forma? — *Do you keep fit?*

mantenerse en forma	*to keep fit / in shape*	entrenar(se)	*to train*	activo/a	*active*
el ejercicio (físico)	*(physical) exercise*	equilibrado/a	*balanced*	la salud	*health*
el entrenamiento	*training*	estar en forma	*to be fit*	saludable	*healthy*

Question

¿Es importante mantenerse en forma?

Is it important to keep fit?

Grammar — reflexive verbs

'Mantenerse' and 'entrenarse' are reflexive verbs. Check p.92 for a reminder of how to form them.

Simple Answer

Sí, creo que es importante entrenarse y comer bien.

Yes, I think it's important to train and to eat well.

Extended Answer

Diría que es importante entrenarse, pero no tengo tiempo para hacerlo todos los días. Voy al gimnasio dos veces a la semana para mantenerme en forma. Para mí, es importante elegir comida saludable también.

I would say that it's important to train, but I don't have time to do it every day. I go to the gym twice a week to keep myself in shape. For me, it's important to choose healthy food too.

Una vida sana — *A healthy life*

Intento comer una dieta equilibrada todos los días.

I try to eat a balanced diet every day. ← *to avoid junk food —* evitar la comida basura

Para mantenerme en forma, juego al tenis dos veces a la semana.

To keep fit, I play tennis twice a week. ← *I do exercise almost every day —* hago ejercicio casi todos los días

drinking two litres of water every day — beber dos litros de agua todos los días

Vale la pena comer menos comida rápida y más verduras.

It's worth eating less fast food and more vegetables. ←

Para mí, es importante dormir al menos ocho horas.

For me, it's important to sleep for at least eight hours. ← *to relax a bit after school —* relajarme un poco después del colegio

WRITING — *Time to give your Spanish a workout...*

Selina has written an article about healthy living.

La salud es muy importante para mí. Voy al colegio a pie todos los días, y hago deporte tres veces a la semana. Normalmente como bien — tengo una dieta equilibrada. Recientemente he aprendido a cocinar y me encanta la comida saludable. Además es **un buen consejo**[1] beber agua en vez de **bebidas gaseosas**[2] porque contienen mucho azúcar, lo que puede llevar a problemas con los dientes. Para evitar **el estrés**[3], se debe hacer algo que te relaje todos los días. Se puede hacer ejercicio físico o escuchar música o **sencillamente**[4] hablar con tu familia. Por último, es una buena idea acostarte temprano.

Grade 8-9

[1] a good piece of advice
[2] fizzy drinks
[3] stress
[4] simply

Tick list:
- ✓ tenses: present, perfect, subjunctive
- ✓ use of impersonal verbs
- ✓ good topical vocab and time phrases

To improve:
+ give reasons for opinions

Escribe aproximadamente **90** palabras en **español** para una revista. Menciona:

- *lo que haces para mantenerte en forma;*
- *si tienes una dieta equilibrada;*
- *si tienes una vida más o menos sana que hace cinco años;*
- *dos cosas que podrías hacer para llevar una vida más sana* [16 marks]

Unhealthy Living

You'll also need to be able to talk about drinking and smoking in your exams — what joy...

Una vida malsana — *An unhealthy life*

el cigarrillo	*cigarette*	el fumador (pasivo)	*(passive) smoker*
fumar	*to smoke*	el tabaquismo	*addiction to tobacco*
el humo	*smoke*	el síndrome de abstinencia	*withdrawal symptoms*
oler	*to smell*	la droga blanda / dura	*soft / hard drug*
los pulmones	*lungs*	el sobrepeso	*obesity*
respirar	*to breathe*	borracho/a	*drunk*
hacer daño	*to harm*	emborracharse	*to get drunk*
cansarse	*to get tired*	el botellón	*drinking party in the street*

Question

¿Qué piensas de los cigarrillos?
What do you think of cigarettes?

Simple Answer

Los cigarrillos son peligrosos porque es difícil dejar de fumar.
Cigarettes are dangerous because it's difficult to stop smoking.

Grammar — to stop ...ing

To say '<u>to stop ...ing</u>', use '<u>dejar de</u>' followed by the <u>infinitive</u>.

Quiero <u>dejar de fumar</u>.
I want <u>to stop smoking</u>.

Extended Answer

Estoy convencido/a de que los cigarrillos perjudican la salud. Incluso cuando una persona ha dejado de fumar, los cigarrillos causan una variedad de problemas debido al síndrome de abstinencia.
I am convinced that cigarettes damage your health. Even when a person has stopped smoking, cigarettes cause a variety of problems due to withdrawal symptoms.

No quiero probar las drogas porque son peligrosas.

I don't want to try drugs because they are dangerous.

to smoke because it smells really horrible — fumar porque huele fatal
'<u>Oler</u>' (*to smell*) is an <u>irregular</u> verb.

Una vez, me emborraché, pero no me gustó.

Once, I got drunk, but I didn't like it.

I went to a drinking party in the street — fui a un botellón

No se puede fumar en espacios públicos.

You can't smoke in public spaces.

buy cigarettes if you're under 18 — comprar cigarrillos si tienes menos de 18 años

---

 SPEAKING *Last night, I had four and a half pints (of tea)...*

Have a look at Karima's answer to this question.

¿Piensas que el alcohol es peligroso?

Desde mi punto de vista, no hay ningún problema si alguien quiere beber una cerveza o un poco de vino. A mis padres les gusta probar vinos de varios países y no se emborrachan. Sin embargo, creo que hay problemas con el alcohol cuando los jóvenes se emborrachan sin pensar en las consecuencias. Es peligroso porque no saben ni dónde están ni cuánto han bebido. Hace unos meses, mi amigo bebió demasiado y tuvo que ir al hospital. Es muy irresponsable beber tanto alcohol.

Grade 8-9

Tick list:
✓ tenses: present, preterite
✓ good use of quantifiers
✓ lots of opinions

To improve:
+ include another tense e.g. future
+ use more topical vocab

Now answer the following questions.
Try to speak for about 2 minutes. [10 marks]

- ¿Qué piensas de las drogas?
- ¿Piensas que el alcohol es más peligroso que las drogas? ¿Por qué?
- ¿Qué le dirías a un joven que toma drogas?

Illnesses

Talking about feeling ill might put you off your lunch, but it'll be well worth it if it comes up in your exam.

Las enfermedades — *Illnesses*

encontrarse / sentirse mal	*to feel ill*	doler	*to hurt*	el cerebro	*brain*
encontrarse / estar enfermo/a	*to be ill*	el dolor	*pain*	el ataque cardíaco	*heart attack*
mejorarse	*to get better*	el cuerpo	*body*	el estrés	*stress*
los primeros auxilios	*first aid*	el corazón	*heart*	el sida	*AIDS*
tener dolor (de)...	*to have a pain (in)...*	el hígado	*liver*	seropositivo/a	*HIV-positive*

Question

¿Cómo te sientes?
How do you feel?

Simple Answer

Me duele la garganta.
My throat hurts.

Poor Eric was feeling even greener than normal.

Extended Answer

Me duelen el pie y el brazo, y tengo dolor de espalda.
My foot and arm hurt, and I have backache.

Grammar — 'doler' — to hurt

'Doler' works in a similar way to 'gustar' — to say what's hurting you, you need to use an indirect object pronoun (see p.77) before the verb.
You also need to add an 'n' in the plural.

Me duele la pierna. *My leg hurts.* — Literally, 'the leg hurts me'.
Me duelen los pies. *My feet hurt.*

Le duelen el brazo y la mano. *His / her arm and hand hurt.*

You also need to remember that 'doler' is a radical-changing verb. See p.84.

Necesito ir al médico — *I need to go to the doctor*

Hace un mes, me encontré enfermo y tuve que ir al médico.
A month ago, I felt ill and I had to go to the doctor.
the doctor gave me a prescription — el médico me dio una receta

De niño, tenía muchos problemas respiratorios.
As a child, I had a lot of respiratory problems.
problems with my liver — problemas con el hígado

Creo que todos deberían hacer un curso de primeros auxilios.
I think everyone should do a first aid course.
learn about what you should do if someone has a heart attack — aprender lo que se debe hacer si alguien tiene un ataque cardíaco

El sida es un problema muy grave en algunos países.
AIDS is a very serious problem in some countries.
The lack of doctors — La falta de médicos

Muchos jóvenes se preocupan por su peso y su apariencia.
Many young people worry about their weight and their appearance.
their exams, which causes a lot of stress — sus exámenes, lo que causa mucho estrés

A practice translation — just what the doctor ordered...

Translate this text into **English**. [9 marks]

Me siento muy mal. La semana pasada, fui al campo, pero desafortunadamente estaba lloviendo y no había traído mi paraguas. Me duele muchísimo la garganta y apenas puedo hablar. He tenido que beber muchos líquidos durante unos días y no tengo ganas de comer. Tendré que ir al médico si no me mejoro pronto. Lo peor es que si todavía estoy enfermo el sábado, no podré ir a la fiesta de mi amigo.

Where to Go

Grab some sun cream and pack your suitcase because you're off on holiday...

Los países y las nacionalidades — *Countries and nationalities*

España	*Spain*	español	*Spanish*
Inglaterra	*England*	inglés	*English*
Escocia	*Scotland*	escocés	*Scottish*
Gales	*Wales*	galés	*Welsh*
Irlanda	*Ireland*	irlandés	*Irish*
Irlanda del Norte	*Northern Ireland*	norirlandés	*Northern Irish*
Gran Bretaña	*Great Britain*	británico	*British*
Francia	*France*	francés	*French*
Alemania	*Germany*	alemán	*German*
Portugal	*Portugal*	portugués	*Portuguese*
Italia	*Italy*	italiano	*Italian*
Grecia	*Greece*	griego	*Greek*
Europa	*Europe*	europeo	*European*

los Estados Unidos	*United States*
Canadá	*Canada*
la India	*India*
Australia	*Australia*
Rusia	*Russia*
Brasil	*Brazil*
México	*Mexico*
Argentina	*Argentina*
Perú	*Peru*
Chile	*Chile*
Colombia	*Colombia*
Cuba	*Cuba*

Mi padre es medio irlandés, así que vamos de vacaciones a Irlanda a menudo.

My father is half Irish, so we often go on holiday to Ireland.

Mi padre es griego y solía ir a Grecia para quedarme con mi familia.

My father is Greek and I used to go to Greece to stay with my family.

Luisa fue a Londres el año pasado y le gustó mucho la comida británica.

Luisa went to London last year and she really liked British food.

Grammar — nationalities

Nationalities are <u>adjectives</u> — some have an <u>accent</u> when they're used in the <u>masculine singular</u> form, but drop the accent and add 'a' in the <u>feminine</u> form.

ingl<u>és</u> (m., sing.) — **ingl<u>esa</u>** (f., sing.)
ingl<u>eses</u> (m., pl.) — **ingl<u>esas</u>** (f., pl.)

Las chicas <u>son inglesas</u>.
The girls <u>are English</u>.

Remember — always use the verb '<u>ser</u>' with nationalities (p.85).

Question	**Simple Answer**	**Extended Answer**
¿Adónde quisiera ir de vacaciones?	Quisiera ir al norte de España.	Me gustaría ir al norte de España porque mi tía nació en Asturias. Quisiera visitar el pueblo donde vivía.
Where would you like to go on holiday?	*I would like to go to the north of Spain.*	*I would like to go to the north of Spain because my aunt was born in Asturias. I would like to visit the town where she used to live.*

 READING ***This page about countries will have you going places...***

Arturo has written a leaflet to help promote his region.

¡Ven a visitar la región bellísima de Galicia! Está situada en la costa del Océano Atlántico en el norte de España. Aquí se puede conocer las ciudades famosas de Vigo, Pontevedra, Ourense, o Santiago de Compostela, que es más conocida por su catedral y sus **peregrinaciones**[1] todos los años. ¡Hay tantas cosas que hacer! Por ejemplo, se puede **alquilar**[2] un barco en Pontevedra, explorar las calles antiguas de Vigo, o nadar en uno de los **ríos**[3] en Ourense!

[1]pilgrimages   [2]to rent, hire   [3]rivers

Lee este texto, y luego contesta a las preguntas en **español**.

e.g. ¿Qué región se menciona?   ***Galicia.***

1. ¿Dónde está Galicia? Da dos detalles. [2]

2. ¿Por qué es la ciudad de Santiago de Compostela famosa? Da dos razones. [2]

3. ¿Qué se puede hacer en Ourense? [1]

Accommodation

So you've chosen which country you're going to visit — now all you need is somewhere to stay...

Busco alojamiento... — *I'm looking for accommodation...*

alojarse / quedarse	*to stay*	las instalaciones	*facilities*
el albergue juvenil	*youth hostel*	media pensión	*half board*
la pensión	*boarding house (B&B)*	pensión completa	*full board*
el parador	*state-owned hotel*	la habitación doble	*double room*
(irse de) camping	*(to go) camping*	la habitación individual	*single room*
la tienda	*tent*	la cama de matrimonio	*double bed*
el crucero	*cruise*	el aire acondicionado	*air-conditioning*

Juliet was desperate for a room with a balcony...

Quisiera quedarme aquí cuatro noches.

I would like to stay here for four nights.

a room with a balcony — una habitación con balcón

Siempre nos quedamos en una pensión.

We always stay in a boarding house.

a luxury hotel — un hotel de lujo

Es esencial encontrar una habitación que tenga aire acondicionado.

It's essential to find a room that has air-conditioning.

that has a bathroom — que tenga cuarto de baño

Question	**Simple Answer**	**Extended Answer**
¿Qué tipo de habitación quisiera usted?	Quisiera una habitación con vista al mar.	Somos una familia de tres, así que quisiéramos dos habitaciones — una individual y una doble.
What type of room would you like?	*I would like a room with a sea view.*	*We are a family of three, so we would like two rooms — a single and a double.*

Quisiera alojarme en... — *I would like to stay in...*

Mi amigo/a quisiera encontrar alojamiento de media pensión.

My friend would like to find half-board accommodation.

full-board — pensión completa

Preferiríamos alojarnos en un parador porque tienen buenas instalaciones.

We would prefer to stay in a state-owned hotel because they have good facilities.

on a campsite because we have a caravan and like nature — en un camping porque tenemos una caravana y nos gusta la naturaleza

Nos gustaría quedarnos en un albergue juvenil para conocer a gente nueva.

We would like to stay in a youth hostel in order to meet new people.

to save money — ahorrar dinero

Yep, 'shop' and 'tent' are both 'la tienda' in Spanish...

TRACK LISTENING 10

Listen to this extract about hotels in Rio de Janeiro from a book by Gorgonio Petano y Mazariegos.

1. How are the hotels in general described?

   A) average   B) fantastic *[1]*

2. How many hotels are mentioned when discussing the best hotels in the city? *[1]*

3. How is the *Hotel de los Extranjeros* described? Choose the two correct adjectives from the list below.

   small   old-fashioned

   modern   strange

   elegant   ugly   *[2]*

4. What do the people of the *Cuerpo Diplomático extranjero* do at the hotel?

   A) eat dinner

   B) live

   C) have meetings   *[1]*

Getting Ready to Go

That holiday won't book itself. Thankfully, there's plenty of vocab here to help you get something sorted.

Reservando unas vacaciones — *Booking a holiday*

la agencia de viajes	*travel agent's*	el folleto	*leaflet*
libre / disponible	*available*	el regreso	*return*
el pasaporte	*passport*	el guía	*guide*
el carnet de conducir	*driving licence*	la guía	*guidebook*
la maleta	*suitcase*	buscar	*to look for*
el equipaje	*luggage*	informarse	*to find out*
la ficha / el formulario	*registration form*	el lugar / sitio	*place*

Grammar — I need...

When talking about the features of something you <u>require</u>, use the <u>subjunctive</u> (p.97).

Busco un hotel grande que <u>tenga</u> una piscina.

I'm looking for a big hotel that <u>has</u> a pool.

Question	**Simple Answer**	**Extended Answer**
¿Estás listo/a para tus vacaciones?	Sí, he hecho mi maleta.	Sí, he hecho mi maleta, pero todavía no he comprado una guía. Necesito una guía que incluya información sobre España e Italia.
Are you ready for your holidays?	*Yes, I have packed my suitcase.*	*Yes, I've packed my suitcase, but I haven't bought a guidebook yet. I need a guidebook that includes information about Spain and Italy.*

¿En qué puedo servirle? — *How can I help you?*

Por favor, ¿puedo reservar la mejor habitación disponible?

Please can I reserve the best room available?

Quisiera ir a un lugar donde pueda nadar.

I would like to go to a place where I can swim.

¿Puede usted darnos unos folletos? Queremos informarnos sobre lo que hay en esta región.

Can you give us some leaflets? We want to find out about what there is in this region.

a room on the ground floor — una habitación en la planta baja

canoe — hacer piragüismo

tell us if there are rooms available — decirnos si hay habitaciones libres

to know what time the museum opens — saber cuándo abre el museo

---

WRITING

You shouldn't have reservations when it comes to booking...

Read the following scene from a Spanish TV show script. A travel agent is speaking to Bea.

Agente de Viajes (AV): Dígame, Señora.

Grade 6-7

Bea: Buenos días. Quisiera reservar unas vacaciones en España pero no sé el mejor lugar para quedarnos. Quiero ir con cuatro amigos.

AV: Bueno. Pues, ¿cuándo quisiera usted venir?

Bea: Preferiríamos ir durante las vacaciones de verano, desde el 3 de agosto hasta el 11 de agosto. Nos gustan las montañas.

AV: Hace buen tiempo durante agosto. Le recomendaría ir a Gijón, en el norte de España, porque se puede visitar la costa y los Picos de Europa, que son estupendos.

Tick list:
✓ tenses: present, imperfect subjunctive, conditional
✓ superlative

To improve:
+ use subjunctive to say what you require
+ include more adjectives
+ use more conjunctions

Escribe un diálogo con un agente de viajes y menciona:

- *el tipo de lugar donde te gustaría ir;*
- *cuándo quieres ir;*
- *qué actividad quieres poder hacer;*
- *que te gustaría alquilar un coche.*

Escribe aproximadamente **90** *palabras en* **español**. *[16 marks]*

How to Get There

Boats, buses, cars, coaches, trains and trams — this page will get you from A to B.

Cómo llegar a tu destino — *How to get to your destination*

el avión	*aeroplane*	el pasajero / viajero	*passenger / traveller*
el aeropuerto	*airport*	hacer transbordo	*to change, transfer*
el vuelo	*flight*	el billete (de ida / de ida y vuelta)	*(single / return) ticket*
el barco	*boat*	la estación (de autobuses / de trenes)	*(bus / train) station*
conducir	*to drive*	el andén	*platform*
la autopista	*motorway*	la red de ferrocarril	*railway network*
el tranvía	*tram*	la estación de servicio	*service station*
el viaje	*journey*	la gasolina (sin plomo)	*(unleaded) petrol*

Preferiría ir a España en avión porque me encuentro mal cuando voy en barco.

I would prefer to go to Spain by plane because I feel ill when I go by boat.

by car because it's cheaper — en coche porque es más barato

Fuimos a la playa a pie ya que está cerca de nuestro hotel.

We went to the beach on foot since it's near our hotel.

by taxi because our feet were hurting — en taxi porque nos dolían los pies

Viajaremos en autobús porque siempre nos perdemos cuando vamos en coche.

We will travel by bus because we always get lost when we go by car.

the airport workers are on strike — los empleados del aeropuerto están en huelga

Is it a boat?
Is it a car? It would appear to be both...

El tren está retrasado — *The train is delayed*

¿A qué hora sale el tranvía?

At what time does the tram leave?

does the train arrive — llega el tren

Necesito reservar un coche. ¿Tengo que rellenar una ficha?

I need to reserve a car. Do I have to fill in a registration form?

have my driving licence with me — tener mi carnet de conducir conmigo

Coge el metro porque hay un atasco en la autopista.

Take the underground because there's a traffic jam on the motorway.

the train has been cancelled — el tren ha sido cancelado

No me importa viajar en autocar, pero prefiero ir en tren porque es más cómodo.

I don't mind travelling by coach, but I prefer to go by train because it's more comfortable.

by plane because it's faster — en avión porque es más rápido

This transport stuff is driving me crazy...

*Translate this text into **English**.* [9 marks]

Mi ciudad tiene varios tipos de transporte. El metro, que abrió en 1924, es muy limpio y rápido. Además, existe una red de tranvías en la que se puede visitar la mayoría de los barrios de la ciudad. Desde el aeropuerto, es posible volar a todas las ciudades importantes de Europa y no está muy lejos del centro. Pronto, van a mejorar la red de autobuses, lo que será fenomenal.

What to Do

Accommodation? Check. Transport? Check. Now the fun can begin...

Hay varias actividades... — *There are various activities...*

la excursión	*trip, excursion*	caminar	*to walk*
el mar	*the sea*	esquiar	*to ski*
bañarse	*to swim*	sacar / hacer fotos	*to take photos*
tomar el sol	*to sunbathe*	el parque de atracciones	*fairground*
broncearse	*to get a tan*	el parque temático	*theme park*
los deportes acuáticos	*water sports*	el recuerdo	*souvenir*

Question

¿Qué actividades hiciste durante tus vacaciones?
What activities did you do during your holiday?

Simple Answer

Fuimos a la playa — fue muy relajante.
We went to the beach — it was very relaxing.

Extended Answer

Pasamos mucho tiempo en la playa porque hacía sol. Me bañé y tomé el sol con mis primos.
We spent a lot of time on the beach because it was sunny. I swam and sunbathed with my cousins.

Grammar — la foto

Watch out for nouns that don't fit the masculine / feminine rule of ending with an '-o' or '-a' (p.66):

la fot**o**   *the photo*
el agu**a**   *the water*

('Water' is actually a feminine noun, but it takes '<u>el</u>' as its article because 'la agua' is too awkward to pronounce.)

Estamos de vacaciones — *We're on holiday*

Para mí, lo importante es encontrar un parque de atracciones.

For me, the important thing is to find a fairground.

> to buy souvenirs — comprar recuerdos
> to go to a museum — visitar un museo

Nos gusta nada más que dar un paseo por las calles.

We like nothing more than to go for a stroll around the streets.

> to try the region's typical food — probar la comida típica de la región

Cuando estoy de vacaciones, suelo sacar muchas fotos.

When I'm on holiday, I usually take lots of photos.

> go on various excursions — hacer varias excursiones

SPEAKING — *So much to do, so little time...*

Tom and his teacher are discussing holiday activities. Look at Tom's response to this question:
¿Te gusta ir de vacaciones a lugares donde se puede practicar deportes acuáticos?

Depende del lugar. Cuando voy a un país donde hace calor, como España, tengo ganas de hacer deportes acuáticos. Voy a ir a **Noruega**[1] el año que viene. Practicaremos el piragüismo, pero pienso que el agua estará muy fría.

Grade 6-7

[1]Norway

Tick list:
✓ tenses: present, immediate future, proper future

To improve:
+ be more descriptive
+ more tenses
+ more topic vocab

*Now answer these questions in **Spanish**. Try to talk for **2** minutes. [10 marks]*

- *¿Qué hay en la foto?*
- *¿Cómo fueron tus últimas vacaciones?*
- *¿Cuáles serían tus vacaciones ideales?*

Practical Stuff

Picture this: you're on a motorway in Spain and suddenly your car breaks down — very inconvenient. But help is at hand... after reading this page, you'll be able to sort it out in Spanish.

¡He perdido mi billete! — *I've lost my ticket!*

la comisaría	*police station*
el monedero	*purse*
la cartera	*wallet*
robar	*to steal / rob*
el garaje	*garage*
la gasolina	*petrol*
la avería	*breakdown*
el desvío	*diversion*
el cajero automático	*ATM / cashpoint*
confirmar	*to validate (ticket)*

Question

¿Usted ha perdido su billete?
Have you lost your ticket?

Simple Answer

Sí, lo perdí en el andén.
Yes, I lost it on the platform.

Extended Answer

No sé dónde está. Lo he buscado por todas partes pero no lo he encontrado.
I don't know where it is. I've looked for it everywhere but I haven't found it.

When you use public transport in Spain, you often have to validate your ticket in a machine before you travel.

Grammar — the perfect tense

Say what you 'have done' using the perfect tense. To make the perfect tense, you need the right form of the verb 'haber' in the present tense for the 'have' bit and the past participle of the verb for the 'done' bit.

He confirmado mi billete.   *I have validated my ticket.*

El coche ha chocado contra un árbol.   *The car has crashed into a tree.*

For more information, have a look at p.89.

Tengo un problema — *I have a problem*

El coche de mi madre tiene una avería. ¿Hay un garaje por aquí?

My mother's car has broken down. Is there a garage around here?

a service station — una estación de servicio

Tengo que ir a la comisaría porque alguien me ha robado la cartera.

I have to go to the police station because someone has stolen my wallet.

I left my keys on the bus — dejé mis llaves en el autobús

Cuando estaba de vacaciones en Francia tuve un accidente y me llevaron al hospital.

When I was on holiday in France I had an accident and they took me to hospital.

I broke my arm — me rompí el brazo

WRITING — *Time to confirm your one-way ticket to exam success...*

Gael has written about a problem that occurred last weekend.

El fin de semana pasado estaba viajando a Liverpool en tren cuando **me di cuenta de que**[1] había dejado mi cartera en el andén. Cuando vino **el revisor**[2], le expliqué que no tenía mi billete porque lo había perdido. Yo estaba muy preocupado porque pensé que él no me creería, pero **sonrió**[3] y me dio mi cartera. Alguien lo había encontrado en la estación y **se lo había entregado**[4] al revisor. ¡Qué suerte!

Grade 8-9

[1] I noticed that
[2] the ticket inspector
[3] he smiled
[4] he/she had handed it in

Tick list:
✓ tenses: preterite, imperfect, pluperfect, conditional
✓ good subject-specific vocab
✓ good use of pronouns

To improve:
+ use more varied conjunctions e.g. ya que, por eso

Escriba usted un artículo sobre los problemas que tuvo cuando estaba de vacaciones el año pasado:

Debe incluir los puntos siguientes:

- dónde estaba usted y con quién
- qué le pasó
- cómo usted solucionó el problema
- sus planes de vacaciones para el año que viene.

Escriba aproximadamente **150** palabras en **español**. [32 marks]

School Subjects

School subjects — as if you don't get enough of that at school. However, it's important to learn them and to be able to say what you think about them.

Las asignaturas — *School subjects*

el español	*Spanish*		el dibujo	*art*
el alemán	*German*		el arte dramático	*drama*
el francés	*French*		la música	*music*
el inglés	*English*		las matemáticas	*maths*
las ciencias	*science*		las ciencias económicas	*economics*
la biología	*biology*		el comercio	*business studies*
la química	*chemistry*		la informática	*IT*
la física	*physics*		la cocina	*food technology*
la geografía	*geography*		los trabajos manuales	*handicrafts*
la historia	*history*		la gimnasia	*gymnastics*
la religión	*RE*		la educación física	*PE*

The thought of so many different subjects gave David a real fright.

Mi asignatura preferida es... — *My favourite subject is...*

Question	Simple Answer	Extended Answer
¿Cuál es tu asignatura preferida? *What's your favourite subject?*	Mi asignatura preferida es la música. Me encanta tocar la guitarra. *My favourite subject is music. I love to play the guitar.*	El español es mi asignatura preferida ya que es muy interesante. Es útil también porque espero ir a España el verano que viene. *Spanish is my favourite subject as it's very interesting. It's useful too because I hope to go to Spain next summer.*

Me encanta la historia. Es interesante aprender sobre el pasado.

I love history. It's interesting to learn about the past.

Nos gustan mucho las matemáticas. Es fascinante trabajar con números.

We really like maths. It's fascinating to work with numbers.

Miguel odia la química porque es tan difícil.

Miguel hates chemistry because it's so difficult.

I hate — Odio

boring — aburrido

useful — útil

José finds art awful — José encuentra el dibujo horrible

WRITING *I'm subjected to school every day...*

Gabriela has written about her school subjects in a chat room.

Generalmente, me gustan mis asignaturas. Me encantan las lenguas porque son divertidas, así que **opté por estudiar**[1] el francés y el inglés este **curso**[2]. Sin embargo, lo malo es que son difíciles. Por otro lado, me fastidia la profesora de ciencias porque es demasiado estricta. Pero a decir verdad, mi asignatura preferida es la educación física porque me gusta jugar al baloncesto.

Grade 6-7

[1] I chose to study [2] school year

Tick list
✓ adjectives agree
✓ range of vocabulary and conjunctions

To improve...
+ use different tenses
+ more complex adjectives
+ extend opinions

Escribe tu propio comentario. Menciona:
- *qué asignaturas (no) te gustan, y por qué;*
- *qué asignaturas quieres estudiar el curso que viene, y por qué.*

*Escribe aproximadamente **150** palabras en **español**.*
Responde a los dos aspectos de la pregunta. [32 marks]

School Routine

Same old routine, day in, day out. At least routines are quite easy to talk about in the exam...

Mi rutina escolar — *My school routine*

el trimestre	*(school) term*
la agenda	*diary*
el horario	*timetable*
la clase	*lesson*
el recreo	*break*

Grammar — telling the time

If you're saying what time something is at, remember to put '<u>a</u>' first.
La hora de comer es <u>a la una</u>. *Lunchtime is <u>at one o'clock</u>.*
For more about time, see p.2.

Mi colegio empieza a las nueve, y a las nueve y cinco, el profesor pasa la lista.

My school starts at nine o'clock, and at five past nine, the teacher calls the register.

> at twenty to nine — a las nueve menos veinte

> we go to the assembly room — vamos al salón de actos

Tengo cinco clases por día, y cada clase dura cuarenta minutos. El día escolar termina a las tres y media.

I have five lessons a day, and each lesson lasts forty minutes. The school day finishes at half past three.

> I return home at quarter past three. — Vuelvo a casa a las tres y cuarto.

¿Qué haces durante el recreo? —*What do you do during break?*

Durante el recreo, juego al fútbol con mis amigos, y a la hora de comer, vamos a la cantina para almorzar.

During break, I play football with my friends, and at lunchtime, we go to the canteen to eat lunch.

> I chat — charlo

> we sit outside and eat lunch — nos sentamos afuera y almorzamos

Prefiero pasar el recreo en la biblioteca porque mis amigos van al club de tenis, que a mí no me gusta.

I prefer to spend my break in the library because my friends go to tennis club, which I don't like.

> go to gymnastics club — van al club de gimnasia

En mi mochila, pongo... — *In my rucksack, I put...*

el bolígrafo	*pen*	la regla	*ruler*	el cuaderno	*exercise book*
el lápiz	*pencil*	las tijeras	*scissors*	el libro	*book*

Eduardo was ready for whatever maths could throw at him.

En mi mochila, hay un estuche.

In my rucksack, there's a pencil case.

Se me ha olvidado mi lápiz.
¿Me puedes prestar un boli por favor?

I have forgotten my pencil.
Can you lend me a pen please?

> In Spanish, '<u>bolígrafo</u>' (*pen*) is often shortened to '<u>boli</u>'.

TRACK LISTENING 11

Una clase — *let that be a lesson to you...*

Juan y Marta hablan de su horario. Completa la tabla con las asignaturas en **español**. *[3 marks]*

día / hora	08.30 — 09.20	09.20 — 10.10	10.10 — 10.30	10.30 — 11.20
lunes	las matemáticas	1)	RECREO	el inglés
martes	las ciencias	el francés	RECREO	2)
miércoles	los trabajos manuales	el español	RECREO	3)

School Life

Now's your chance to talk about what your school's like and what it has and hasn't got.

¿A qué tipo de colegio asistes? — *What type of school do you attend?*

el instituto	*secondary school*	mixto	*mixed*	privado	*private*
la escuela primaria	*primary school*	religioso	*religious*	público	*state*

Mi instituto es un colegio mixto. Está a unos cinco kilómetros de mi casa.

Hay quinientos alumnos en mi instituto y llevamos uniforme.

Soy alumno/a aquí desde hace tres años. Me gusta este colegio y me llevo bien con los profesores.

My school is a mixed school. It's about five kilometres from my house.

There are 500 students at my school and we wear a uniform.

I've been a student here for 3 years. I like this school and I get on well with the teachers.

modern state — público y moderno

about 400 — unos cuatrocientos
950 — novecientos cincuenta

we don't have to wear a uniform — no tenemos que llevar uniforme

the teachers are very nice — los profesores son muy simpáticos

¿Cómo es tu instituto? — *What's your school like?*

las instalaciones	*facilities*	el taller	*workshop*
el aula (f)	*classroom*	el campo de deportes	*sports field*
la pizarra interactiva	*smart board*	el gimnasio	*gymnasium*
la sala de profesores	*staffroom*	los vestuarios	*changing rooms*

Grammar — el aula

'Aula' is feminine, but it uses 'el' when it's singular. Any adjectives must be in the feminine form.

El aula es estupenda.
The classroom is fantastic.

Mi colegio tiene un campo de deportes grande donde podemos jugar al hockey.

En general, mi instituto es muy moderno. Encuentro las aulas maravillosas porque tienen pizarras interactivas.

My school has a big sports field where we can play hockey.

In general, my school is very modern. I find the classrooms marvellous because they have smart boards.

a small gym where we can keep fit — un gimnasio pequeño donde podemos mantenernos en forma

quite old — bastante antiguo

horrible because the heating doesn't work well — horribles porque la calefacción no funciona bien

READING — *My school just had lots of fish...*

Read what Sofía has written about her school below. Then in the table, indicate the three sentences that are true by ticking the correct boxes. [3 marks]

¡Hola! Soy Sofía. Te escribo para hablarte de mi colegio. Está situado en Madrid a unos siete kilómetros de mi casa y hay ochocientos alumnos. Normalmente, mi padre me lleva en coche al colegio. Tengo suerte porque puedo coger el metro también — es muy eficaz si hay atascos en las carreteras. El día empieza a las ocho menos diez. Las clases duran unos cuarenta minutos y tengo un recreo de quince minutos. El descanso para comer empieza a la una y media y dura una hora y media. Generalmente las instalaciones en mi colegio son modernas, pero lo malo es el gimnasio. Es muy sucio. ¡Qué horror! ¿Cómo es tu colegio? ¡Adiós!

1. Sofía usually takes the underground to school.	
2. Sofía is positive about the underground.	
3. Sofía is negative about the underground.	
4. The facilities are old.	
5. The facilities are modern.	
6. Sofía dislikes the gym.	

School Pressures

A chance to vent your frustrations now — should be refreshing after all this stressful revision...

Las reglas — *The rules*

(no) hay que...	*you (don't) have to...*
(no) tienes que...	*you (don't) have to...*
(no) se debe...	*you must (not)...*
(no) es obligatorio...	*it's (not) compulsory...*
(no) deberías...	*you shouldn't...*

No deberías **comer chicle ni beber bebidas gaseosas.** *You shouldn't eat chewing gum nor drink fizzy drinks.*

Hay que **levantar la mano antes de hablar.** *You have to raise your hand before speaking.*

Estoy muy estresado/a por... — *I'm really stressed about...*

estresante	*stressful*	el éxito	*success*	suspender	*to fail*	el apoyo	*support*
la presión	*pressure*	aprobar	*to pass*	repasar	*to revise*	apoyar	*to support*

La vida escolar es estresante. Hay mucha presión y tengo muchos deberes. Afortunadamente, los profesores apoyan a los alumnos estresados.

School life is stressful. There's a lot of pressure and I have a lot of homework. Luckily, the teachers support stressed students.

I'm afraid of failing my exams — tengo miedo de suspender mis exámenes

get good marks — saco buenas notas

Si no saco sobresalientes, no podré ir a la universidad.

If I don't get outstanding marks, I won't be able to go to university.

pass this exam — apruebo este examen

El acoso (escolar) — *(School) bullying*

El acoso es un problema muy grave en mi colegio.

Bullying is a serious problem in my school.

Bullying doesn't happen much — La intimidación no ocurre mucho

El mal comportamiento arruina las clases.

Bad behaviour ruins lessons.

is a distraction — es una distracción

SPEAKING — *It's compulsory to answer these questions carefully...*

Have a look at this photo question. Use the example to give you some inspiration.

¿Hay mucha violencia en los institutos hoy en día?

En mi instituto, la violencia no es un problema. Si la conducta de un alumno es peligrosa, el director **castigará**[1] a ese alumno. Pero a mi modo de ver, muchos institutos tienen problemas con peleas y **falta de respeto**[2]. Sería difícil estudiar en esos colegios.

Grade 6-7

[1] will punish [2] lack of respect

Tick list:
✓ tenses: present, future, conditional
✓ varied vocab

To improve:
+ more opinion phrases with explanations
+ use past tenses, e.g. preterite and imperfect

*Now answer these questions — talk for about **3** minutes.*

- *¿Qué hay en la foto?*
- *¿Cómo era la vida escolar en tu escuela primaria?*
- *¿Hay mucha violencia en los institutos hoy en día?*
  [15 marks]

After you've answered the questions you've prepared, your teacher will ask you some questions that you haven't seen. See p.100 for more tips for doing well in the speaking exam.

School Events

Every year, schools up and down the country hold exciting events, like trips and... err... parents' evenings.

¿Qué pasa en tu colegio? — *What's happening at your school?*

participar en	*to participate in*	la vuelta al colegio	*first day back at school*
la excursión (del colegio)	*(school) trip*	el autobús escolar	*school bus*
el intercambio	*exchange*	el grupo escolar	*school group*
(al) extranjero	*abroad*	la reunión de padres	*parents' evening*

Question

¿Qué pasa en tu colegio esta semana?
What's happening at your school this week?

Simple Answer

Esta semana hay una excursión del colegio al campo.
This week there's a school trip to the countryside.

Extended Answer

Esta semana hay reunión de padres. Mis padres hablarán con mis profesores sobre mi rendimiento escolar.
This week it's parents' evening. My parents will talk to my teachers about my academic achievement.

Grammar — saying what's happening

In Spanish, you can use the normal present tense to say things like 'I am doing' as well as 'I do'.

You only have to use the present continuous form (see p.93) when you really want to emphasise that something's happening right now.

Participo en un intercambio.
I'm participating in an exchange (soon).

Estoy participando en un intercambio.
I'm participating in an exchange (right now).

El año pasado hice un intercambio al extranjero. Me quedé con Miguel durante una semana y ahora somos amigos por correspondencia.

Last year I did an exchange trip abroad. I stayed with Miguel for a week and now we're penfriends.

I participated in — participé en

Pronto haremos una excursión a un museo. Ya que somos un grupo escolar, nos darán una visita guiada.

Soon we will go on a trip to a museum. As we're a school group, they'll give us a guided tour.

a discount — un descuento

A veces hay ventas de pasteles durante el recreo. Damos todo el dinero a organizaciones caritativas.

Sometimes there are cake sales during break time. We give all the money to charities.

there is a fancy dress day — hay un día de disfraces

Todos los años el instituto realiza una entrega de premios. Los profesores dan premios a los alumnos que han sacado las mejores notas.

Every year the school holds a prize-giving ceremony. The teachers give prizes to the students who have got the best marks.

who have tried the hardest — que se han esforzado más

Prepare for any event-uality with this question...

Yann ha escrito una carta sobre un evento en su colegio.

El 3 de septiembre, mi instituto **cumplirá setenta años**[1] y habrá una gran fiesta para toda la comunidad. Cualquier persona que asistía al instituto podrá venir para celebrar con nosotros. Mis amigos van a hacer un pastel, y yo voy a ayudar con las visitas guiadas. Lo mejor es que han cancelado las clases ese día. ¡Qué suerte!

Grade 6-7

[1]will be seventy years old

Tick list
✓ tenses: present, imperfect, perfect and future
✓ 'lo' + adjective
✓ good use of exclamation

To improve...
+ use more varied conjunctions
+ add more opinions

Ahora escribe una carta sobre una excursión del colegio reciente. Debes incluir los puntos siguientes:
• lo que hiciste
• lo bueno de las excursiones
• alguna desventaja de las excursiones
• una excursión del colegio que te gustaría hacer

Escribe aproximadamente **90** palabras en **español**. [16 marks]

Education Post-16

It might not be something you've thought a lot about, but your future plans could come up in the exam. Learn this page and it might even give you some ideas...

Cuando tenga 16 años... — *When I'm 16...*

el/la aprendiz/a	*apprentice*	la academia	*academy, school post-16 (for certain careers)*
la experiencia laboral	*work experience*		
la práctica	*work placement*	las perspectivas	*employment*
hacer el bachillerato	*to do A-levels*	laborales	*prospects*

Apparently this wasn't what Mrs Adams meant when she told me to look for some work experience...

Quiero seguir mis estudios y hacer el bachillerato **porque espero** estudiar Derecho en la universidad.

I want to continue my studies and do my A-levels because I hope to study law at university.

Para mejorar nuestras perspectivas laborales, el profesor **recomienda que** busquemos experiencia laboral.

In order to improve our employment prospects, the teacher recommends that we look for work experience.

to do a work placement — hacer una práctica

to become a plumber's apprentice — hacerme aprendiz/a de fontanero

to get a degree — conseguir un título

You often need to use the subjunctive when someone wants someone else to do something. See p.97.

Después del bachillerato... — *After A-levels...*

el año libre / sabático	*gap year*	la carrera	*career, profession*
la formación (profesional)	*vocational training*	calificado	*competent, skilled*

Question
¿Qué quieres hacer después de terminar el bachillerato?
What do you want to do after you finish your A-levels?

Simple Answer
Después de terminar el bachillerato, quiero empezar a trabajar.
After finishing my A-levels, I want to start working.

Extended Answer
Voy a dedicarme a mis estudios porque quiero ser traductor/a. Si quiero ser traductor/a calificado/a, tendré que estudiar mucho.
I'm going to focus on my studies because I want to be a translator. If I want to be a competent translator, I'll have to study a lot.

Quisiera tomarme un año sabático, **luego** me gustaría ir a la universidad porque quiero hacer carrera en medicina.

I would like to take a gap year, then I would like to go to university because I want to have a career in medicine.

Me gustaría ser electricista, **pero primero,** necesito formación profesional.

I would like to be an electrician, but first, I need vocational training.

Grammar — conditional

To talk about something that could, should or would happen, use the conditional tense (p.91).

Me gustaría estudiar música.
I would like to study music.

Remember that 'quisiera' can be used to say 'I would like' too (p.91).

After school I want to have my tea and watch Hollyoaks...

Translate this text into **Spanish**. [12 marks]

When I was young, I thought I would like to be a teacher. My parents are teachers and although they find the work interesting, my father says that it is quite stressful. Now I have decided that I'm going to go to an academy to study photography. I would love to take photos of weddings!

Career Choices and Ambitions

All this revising is hard work and now you've got another job to do — learn about careers.

Los empleos — *Jobs*

el/la empleado/a	*employee*	el/la fontanero/a	*plumber*	
el/la abogado/a	*lawyer*	el/la ingeniero/a	*engineer*	
el/la arquitecto/a	*architect*	el/la mecánico/a	*mechanic*	
el/la bombero/a	*firefighter*	el/la médico/a	*doctor*	
el/la cocinero/a	*chef*	el/la oficial de policía	*police officer*	
el/la constructor/a	*builder*	el/la periodista	*journalist*	
el/la contable	*accountant*	el/la veterinario/a	*vet*	
el/la enfermero/a	*nurse*	estar en paro	*to be unemployed*	

> **Grammar** — I'm a...
>
> When talking about jobs, <u>usually</u> you <u>don't</u> need the article '<u>un(a)</u>' (p.67).
>
> **Quiero ser funcionario/a**
> *I want to be a civil servant*.
>
> You <u>do</u> though if you use an <u>adjective</u>.
>
> **Soy <u>un(a) buen(a)</u> técnico/a.**
> *I'm <u>a good</u> technician*.

a tiempo completo	*full-time*	ganar	*to earn*	
a tiempo parcial	*part-time*	el sueldo	*salary*	

> For more jobs, have a look at the vocab list starting on p.116.

Mi empleo ideal sería periodista. Trabajaría en una oficina y escribiría artículos interesantes.

My ideal job would be a journalist. I would work in an office and I would write interesting articles.

full time — a tiempo completo

Para mí, es importante tener un empleo desafiante.

For me, it's important to have a challenging job.

stimulating — estimulante
rewarding — gratificante
varied — variado

Mi madre es enfermera. Es un trabajo difícil porque tiene mucha responsabilidad, pero a ella le encanta ayudar a la gente.

My mother is a nurse. It's a difficult job because she has a lot of responsibility, but she loves helping people.

there's a lot of pressure — hay mucha presión

Tengo un empleo a tiempo parcial — *I have a part-time job*

Soy dependiente en una tienda de ropa. Lo mejor es charlar con los clientes.

I'm a shop assistant in a clothes shop. The best thing is chatting with customers.

waiter/waitress in a restaurant — camarero/a en un restaurante

that there are discounts for employees — que hay descuentos para los empleados

No tengo empleo a tiempo parcial, pero a veces cuido a mi hermana y recibo paga.

I don't have a part-time job, but sometimes I look after my sister and I receive pocket money.

Trabajo en una peluquería los sábados. Me gusta el empleo pero no gano mucho.

I work in a hairdresser's on Saturdays. I like the job, but I don't earn a lot.

I hope to find another job and earn more money — espero conseguir otro empleo y ganar más dinero

Before you go careering into the next section...

Translate this text into **English**. [9 marks]

> — Cuando yo tenía quince años, era difícil conseguir un trabajo — dijo mi madre.
>
> — Sí, pero mucho ha cambiado en los últimos años — le respondí. — Quiero ser abogada. Ganan un buen sueldo y me gustaría ayudar a la gente. ¡El trabajo sería tan variado!

Languages for the Future

There's life beyond GCSE — your Spanish might help you make friends, or even land you a job. Bullseye.

¿Hablas otro idioma? — *Do you speak another language?*

la lengua / el idioma	*language*
conocer a alguien	*to get to know someone*
viajar por el mundo	*to travel the world*
expresarse	*to express yourself*
comunicarse	*to communicate*
traducir	*to translate*
pronunciar	*to pronounce*
el/la auxiliar de lengua	*foreign language assistant*
el laboratorio de idiomas	*language lab*

Grammar — articles + languages

When a <u>language</u> is the <u>subject</u> of the sentence, you need to <u>use the definite article</u> with it.

El español es fácil.   *Spanish is easy.*

However, when you use a language as the <u>object</u> of the verbs '<u>saber</u>', '<u>aprender</u>' or '<u>hablar</u>', you <u>don't</u> need to use the <u>article</u>.

Aprendo árabe.   *I'm learning Arabic.*

Have a look at p.76-77 for a reminder about subjects and objects.

Quiero trabajar por una empresa internacional, así que los idiomas son importantes para mí.

I want to work for an international company, so languages are important to me.

En mi instituto tenemos auxiliares de lenguas. Me parece un trabajo muy divertido. Me gustaría hacer algo parecido en el futuro.

In my school we have foreign language assistants. It seems like a very fun job. I'd like to do something similar in the future.

Voy a viajar por Asia después del bachillerato, así que he aprendido algunas frases útiles para poder comprar cosas y pedir comida.

I'm going to travel around Asia after my A-Levels, so I have learnt some useful phrases so I can buy things and order food.

Aprender una lengua extranjera — *To learn a foreign language*

Question

¿Es importante aprender otro idioma?
Is it important to learn another language?

Simple Answer

Sí, porque no todo el mundo habla inglés.
Yes, because not everyone speaks English.

Extended Answer

Sí, es importante que aprendamos idiomas extranjeros porque vivimos en una sociedad multicultural.
Yes, it's important that we learn foreign languages because we live in a multicultural society.

En mi opinión es una pérdida de tiempo aprender una lengua extranjera. Si necesitas comunicarte en el extranjero, hay aplicaciones que te pueden ayudar.
In my opinion it's a waste of time to learn a foreign language. If you need to communicate abroad, there are apps that can help you.

Whilst in Athens, this guy offered to paint me a vase. At least, I <u>think</u> that's what he said — it was all Greek to me...

 ## I'm always Russian around learning other languages...

Read what David says about the languages he speaks and then answer the questions in English.

Me llamo David y soy **azafato**[1]. Para nosotros es esencial saber por lo menos tres lenguas para poder comunicarnos con los clientes. Aprendí inglés y francés en el instituto, y pronto asistiré a **clases nocturnas**[2] de alemán en una escuela donde hay laboratorios de idiomas. Creo que la parte más difícil para mí será la pronunciación.

[1]flight attendant   [2]evening classes

1. Give one requirement of David's job. [1]
2. What will he do in the near future? [1]
3. What will the venue be like? [1]
4. What does he think will be challenging? [1]

Applying for Jobs

Trawling through job adverts isn't exactly entertaining — but actually getting a job's a pretty good reward.

Solicitar un puesto de trabajo — *To apply for a job*

el anuncio de trabajo	*job advertisement*	las condiciones de empleo	*terms of employment*
la vacante	*vacancy*	las posibilidades de promoción	*promotion prospects*
la carta de solicitud	*application letter*	el sueldo	*salary*
la solicitud	*application form*	bien pagado	*well-paid*
adjuntar	*to attach*	por hora	*per hour*
la entrevista	*interview*	el/la jefe	*boss*

Question

¿Por qué decidió usted solicitar este puesto de trabajo?
Why did you decide to apply for this job?

Simple Answer

Cuando leí el anuncio de trabajo, me interesó mucho.
When I read the job advertisement, it really interested me.

Extended Answer

Es un trabajo bien pagado y las condiciones de empleo me parecen justas. Además, hay buenas posibilidades de promoción.
It's a well-paid job and the terms of employment seem fair to me. Moreover, there are good promotion prospects.

Mi amigo me dijo que había vacantes en su empresa, así que decidí rellenar el formulario y mandarles mi currículum.

My friend told me that there were vacancies in his company, so I decided to fill in the form and send them my CV.

> to write an application letter — escribir una carta de solicitud

La semana que viene tengo una entrevista de trabajo. Tendré que prepararme bien, porque conoceré al director.

Next week I have a job interview. I'll have to prepare myself well because I'll meet the manager.

> it's a very well-paid job — es un trabajo muy bien pagado

Cuando buscas un trabajo, es una buena idea pensar en las condiciones de empleo y el sueldo.

When you're looking for a job, it's a good idea to think about the terms of employment and the salary.

> the skills you have — las habilidades que tienes

 ## I applied to be an astronaut, but they said there was no space...

Read this role play. Blanca is having an interview with Carlos, a careers adviser.

Carlos: ¿Qué tipo de trabajo le gustaría hacer?

Blanca: No sé exactamente. Ese es el problema que tengo.

Carlos: ¿Qué habilidades tiene usted?

Blanca: Aprendo rápidamente y me gusta trabajar con los ordenadores.

Carlos: ¿Tiene usted alguna experiencia laboral?

Blanca: Sí, hice una práctica en una oficina hace un año.

Carlos: ¿Ha visto este anuncio? Lo acabamos de recibir. Buscan individuos que tengan buenas **habilidades informáticas**[1] y que sepan trabajar en grupo. ¿Le interesa?

Blanca: Sí. A lo mejor les mandaré un correo. Gracias.

Grade 8-9

[1] computer skills

Tick list:
✓ good variety of tenses
✓ correct use of 'usted'

To improve:
+ try to use more subject-specific vocab

Usted está hablando con el director de su instituto.
- trabajo ideal — opinión
- experiencia laboral
- !
- ? ser profesor — opinión
- ? consejos para encontrar un trabajo

*Now prepare the role-play on the right. You must address the head teacher as 'usted', and try to speak for about **two** minutes. [15 marks]*

Section 10 — Current and Future Study and Employment

| Nouns | **Words for People and Objects** |

Nouns are like the building blocks of a language — it's really important to know how to use them.

Every Spanish noun is masculine or feminine

When you learn a new noun, learn its gender too.

1) Whether a word is masculine, feminine or plural affects lots of things.

2) All 'the' and 'a' words change depending on the word's gender, and so do any adjectives which describe the noun.

el árbol alto (m.)   *the tall tree*
la casa alta (f.)   *the tall house*

These rules help you guess what gender a word is

1) If you see a word with 'el' or 'un' before it, it's usually masculine.

2) 'La' or 'una' in front of a word means it's feminine.

3) If you don't have these clues, there are other tricks you can use to help you guess.

MASCULINE	Most nouns that end in: -o -l -n -r -s -ta -aje	AND	Male people, days, months, languages, seas, rivers, oceans and mountains.
FEMININE	Most nouns that end in: -a -ción -sión -tad -tud -dad -umbre	AND	Female people, letters of the alphabet.

4) You can't tell whether a noun ending in 'e' or 'ista' is masculine or feminine — you have to learn them.

| el coche *the car* | la gente *the people* | el turista *the tourist (male)* | la turista *the tourist (female)* |

These are some of the exceptions to the rules. You'll just need to learn these ones off by heart.

el día	*day*	la foto	*photo*
el problema	*problem*	la moto	*motorbike*
el mapa	*map*	la mano	*hand*

Making nouns plural

1) Some nouns in Spanish end in a vowel. To make them plural, just add 's' — 'una cama' (*one bed*) becomes 'dos camas' (*two beds*).

2) There are some exceptions to these rules though:

Type of noun	To make it plural...	Example
ends in a consonant except 'z'	add 'es'	una flor *one flower* ⟶ dos flores *two flowers*
ends in 'z'	drop the 'z' and add 'ces'	un lápiz *one pencil* ⟶ dos lápices *two pencils*
days ending in 's'	make the article plural but keep the noun the same	el viernes *Friday* ⟶ los viernes *Fridays*
family surnames		Los Simpson *The Simpsons*

Sometimes you need to add or remove an accent in the plural to avoid changing the pronunciation of the word. Here are a couple of common examples.

un inglés *one English person* ⟶ dos ingleses *two English people*
un joven *one young man* ⟶ dos jóvenes *two young men*

Ignore genders at your peril...

Write 'el' or 'la' for each of these words. Then write each one in the plural form with 'los' or 'las'.

| 1. sombrero | 3. tradición | 5. porcentaje | 7. tensión | 9. ciudad |
| 2. problema | 4. viernes | 6. francés | 8. dificultad | 10. mapa |

'The', 'A', 'Some' and Other Little Words

In Spanish, 'the' and 'a' change depending on the gender of the noun and whether it's singular or plural.

El, la, los, las — *the*

'El', 'la', 'los' and 'las' are definite articles.

	Masculine	Feminine
singular	el	la
plural	los	las

1) The word for 'the' changes depending on the gender of the noun, and whether it's singular or plural.

2) Use 'el' before feminine nouns which start with a stressed 'a'. → El agua está fría.   *The water is cold.*

3) Sometimes you need a definite article in Spanish where you wouldn't use one in English...

   a) with nouns used in a general sense: No me gusta el café. *I don't like coffee.*
   b) in front of the days of the week and times: los lunes a las seis *Mondays at six o'clock*
   c) in front of weights and measurements: dos euros el kilo *two euros a kilo*
   d) when you use a person's title: ¿Cómo está el señor Gómez? *How is Mr Gómez?*

4) There's a neuter article 'lo' for things that aren't masculine or feminine.

   lo mejor / peor / aburrido es que...   *the best / worst / boring thing is that...*

   When you use 'lo' in front of an adjective, the adjective has to be in the masculine form — see p.68.

Un, una, unos, unas — *a and some*

'Un', 'una', 'unos' and 'unas' are indefinite articles.

1) 'Un' and 'una' mean 'a'.

2) 'Un' is used for masculine words and 'una' is used for feminine words. → un gato   *a cat*   una casa   *a house*

3) When you make 'un' or 'una' plural, they become 'unos' and 'unas' — they mean 'some' or 'a few'. → unos gatos   *some cats*   unas casas   *some houses*

4) Watch out, though — 'a' is left out...

   a) ...after the verb 'ser' when talking about someone's occupation or nationality: Soy estudiante. *I'm a student.*
   b) ...after a negative verb: No tengo perro. *I haven't got a dog.*

Any, another, each, all

These are known as indefinite adjectives. See p.68-70 for more adjectives.

1) There's no special word for 'any' in Spanish.   ¿Tienes manzanas?   *Have you got any apples?*

2) Use 'otro' or 'otra' for 'another'.   Lo haré otro día.   *I'll do it another day.* ← You don't need to write 'un' or 'una' before 'otro/a'.

3) 'Cada' means 'each'. It's the same for masculine and feminine nouns.   Cada otoño voy a Gales.   *Each autumn I go to Wales.*

4) 'Todo/a/os/as' means 'all'.   Compré todos los libros en la librería.   *I bought all the books in the bookshop.*

Articles are most definitely important...

Translate these sentences into Spanish.

1. I like chocolate.
2. I don't have any water.
3. She is a teacher.
4. He wants some potatoes.
5. I want to speak to Mrs López.
6. Each person has two dogs.

Adjectives	# Words to Describe Things

Jazz up your work with some flashy describing words — and collect more marks while you're at it.

Adjectives describe things — *learn these common ones*

grande	*big*	guapo/a	*good-looking*		
pequeño/a	*small*	feliz	*happy*		
alto/a	*tall / high*	triste	*sad*		
bajo/a	*short / low*	fácil	*easy*		
largo/a	*long*	difícil	*difficult*		
gordo/a	*fat*	malo/a	*bad*		
delgado/a	*slim*	nuevo/a	*new*	interesante	*interesting*
viejo/a	*old*	rápido/a	*fast*	simpático	*kind*
joven	*young*	lento/a	*slow*	aburrido	*boring*

When you look up an adjective in the dictionary, it'll be in the masculine singular form.

Adjectives need to agree with the noun

1) Adjectives have to <u>agree</u> with the <u>noun</u> they refer to, <u>even if they aren't right next to it</u>.

2) This means the <u>adjective changes</u> depending on the <u>gender</u> of the <u>noun</u> and whether it's <u>singular</u> or <u>plural</u>.

3) Adjectives that end in '<u>o</u>' in the <u>masculine singular</u> form change the '<u>o</u>' to '<u>a</u>' in the <u>feminine</u> form. When <u>plural</u>, the adjective ends in '<u>os</u>' (masculine) or '<u>as</u>' (feminine).

Masculine singular	Feminine singular	Masculine plural	Feminine plural
el chico pequeño	la chica pequeña	los chicos pequeños	las chicas pequeñas
the small boy	*the small girl*	*the small boys*	*the small girls*

4) Adjectives which <u>don't</u> end in '<u>o</u>' or '<u>a</u>' <u>don't change</u> in the singular. If the noun is <u>plural</u>, add '<u>s</u>' if it ends in a vowel, or '<u>es</u>' if it ends in a consonant.

Masculine singular	Feminine singular	Masculine plural	Feminine plural
el hombre triste	la mujer triste	los hombres tristes	las mujeres tristes
the sad man	*the sad woman*	*the sad men*	*the sad women*

If the adjective ends in 'z', remove the 'z' and add 'ces'. See p.66 for nouns that work in a similar way.

Some adjectives don't change to agree

Some adjectives <u>don't change at all</u>.

Most adjectives that don't change are colours.

beis	*beige*	rosa	*pink*
lila	*lilac*	turquesa	*turquoise*
naranja	*orange*	violeta	*violet*

tres coches naranja   *three orange cars*
siete trenes rosa   *seven pink trains*

Adjectives agree (and I'm sure you do too) that this page is great...

Translate these phrases, making sure the adjectives agree with the nouns (where they need to).

1. the happy dog	**3.** the blue cars	**5.** five small cats	**7.** four beige books
2. seven red skirts	**4.** two short women	**6.** nine violet chairs	**8.** one sad person

Words to Describe Things

Once you know loads of adjectives, you need to know where to put them.

Most adjectives go after the word they describe

1) In Spanish, <u>most adjectives go after the noun</u> (the word they describe).

2) But that's not always the case — some adjectives always go <u>in front of the noun</u> they're describing, like these ones:

Es un vestido horrible.
It's a horrible dress.

mucho/a	*a lot of*	tanto/a	*so much*	primero/a, segundo/a...	*first, second...*
muchos/as	*lots of*	tantos/as	*so many*	próximo/a	*next*
otro/a	*another*	poco/a	*little*	último/a	*last*
otros/as	*other*	pocos/as	*few*		
alguno/a	*some*	cada	*each*		

'Otro', 'cada', and 'alguno/a' are all indefinite adjectives. For more on indefinite adjectives, see p.67.

Some adjectives change before masculine nouns...

Some adjectives <u>lose</u> the final '<u>o</u>' when they go in front of a <u>masculine noun</u>.

bueno/a	*good*	tercero/a	*third*	ninguno/a	*none*
primero/a	*first*	alguno/a	*some*	malo/a	*bad*

un buen día   *a good day*   el tercer libro   *the third book*   algún día   *some day*

① '<u>Alguno</u>' and '<u>ninguno</u>' <u>drop</u> the final '<u>o</u>' and <u>add an accent</u>.	No hay ningún taxi libre.	*There's no taxi free.*
② '<u>Grande</u>' is the only adjective that <u>drops</u> '<u>de</u>' in front of both <u>masculine and feminine</u> words.	una gran señora	*a great lady*

...and some change their meaning depending on their position

Paloma couldn't wait to try out the power steering in her new car.

Adjective	Before the noun...	After the noun...
grande	un gran hombre *a great man*	un hombre grande *a big man*
mismo	el mismo día *the same day*	yo mismo *I myself*
nuevo	un nuevo coche *a new (to owner) car*	un coche nuevo *a brand new car*
viejo	un viejo amigo *a long-standing friend*	un amigo viejo *an old (elderly) friend*

Don't let those adjectives trip you up — learn where they go...

Translate these phrases and sentences into Spanish, making sure the adjectives go in the right place.

1. There are lots of cats.
2. the first day
3. the same dog
4. the other pupils
5. Some people think that...
6. He's a great teacher.

| Adjectives | **Words to Describe Things** |

Adjectives are also really useful for saying what's yours and for pointing things out.

Mi, tu, nuestro — *my, your, our*

'Mi', 'tu', 'nuestro' etc. are possessive adjectives.

Words like '<u>my</u>' and '<u>your</u>' in Spanish have to <u>agree</u> with the <u>noun</u> they're describing — <u>not the owner</u>.

Possessive	Masculine singular	Feminine singular	Masculine plural	Feminine plural
my	mi (mío)	mi (mía)	mis (míos)	mis (mías)
your (inf., sing.)	tu (tuyo)	tu (tuya)	tus (tuyos)	tus (tuyas)
his/her/its/your (form., sing.)	su (suyo)	su (suya)	sus (suyos)	sus (suyas)
our	nuestro	nuestra	nuestros	nuestras
your (inf., pl.)	vuestro	vuestra	vuestros	vuestras
their/your (form., pl.)	su (suyo)	su (suya)	sus (suyos)	sus (suyas)

'Su(s)' can mean 'his', 'her', 'its', 'their' and 'your' (formal). Use the rest of the information in the sentence to work out which of these it is.

mi libro
my book

su perro
his dog

The forms <u>in pink</u> (in brackets) are the <u>special long forms</u> — put them <u>after the noun</u>:

las casas tuyas   *your houses*

el gato nuestro   *our cat*

The '<u>our</u>' and '<u>your (inf., pl.)</u>' forms are the <u>same</u> in the <u>short</u> and <u>long</u> forms.

Este, ese, aquel — *this, that, that over there*

'Este', 'ese' and 'aquel' are demonstrative adjectives.

1) Use '<u>este</u>' to say '<u>this</u>'. It's an adjective, so it <u>changes to agree</u> with the noun. When the noun is <u>feminine</u>, use '<u>esta</u>', and when it's <u>plural</u>, use '<u>estos</u>' (masculine) or '<u>estas</u>' (feminine).

este tigre   *this tiger*   esta leche   *this milk*   estos huevos   *these eggs*   estas caras   *these faces*

2) In Spanish, there are <u>two words</u> for '<u>that</u>', but their meanings are slightly different. '<u>Ese</u>' is used when you'd normally say '<u>that</u>' in English. Use '<u>esa</u>' for feminine nouns, and '<u>esos</u>' or '<u>esas</u>' for plural nouns.

ese tigre   *that tiger*   esa leche   *that milk*   esos huevos   *those eggs*   esas caras   *those faces*

3) '<u>Aquel</u>' is used for things that are <u>even further away</u> — in English, you might say '<u>that over there</u>'. 'Aquel' changes to '<u>aquella</u>' in the <u>feminine</u> form and '<u>aquellos</u>' and '<u>aquellas</u>' for the <u>plural</u> forms.

aquel tigre   *that tiger over there*   aquellos huevos   *those eggs over there*
aquella leche   *that milk over there*   aquellas caras   *those faces over there*

Cuyo — *whose*

'Cuyo' is a relative adjective.

To say '<u>whose</u>' in Spanish, use '<u>cuyo/a/os/as</u>'. The <u>ending</u> agrees with the <u>noun following</u>, <u>not with its owner</u>.

	Masculine singular	Feminine singular	Masculine plural	Feminine plural
whose	cuyo	cuya	cuyos	cuyas

Eva es la chica cuyo gato está allí.
Eva is the girl whose cat is there.

It's your turn now — help yourself to these quick questions...

Translate these sentences into Spanish.

1. Their books are new.
2. I want that apple.
3. That lion over there is eating.
4. These pears are good.
5. That man, whose wife is Spanish, is tall.
6. Lucas is the boy whose parents are nice.

Words to Describe Actions

Adverbs describe verbs by adding more information about how an action is done. Using them makes your Spanish much more interesting and complex, which can only be a good thing...

Adverbs help you describe how actions are done

1) If you wanted to <u>describe how you run</u>, you could say 'I run <u>slowly</u>' — '<u>slowly</u>' is an <u>adverb</u>.

2) In English, you add '-<u>ly</u>' to the adjective '<u>slow</u>' to make '<u>slowly</u>'.

3) It's similar in Spanish — to form an adverb, you add '-<u>mente</u>' to the end of the <u>adjective</u>. <u>But</u>, you need to make sure the adjective is in the <u>feminine form</u> first.

> lento (*slow*) ⟶ lenta (*feminine form of 'slow'*) **+** -mente ⟶ lentamente (*slowly*)

4) With adjectives that <u>don't end</u> in '<u>o</u>', you can just add '-<u>mente</u>'.

> fácil (*easy*) **+** -mente ⟶ fácilmente (*easily*)

5) Unlike with adjectives (see p.68), adverbs don't need to <u>agree</u>. This is because they're <u>describing</u> an <u>action</u>, not the <u>person</u> doing the action.

> Hablamos sinceramente.   *We speak sincerely.*
> Habla alegremente.   *She speaks happily.*

6) Adverbs come <u>after</u> the <u>verb</u>.

> Estudio tranquilamente.   *I study quietly.*

Alexa spoke happily of the time she managed to take off her skis without falling over.

Some adverbs are formed differently

1) Just like in English, there are a couple of <u>exceptions</u>.

2) You don't say 'I sing <u>goodly</u>' in English, and you can't say '<u>buenamente</u>' in Spanish either.

> bueno/a   *good* ⟶ bien   *well*
> malo/a   *bad* ⟶ mal   *badly*

> Canto bien. ⟶ *I sing well.*
> Canto mal. ⟶ *I sing badly.*

3) Even though you can use '<u>rápidamente</u>' and '<u>lentamente</u>' for '<u>quickly</u>' and '<u>slowly</u>', you can also use the <u>irregular</u> forms — '<u>deprisa</u>' (*quickly*) and '<u>despacio</u>' (*slowly*). They <u>don't</u> add '-<u>mente</u>' or <u>change their ending</u>.

> Escribes deprisa.   *You write quickly.*

> Escribes despacio.   *You write slowly.*

Just like regular adverbs, these ones come after the verb.

Make sure you're speaking Spanish maravillosamente...

Try translating these sentences into Spanish.

1. They cry noisily.
2. He lives healthily.
3. She speaks clearly.
4. We speak intelligently.
5. The baby sleeps well.
6. I run quickly.
7. You dance badly.
8. I read slowly.

Adverbs	# Words to Describe Actions

And here's another page on adverbs. This time, it's how to form adverbs using 'con', and some handy lists of adverbs that help you say where or when something is happening.

You can also form adverbs using 'con' + noun

1) In English, you can say someone did something 'with ease' instead of saying 'easily'.

2) You can do the same in Spanish by putting 'con' with a noun.

Lo hago con facilidad. *I do it with ease / easily.*	Hablaste con arrogancia. *You spoke with arrogance / arrogantly.*	¡Con cuidado! *With care! / Carefully!*

Adverbs can tell you where something is done...

You can put these handy words into sentences to say where things happen.

aquí	here
ahí	(just) there
allá / allí	(over) there
cerca	near
lejos	far away
en / por todas partes	everywhere

Mi tía trabaja aquí.   *My aunt works here.* ← *just there — ahí*

Hay gatos por todas partes.   *There are cats everywhere.*

Está muy cerca.   *It's very near.* ← *far away — lejos*

To say where something is, you need the verb 'estar' (p.85).

...or when it's happening

1) Use these adverbs to help you say when something is being done.

ahora	now / nowadays	antes (de)	before
ya	already	después (de)	after(wards)
al mismo tiempo	at the same time	en seguida	straightaway
de momento	at the moment	mientras tanto	meanwhile
de repente	suddenly	pronto	soon
de nuevo	again	todavía	still, yet

Ya tengo un reloj. *I already have a watch.*

Estaré allí pronto. *I'll be there soon.*

2) These ones are really useful for saying how often something is done.

a diario	daily
a menudo	often
a veces	sometimes
de vez en cuando	from time to time
pocas veces	rarely, a few times
siempre	always

Siempre juego al fútbol en el parque con mis amigos. *I always play football in the park with my friends.*

A veces voy a la tienda. *I sometimes go to the shop.*

Use loads of adverbs and start raking in the marks with ease...

Translate these sentences into Spanish using all your adverb knowledge.

1. My shoes are here.   **3.** I did it patiently. (Use 'con'.)   **5.** She did it straightaway.

2. I want to do it again.   **4.** We live far away.   **6.** He danced enthusiastically. (Use 'con'.)

Words to Compare Things

To make your Spanish even more brilliant, learn how to compare things.

Más, el más — *more, the most*

'More' is a comparative and 'the most' is a superlative.

1) In Spanish you can't say 'cheaper' or 'cheapest' — you have to say '<u>more cheap</u>' or '<u>the most cheap</u>'.

Este piso es barato.	Este piso es más barato.	Este piso es el más barato.
This flat is cheap.	*This flat is cheaper.* i.e. 'more cheap'	*This flat is the cheapest.* i.e. 'the most cheap'

2) To say '<u>less cheap</u>' or '<u>the least cheap</u>', use '<u>menos</u>'.

Este piso es barato.	Este piso es menos barato.	Este piso es el menos barato.
This flat is cheap.	*This flat is less cheap.*	*This flat is the least cheap.*

3) To say 'the most / least' if the word you're describing is <u>feminine</u>, use 'la más / menos'. For <u>plural</u> words, use 'los/las más / menos'.

Laura es la más baja.	*Laura is the shortest.*
Jo y Ed son los menos altos.	*Jo and Ed are the least tall.*

Más / menos ... que — *more / less ... than*

1) Use '<u>más</u> ... <u>que</u>' (*more ... than*) and '<u>menos</u> ... <u>que</u>' (*less ... than*) to <u>compare</u> two things <u>directly</u>.

Catalina es más inteligente que Jorge.	*Catalina is more intelligent than Jorge.*
Jorge es menos inteligente que Catalina.	*Jorge is less intelligent than Catalina.*

2) Or to say two things are <u>as</u> young or old or brilliant <u>as</u> each other, use '<u>tan</u> ... <u>como</u>' (*as ... as*).

Catalina es tan feliz como Jorge.	*Catalina is as happy as Jorge.*

There are some exceptions...

As usual, there are a few trickier ones — learn these exceptions.

If the noun is feminine or plural, you'll need to change the 'el' to 'la', 'los' or 'las'.

bueno	*good*	→	mejor	*better*	→	el mejor	*the best*
malo	*bad*	→	peor	*worse*	→	el peor	*the worst*
viejo	*old (for people only)*	→	mayor	*older*	→	el mayor	*the oldest*
joven	*young (for people only)*	→	menor	*younger*	→	el menor	*the youngest*

All the comparatives and superlatives stay the same for the masculine and feminine forms, but they add 'es' for the plural forms.

Manuela es la mayor de mis hermanas.	*Manuela is the oldest of my sisters.*

Blanca y Renata son las menores.	*Blanca and Renata are the youngest.*

El gorro azul es el mejor.	*The blue cap is the best.*

Making comparisons is the best thing ever...

Translate these sentences into Spanish — watch out for the irregular adjectives though.

1. My cat is the fattest.   **3.** Juan is older than Marta.   **5.** The film is better than the book.
2. I am as tall as my father.   **4.** It was the worst day of the week.   **6.** Our magazine is the most interesting.

Words to Compare Actions

Now you've got to grips with comparing things, you can use some of the same techniques to compare actions.

Using adverbs to say 'more ...ly' and 'less ...ly'

Adverbial phrases like this are called comparatives.

1) To say that something is done '<u>more ...ly</u>', use '<u>más ... que</u>'.

Eva trabaja más alegremente que Inés.	*Eva works more happily than Inés.*

2) If you want to say that something is done '<u>less ...ly</u>', use '<u>menos ... que</u>'.

Inés trabaja menos alegremente que Eva.	*Inés works less happily than Eva.*

3) To say that someone does something '<u>as ... as</u>' someone else, use '<u>tan ... como</u>'.

Eva trabaja tan alegremente como Inés.	*Eva works as happily as Inés.*

Using adverbs to say the 'most ...ly'

This kind of construction is called a 'superlative'.

To say someone does something '<u>the most ...ly</u>', follow this pattern.

(Make sure you remember to change '<u>el</u>' to '<u>la</u>' if the subject is <u>feminine</u>, '<u>los</u>' if it's a <u>masculine plural</u> subject, and '<u>las</u>' for a <u>feminine plural</u> subject.)

Daniela es la que trabaja más alegremente.	*Daniela works the most happily.*
Juan es el que baila menos rápidamente.	*Juan dances the least quickly.*

Watch out for irregular comparatives and superlatives

Yes, you guessed it — there are some more <u>lovely irregular forms</u>.

bien (*well*)	→	mejor (*better*)	→	el que mejor ... (*the one who ... the best*)
mal (*badly*)	→	peor (*worse*)	→	el que peor ... (*the one who ... the worst*)

Cocino mejor que mis amigos.	*I cook better than my friends.*
Escribes peor que un niño.	*You write worse than a child.*
Él es el que peor juega.	*He's the one who plays the worst.*
Ellas son las que mejor bailan.	*They are the ones who dance the best.*

Use adverbs and you'll be speaking Spanish the most fluently...

Have a go at using what you know about adverbs to translate these sentences.

1. Carmen eats more quickly.
2. Luis sings as well as Adela.
3. Selina drives the best.
4. I study better than my friends.
5. We walk more slowly than Rob.
6. Ed is the one who runs the worst.

Words to Say How Much

You can use quantifiers and intensifiers with other words to give more detailed descriptions.

Use quantifiers to say how many or how much

1) Just saying 'I have apples' is boring. Use quantifiers to say you only have a few apples — or loads.

2) Quantifiers go before the noun, and most change their endings to agree with it, just like adjectives do.

mucho	a lot/lots of
poco	only a little/only a few
un poco de	a bit of
demasiado	too much/too many
tanto	so much/so many
bastante	enough

'Un poco de' doesn't change its ending.

Tengo muchos deberes.	I have a lot of homework.
Tengo pocas cartas.	I only have a few letters.
Haces demasiado ruido.	You make too much noise.
Hay tanta gente.	There are so many people.
Tienes bastantes zapatos.	You have enough shoes.
Comí un poco de chocolate.	I ate a bit of chocolate.

3) You don't just have to use these quantifiers with nouns — you can also use them with verbs. When you use them with verbs, they work like adverbs, so they go after the verb and don't change their endings.

Hablas demasiado.	You talk too much.
Come mucho.	She eats a lot.

Use intensifiers to strengthen what you're saying

1) You can use intensifiers like 'very' and 'quite' to add detail to what you're saying.

2) Intensifiers go before the word they're modifying, but their endings don't change at all.

muy	very
poco	not very
demasiado	too
bastante	quite

Simón está muy feliz.	Simón is very happy.
Es poco cortés.	He's not very polite.
Habla demasiado tranquilamente.	She speaks too quietly.
Comes bastante bien.	You eat quite well.

Add '-ito' or '-ísimo' to make adjectives smaller or stronger

1) You can add 'ito/a/os/as' to the end of most adjectives to make something seem smaller or cuter.

El bebé está enfermito.	The baby is poorly.

2) Add 'ísimo/a/os/as' to make the meaning of what you're saying stronger. It's as if you're adding 'really' to the adjective — so if 'bueno' is 'good', then 'buenísimo' would mean 'really good' or 'wonderful'.

La película es malísima.	The film is terrible.

That's enough of quantifiers and intensifiers for now...

Translate these sentences into Spanish.

1. There are too many cats here.
2. It's quite interesting.
3. I have lots of friends.
4. They speak too slowly.
5. There are so many beaches in Spain.
6. The book is really good.

| Subject Pronouns | **I, You, We** |

Pronouns are really handy little words that save you from needing to repeat nouns all the time.

Subject and object

Before you get started on pronouns, you need to know how to find the subject and the object of a sentence.

| The subject of a sentence is the noun doing the action. | → Pau come la pera. | *Pau eats the pear.* ← | The object of a sentence is the noun having the action done to it. |

Yo, tú, él, ella — *I, you, he, she*

1) Pronouns are words that replace nouns — like 'you' or 'them'. You use them to avoid repeating nouns.

| Jessica went to the beach and she sat on the sand. | In English, the pronoun 'she' replaces Jessica's name. 'She' is a 'subject pronoun' because it replaces the subject of the sentence — Jessica. |

2) You don't normally include subject pronouns in Spanish sentences — but you still need to know them.

I	yo	we	nosotros/as
you (inf., sing.)	tú	you (inf., pl.)	vosotros/as
he/it	él	they (masc.)	ellos
she/it	ella	they (fem.)	ellas
you (form., sing.)	usted	you (form., sing.)	ustedes

The masculine 'they' form is also used for groups made up of masculine and feminine nouns.

There's also 'se' which means 'one'. It's used in phrases like 'se puede' (one can / you can). It uses the third person singular form of the verb. See p.95 for more impersonal verbs.

Remember there are four ways to say 'you' in Spanish — see p.7 for more.

Fui a la playa y comí un helado.   *I went to the beach and I ate an ice cream.*

Here, you don't need the pronoun 'yo' because you can see from the first person verb forms 'fui' and 'comí' that the person speaking ('I') is doing the action.

You can use subject pronouns for emphasis

Although you don't usually need subject pronouns in Spanish, they help emphasise exactly who does what:

¿Qué queréis hacer el fin de semana que viene?   *What would you (inf., pl.) like to do next weekend?*

Pues, yo quiero ir de compras, pero él quiere ir al cine.
Well, I want to go shopping, but he wants to go to the cinema.

You include the pronouns here to emphasise who wants what. They're used in Spanish in cases when extra stress is put on pronouns in English.

¿Quieren visitar el museo?   *Do they / you (form., sing.) want to visit the museum?*

Pues, yo sí, pero ella no.   *Well, I do but she doesn't.*

Remember that if you're using 'ustedes', you need the 'they' form of the verb.

Pronouns make your writing sound smoother — use them...

Write down the Spanish subject pronoun you'd use to replace each of these subjects.

1. Juan y Jorge
2. Anabel
3. Pedro y yo
4. Alberto y tú
5. Ramón
6. el señor Pérez y usted
7. Miranda, Alicia y Lina
8. Alberto y Tania

Me, You, Them

Now you've got to grips with subject pronouns, it's time for object pronouns — bet you didn't see that coming.

Me, te, lo — *me, you, him*

> 'Me', 'you', 'him' and 'her' are direct object pronouns. They replace the object of a sentence — the thing having an action done to it.

Use <u>direct object pronouns</u> when you're talking about <u>who</u> or <u>what</u> an action is <u>done to</u>.

me	me	us	nos
you (inf., sing.)	te	you (inf., pl.)	os
him/it	lo	them (masc.)	los
her/it	la	them (fem.)	las
you (form., sing.)	lo/la	you (form., sing.)	los/las

The pronoun usually goes <u>before</u> the verb.

Ricardo lava el perro.
Ricardo washes the dog. → Ricardo lo lava.
Ricardo washes it.

The action is done to <u>the dog</u> ('el perro' — <u>masculine</u>), so the pronoun 'it' needs to be in the <u>masculine singular form</u>.

Me, te, les — *to me, to you, to them*

1) If you want to talk about doing something '<u>to</u>' or '<u>for</u>' <u>someone</u>, you need an <u>indirect object pronoun</u>.

El perro da el cepillo a Ricardo.
The dog gives the brush to Ricardo. → El perro le da el cepillo.
The dog gives the brush to him.

2) These pronouns are the same ones you use with the verb '<u>gustar</u>' when you say you <u>like something</u>. This is because 'me gusta el chocolate' literally means 'chocolate is pleasing <u>to me</u>'.

to me	me	to us	nos
to you (inf., sing.)	te	to you (inf., pl.)	os
to him / her / it / you (form., sing.)	le	to them / you (form., pl.)	les

3) If the thing you like is <u>singular</u>, you need 'gusta'. If it's <u>plural</u>, you need 'gustan'.

¿Te gusta el español?   *Do you like Spanish?*
Le gustan los parques.   *He likes the parks.*

Getting the order right

1) Object pronouns <u>normally</u> come <u>before the verb</u>, but they can go <u>before</u> or <u>after</u> the verb if it's an <u>infinitive</u> (p.83) or a <u>present participle</u> (p.93).

Often you need to <u>add an accent</u> to keep the pronunciation right.

Lo quiero ver. **OR** Quiero verlo.
I want to see it.

Le estamos hablando. **OR** Estamos hablándole.
We're talking to him.

2) With <u>commands</u>, the pronoun is <u>tacked on to the end</u>.   Escríbeme, por favor.   *Write to me, please.*

3) When <u>two object pronouns</u> come together, the <u>indirect</u> one comes <u>first</u>.

4) And if the <u>indirect object pronoun</u> is '<u>le</u>' or '<u>les</u>', it becomes '<u>se</u>' when it's in front of '<u>lo</u>', '<u>la</u>', '<u>los</u>' or '<u>las</u>'.

direct object pronoun

Te la enviaré.   *I'll send it to you.*

indirect object pronoun

direct object pronoun

Debo dárselo.   *I must give it to him/her/them/you (form.).*

indirect object pronoun

Pronouns are tricky — but if you can use them, you'll be flying...

Translate these sentences into Spanish — try to use the correct pronouns and get the order right.

1. She breaks it (the window).
2. I drink it (the milk).
3. He bought a skirt for her.
4. I send him an email.
5. I want to do it.
6. He said it to us.

More Pronouns

Pronouns can be a bit confusing — but they're really useful for adding extra detail and asking questions.

Some pronouns change after certain prepositions

Watch out — 'mí' needs an accent, but 'ti' doesn't.

1) The words for '<u>me</u>' and '<u>you</u>' (inf., sing.) become '<u>mí</u>' and '<u>ti</u>' after <u>prepositions</u> like '<u>a</u>' (*to*), '<u>para</u>' (*for*), and '<u>sobre</u>' / '<u>de</u>' (*about*).

me	mí	us	nosotros/as
you (inf., sing.)	ti	you (inf., pl.)	vosotros/as
him	él/ella	them (masc.)	ellos/as
you (form., sing.)	usted	you (form., sing.)	ustedes

No es para mí, es para él.   *It isn't for me, it's for him.*

2) '<u>With me</u>' becomes '<u>conmigo</u>' and '<u>with you</u>' becomes '<u>contigo</u>':   Está conmigo.   *He's with me.*

Que — *that, which, who*

1) '<u>Que</u>' can mean '<u>that</u>', '<u>which</u>' or '<u>who</u>' — it's a <u>relative pronoun</u>.

2) You can use it to start a <u>relative clause</u>, which is a way of <u>adding detail</u> to a sentence.

Fui a Menorca, que es una isla preciosa.	*I went to Menorca, which is a beautiful island.*
¿Dónde está el pan que compraste ayer?	*Where's the bread that you bought yesterday?*
Allí está el hombre que vive en nuestra calle.	*There's the man who lives on our road.*

3) If you're talking about an <u>idea</u> instead of an object, you need '<u>lo que</u>'.

Van a venir, lo que es maravilloso.   *They're going to come, which is wonderful.*

4) <u>After prepositions</u>, like '<u>con</u>', '<u>a</u>' and '<u>de</u>', use '<u>quien</u>' for 'who' or '<u>el / la que</u>' or '<u>el / la cual</u>' for 'that / which.'

el hombre con quien estoy hablando	el mercado del cual compro flores
the man with whom I'm talking	*the market from which I buy flowers*

If you were talking about a plural noun, you'd need to use 'con quienes' or 'de los / las cuales' instead.

Using pronouns to ask questions

Pronouns for asking questions are called 'interrogative pronouns'.

1) Normally, you can use '<u>¿Qué...</u>' to ask a question that starts with '<u>What...</u>' in English.

¿Qué te gustaría hacer?   *What would you like to do?*

If 'cuál' is being used before a noun, it needs to agree with it. Use 'cuál' for all singular nouns and 'cuáles' for all plural nouns.

2) Use '<u>¿Cuál...</u>' when you'd use '<u>Which...</u>' or '<u>Which one...</u>' in English. But remember — sometimes you need '<u>¿Cuál...</u>' when you'd actually use 'What...' in English — see p.4.

¿Cuál es mejor?   *Which (one) is better?*   ¿Cuál es tu apellido?   *What is your surname?*

3) '<u>¿Quién...</u>' means '<u>Who...</u>'. You often use '<u>¿Quién...</u>' with <u>prepositions</u>.

¿Quién es?   *Who is it?*   ¿Con quién?   *With whom?*   ¿De quién son?   *Whose are they?*

This page, which is very useful, will help you greatly...

Pronouns are tricky — so the best way to tackle them is by practising. Translate these sentences into Spanish.

1. My sister, who is seven, is short.
2. I went to Madrid, which is the capital of Spain.
3. What's your address?
4. Who do you live with?
5. Whose is this dog?
6. Which do you prefer?

More Pronouns

It's well worth being able to use these pronouns, so make sure you get your head around them.

El mío, el tuyo... — *mine, yours...*

'el mío', 'el tuyo', 'el nuestro' etc. are possessive pronouns.

1) Use possessive pronouns to say '<u>mine</u>' or '<u>yours</u>'.

2) Possessive pronouns <u>agree</u> in <u>gender</u> and <u>number</u> with the <u>noun</u> they're replacing.

Possessive pronoun	Masculine singular	Feminine singular	Masculine plural	Feminine plural
mine	el mío	la mía	los míos	las mías
yours (inf., sing.)	el tuyo	la tuya	los tuyos	las tuyas
his/hers/its/yours (form.)	el suyo	la suya	los suyos	las suyas
ours	el nuestro	la nuestra	los nuestros	las nuestras
yours (inf., pl.)	el vuestro	la vuestra	los vuestros	las vuestras
theirs/yours (form., pl.)	el suyo	la suya	los suyos	las suyas

¿Es tu casa?   *Is it your house?*
No, la mía es más alta.   *No, mine is taller.*

¿Es vuestro hotel?   *Is it your (inf., pl.) hotel?*
No, el nuestro está allí.   *No, ours is there.*

Algo, alguien — *something, someone*

'Algo' and 'alguien' are indefinite pronouns.

'<u>Algo</u>' means '<u>something</u>':   ¿Queréis algo?   *Do you (inf., pl.) want something?*

'<u>Alguien</u>' means '<u>someone</u>':   Vi a alguien.   *I saw someone.*

When you 'see someone' in Spanish, you have to add the <u>personal 'a'</u>. See p.81.

Este, ese, aquel — *this one, that one, that one over there*

Sometimes you might see these pronouns written with an accent on the first 'e' — e.g. 'éste'.

1) <u>Demonstrative pronouns</u> are <u>the same as</u> the <u>demonstrative adjectives</u> on p.70.

2) Remember to <u>change the ending</u> to <u>agree</u> with the noun it refers back to.

Demonstrative pronoun	Masculine singular	Feminine singular	Masculine plural	Feminine plural
this/these one(s)	este	esta	estos	estas
that/those one(s)	ese	esa	esos	esas
that/those one(s) over there	aquel	aquella	aquellos	aquellas

Me gustaría este.
I'd like this one.

Prefiere esas.
She prefers those.

3) Use the <u>neuter forms</u> '<u>esto</u>', '<u>eso</u>' and '<u>aquello</u>' if you <u>don't</u> know the <u>gender</u> of the noun.

¿Qué es eso?   *What's that?*

Ahh pronouns — these will get you good marks...

Translate these sentences into Spanish, using the correct pronouns.

1. They're mine. *(cats)*
2. What's that over there?
3. This bed is bigger than that one over there.
4. This book is more interesting than that one.
5. Is it yours (inf., pl.)? *(hat)*
6. Someone's talking quietly.

Prepositions

Prepositions are sneaky little words — but you've got to learn them if you want the highest marks.

Use these words to say where something is...

> Don't forget to use 'estar' (see p.85) to say where something is.

al lado de	next to	bajo / debajo de	below / under	enfrente de	opposite
detrás de	behind	en / sobre	on / upon	en / dentro de	in / into / inside
delante de	in front of	encima de	above / on top of	al fondo de	at the back of
entre	between	contra	against	hacia	towards

A, hasta — to

To say 'to' in Spanish, you normally say 'a'. But when 'to' means 'as far as', use 'hasta'.

Va a Liverpool.	She's going to Liverpool.	Solo va hasta Manchester.	He's only going to Manchester.

En, dentro de — in, inside

'In' is just 'en' and 'inside' is 'dentro de'. The verb 'entrar' (to go in / enter) is normally followed by 'en'.

En Leeds...	In Leeds...	dentro de la caja	inside the box	Entro en la tienda.	I enter the shop.

De — of

You can't say 'de el' or 'a el' in Spanish. Instead, you combine 'a' or 'de' with the definite article (p.67).

'De' is usually 'of'. You can also use 'de' to say what something's made of.

Es de oro.	It's made of gold.	al final del pasillo	at the end of the corridor

	el	la
a	al	a la
de	del	de la

En, a — at

You can normally use 'en' when you want to say 'at'. Sometimes you need 'a' instead...

Está en el colegio.	He's at school.	en casa	at home	a las seis	at six o'clock

Sobre, en — on

> You don't need 'on' for days of the week.

For 'on (top of)', use 'sobre' or 'en'. When you mean 'on' but not 'on top of', use 'en'.

Está sobre la mesa.	It's on the table.	Lo vi en la tele.	I saw it on TV.	El lunes...	On Monday...

De, desde, a partir de — from

'From' is normally 'de'. Use 'desde' when there's a starting and ending point and 'a partir de' for dates.

Es de Kent.	He's from Kent.	desde Fife hasta Ayr	from Fife to Ayr	a partir de julio	from July

Learn these prepositions inside out and back to front...

Use what you know about prepositions to translate these sentences into Spanish.

1. The house is opposite the bank.
2. The train goes as far as Italy.
3. I heard it on the radio.
4. I enter the supermarket.
5. I'm from Hull, but I live in Crewe.
6. From September, I will have a job.

'Por', 'Para' and the Personal 'a'

'Por', 'para' and the personal 'a' are also prepositions, but they don't always translate easily into English.

Use 'para' to...

1) ...say <u>who</u> something is <u>for</u>.

Este dinero es para ti.   *This money is for you.*

2) ...talk about <u>destinations</u>.

el tren para Bilbao   *the train to Bilbao*

3) ...say '<u>to</u>' or '<u>in order to</u>'.

Veo la tele para descansar.   *I watch TV to relax.*

4) ...say '<u>by</u>' in <u>time phrases</u>.

para mañana   *by tomorrow*

5) ...say '<u>for</u>' in phrases like '<u>for X days</u>' when you're talking about the <u>future</u>.

Quiero el coche para un día.   *I want the car for one day.*

6) ...say '<u>in my / your opinion</u>'.

Para mí, es muy bonito.   *In my opinion, it's very pretty.*

7) ...say '<u>about to</u>'.

Según él, está para llover.   *According to him, it's about to rain.*

> 'Según' is another <u>preposition</u>. It means '<u>according to</u>'.

Use 'por' to...

1) ...say '<u>for</u>' in phrases like '<u>for X years / months</u>' in the <u>past</u>.

Vivió allí por un año.   *He lived there for a year.*

> In certain cases, for the future you need to use 'por': Estaré en Galicia por dos años.

2) ...talk about <u>parts of the day</u> when you want to say '<u>in</u>'.

por la mañana   *in the morning*

3) ...say '<u>through</u>'.

Entré por la puerta sin hablar.   *I came through the door without speaking.*

> 'Sin' is a <u>preposition</u> which means '<u>without</u>'.

4) ...say '<u>per</u>' or '<u>a</u>' in <u>number phrases</u>.

tres veces por día   *three times a day*

5) ...talk about <u>exchanges</u>.

Pagó dos euros por el té.   *He paid 2 euros for the tea.*

6) ...say '<u>on behalf of</u>'.

Lo hice por ti.   *I did it for you.*

7) ...say '<u>thank you</u>'.

Gracias por el pastel.   *Thanks for the cake.*

The personal 'a'

> You don't usually use the personal 'a' after 'tener' or 'ser'.

You need an <u>extra</u> '<u>a</u>' <u>before</u> the word for any <u>human being</u> or <u>pet</u> after every single <u>verb</u>.

Estoy buscando a Juan.   *I'm looking for Juan.*   **BUT**   Estoy buscando un taxi.   *I'm looking for a taxi.*

'Por' and 'para' are hard... but they're really useful to know.

Decide whether you need 'por', 'para' or 'a' in each of these sentences.

1. Esta revista es ____ ti.
2. Visito ____ mi abuelo.
3. ____ la tarde, vemos la tele.
4. Gracias ____ la carta.
5. Juego al fútbol dos veces ____ semana.
6. Lo quiero ____ el fin de semana.

Conjunctions

Conjunctions help you link your ideas together to make longer, more complex sentences.

Y — and

1) '<u>Y</u>' means '<u>and</u>' — you use it just like you would in English.

| Me gusta jugar al fútbol. *I like playing football.* | **AND** | Me gusta jugar al rugby. *I like playing rugby.* | **=** | Me gusta jugar al fútbol y al rugby. *I like playing football and rugby.* |

2) '<u>Y</u>' changes to '<u>e</u>' <u>before</u> a word starting with '<u>i</u>' or '<u>hi</u>'.

Hablo español e inglés.   *I speak Spanish and English.*

O — or

1) '<u>O</u>' means '<u>or</u>'.

| Juego al fútbol los sábados. *I play football on Saturdays.* | **OR** | Juego al rugby los sábados. *I play rugby on Saturdays.* | **=** | Juego al fútbol o al rugby los sábados. *I play football or rugby on Saturdays.* |

2) When '<u>o</u>' comes just <u>before</u> a word starting with '<u>o</u>' or '<u>ho</u>', it changes to '<u>u</u>'.

Cuesta siete u ocho euros.   *It costs seven or eight euros.*

Pero — but

1) '<u>Pero</u>' means '<u>but</u>'.

| Me gusta el fútbol. *I like football.* | **BUT** | No me gusta el rugby. *I don't like rugby.* | **=** | Me gusta el fútbol, pero no me gusta el rugby. *I like football, but I don't like rugby.* |

2) When '<u>but</u>' means '<u>but rather</u>', it becomes '<u>sino</u>'.

No es español, sino francés.   *He isn't Spanish, but (rather) French.*

Porque — because

'<u>Porque</u>' helps you <u>give opinions</u>:

Me gusta porque es sabroso.   *I like it because it's tasty.*

There's more about 'porque' and opinions on p.9.

Other conjunctions you need to know

cuando	*when*	así que	*so, therefore*	como	*as, since*
si	*if*	de manera que	*such that*	pues	*well, then*
sin embargo	*however*	mientras	*while*	entonces	*then*

Tiene hambre, así que va a comer.

He's hungry, so he's going to eat.

You don't want to sound like a robot, so start using conjunctions...

Translate these sentences into Spanish, deciding which conjunctions you need to use.

1. Geography is fun, but it's difficult.
2. I like history because it's easy.
3. As I'm ill, I'm staying at home.
4. I go to the park when it's hot.
5. I speak French and Italian.
6. Do you prefer blue or yellow?

Verbs in the Present Tense

There's not a lot you can do without verbs — your Spanish won't make very much sense without them.

Verbs are actions

1) A <u>verb</u> is an <u>action word</u> — for example, '<u>speak</u>', '<u>eat</u>' and '<u>live</u>'.

2) Verbs can be put into <u>different tenses</u>, such as the <u>future</u> or <u>past</u>, for example, 'Yesterday, I <u>ate</u> some cake'.

3) To use a verb, you need to know its <u>infinitive</u> — the form you find in a <u>dictionary</u>, e.g. '<u>hablar</u>' (*to speak*).

Forming the present tense

1) Most <u>regular</u> verbs in Spanish end in '<u>-ar</u>', '<u>-er</u>' or '<u>-ir</u>'. To form the <u>present tense</u> of these regular verbs, you need to find the <u>stem</u>. To do this, <u>remove</u> the <u>last two letters</u> from the <u>infinitive</u>.

Infinitive	Remove last two letters	Stem
hablar	ar	habl-

2) Then <u>add</u> the <u>endings</u> below to the <u>stem</u>.

-ar verbs

I speak	hablo	hablamos	we speak
you (inf., sing.) speak	hablas	habláis	you (inf., pl.) speak
he/she/it/you (form., sing.) speak(s)	habla	hablan	they/you (form., pl.) speak

Cantan bien. *They sing well.*

Toca el piano. *He plays the piano.*

-er verbs

I eat	como	comemos	we eat
you (inf., sing.) eat	comes	coméis	you (inf., pl.) eat
he/she/it/you (form., sing.) eat(s)	come	comen	they/you (form., pl.) eat

Bebes té. *You (inf., sing.) drink tea.*

Vendemos uvas. *We sell grapes.*

-ir verbs

I live	vivo	vivimos	we live
you (inf., sing.) live	vives	vivís	you (inf., pl.) live
he/she/it/you (form., sing.) live(s)	vive	viven	they/you (form., pl.) live

Suben la torre. *They go up the tower.*

Kevin interrumpe. *Kevin interrupts.*

When to use the present tense

For another way to say what you're doing now, see p.93.

① Use the <u>present tense</u> for actions taking place <u>now</u>.

Hablo español. *I speak Spanish / I am speaking Spanish.*

② You also need the <u>present tense</u> for things that take place <u>regularly</u>.

Canto todos los días. *I sing every day.*

③ Use the <u>present tense</u> with '<u>desde hace</u>' to say <u>how long</u> you've been doing something.

Toco el violín desde hace cuatro años. *I've been playing the violin for four years.*

④ You can also use the <u>present tense</u> for things that are <u>about to happen</u>.

Mañana vamos al cine. *Tomorrow we are going to the cinema.*

The present? Oh, you really shouldn't have...

Put each of the infinitives into the form given in brackets, and then translate Q8 into Spanish.

1. bailar (yo)
2. beber (nosotros)
3. nadar (vosotros)
4. correr (usted)
5. aprender (él)
6. visitar (ellos)
7. escribir (tú)
8. She has been living here for a year.

Section 11 — Grammar

Present Tense

Irregular Verbs in the Present Tense

Unfortunately, not all Spanish verbs are regular — and some of the worst offenders are really common verbs...

Radical-changing verbs

These are also known as 'stem-changing verbs'.

1) A radical-changing verb is a verb that changes its spelling in the present tense.

2) Usually, the 'e' in their stem changes to 'ie', or the 'o' or 'u' in their stem to 'ue'. Some verbs like 'pedir' (*to order / ask for*), 'repetir' (*to repeat*) and 'vestirse' (*to get dressed*) change the 'e' in their stem to 'i'.

3) Their stem changes in every form apart from the 'we' and 'you (inf., pl.)' forms.

querer — *to want* (e to ie)

I want	quiero
you (inf., sing.) want	quieres
he/she/it/you (form., sing.) want(s)	quiere
we want	queremos
you (inf, pl.) want	queréis
they/you (form., pl.) want	quieren

These verbs also change their 'e' to 'ie'...

cerrar	*to close*	preferir	*to prefer*
comenzar	*to begin*	sentarse	*to sit down*
despertarse	*to wake up*	sentir(se)	*to feel*
empezar	*to begin*	tener	*to have*
pensar	*to think*	venir	*to come*

Even though their stems change, their endings are regular.

'Tener' and 'venir' have irregular first person singular forms — 'tengo' and 'vengo'.

poder — *to be able to* (o to ue)

I can	puedo
you (inf., sing.) can	puedes
he/she/it/you (form., sing.) can	puede
we can	podemos
you (inf., pl.) can	podéis
they/you (form., pl.) can	pueden

These verbs change their 'o' or 'u' to 'ue'...

acostarse	*to go to bed*	encontrar	*to find*
almorzar	*to have lunch*	jugar	*to play*
costar	*to cost*	llover	*to rain*
doler	*to hurt*	morir	*to die*
dormir	*to sleep*	volver	*to return*

Kevin's perspective on life had changed — radically...

Some common irregular verbs

In Spanish, the verbs 'to go', 'to give', 'to do / make' and 'to know' are irregular.

To say you know a person, use 'conocer' instead. It also has an irregular 1st person — conozco.

ir — *to go*

All of the present tense forms of 'ir' are irregular.

I go	voy	vamos	we go
you (inf., sing.) go	vas	vais	you (inf., pl.) go
he/she/it/you (form., sing.) go(es)	va	van	they/you (form., pl.) go

saber — *to know (something)*

I know	sé
you (inf., sing.) know	sabes
he/she/it/you (form., sing.) know(s)	sabe
we know	sabemos
you (inf., pl.) know	sabéis
they/you (form., pl.) know	saben

Only the 'I' form of 'saber' is irregular.

dar — *to give*

Only the 'I' and 'you (inf., pl.)' forms of 'dar' are irregular.

I give	doy
you (inf., sing.) give	das
he/she/it/you (form., sing.) give(s)	da
we give	damos
you (inf., pl.) give	dais
they/you (form., pl.) give	dan

hacer — *to do*

Only the 'I' form is irregular.

I do	hago	hacemos	we do
you (inf., sing.) do	haces	hacéis	you (inf., pl.) do
he/she/it/you (form., sing.) do(es)	hace	hacen	they/you (form., pl.) do

'Hacer' can also mean 'to make'.

Radical verbs are just so out there...

Find the mistake in each of these Spanish sentences. The subject of the verb is in brackets to help you.

1. Comenza a las tres. (ella)
2. Vís a la tienda. (vosotros)
3. Quieremos leche. (nosotros)
4. Do el libro a Lola. (yo)
5. Podes conducir. (tú)
6. Sabo tu nombre. (yo)

'Ser' and 'Estar' in the Present Tense

In Spanish, there are two verbs for 'to be' — 'ser' and 'estar'. They're used differently, so it's really important to know which you need in each situation. Oh, and one more thing — they're irregular too...

Use 'ser' for permanent things

The verb 'ser' means 'to be'. It's used for permanent things. You need it to...

ser — to be	
I am	soy
you are (inf., sing.)	eres
he/she/it/you (form., sing.) is/are	es
we are	somos
you are (inf., pl.)	sois
they/you (form., pl.) are	son

1) ...talk about nationalities.

> Somos galeses.   *We are Welsh.*

2) ...say someone's name or say who someone is in relation to you.

> Nerea es mi prima.   *Nerea is my cousin.*

3) ...talk about someone's job.

> Mi tío es profesor.   *My uncle is a teacher.*

4) ...describe the physical characteristics of a person or thing.

> Sois altos.   *You (inf., pl.) are tall.*

5) ...describe someone's personality.

> Son alegres.   *They are cheerful.*   Eres muy amable.   *You are very kind.*

Use 'estar' for temporary things and locations

'Estar' also means 'to be'. You use it to...

estar — to be	
I am	estoy
you are (inf., sing.)	estás
he/she/it/you (form., sing.) is/are	está
we are	estamos
you are (inf., pl.)	estáis
they/you (form., pl.) are	están

1) ...talk about things that might change in the future.

> Estoy bastante enfermo.   *I'm quite ill.*
> (But you might not be ill next week.)

> Estás muy triste hoy.   *You are very sad today.*
> (But you might not be sad tomorrow.)

Alba is positively thrilled with her parents' fashion choices.

2) ...talk about where someone or something is.

> Madrid está en España.   *Madrid is in Spain.*   Estamos en casa.   *We are at home.*

To be or to be — that's a question worth asking...

Decide whether you need 'ser' or 'estar' in each of these situations.

1. Es / Está muy hablador hoy.
2. Es / Está muy hablador en general.
3. Somos / Estamos de Escocia.
4. Soy / Estoy en Bradford.
5. Este es / está mi hermano.
6. Mi padre es / está médico.

Preterite Tense	**Talking About the Past**

The preterite tense ('I went' etc.) has quite a few tricky irregular forms — so pay close attention to this page.

I went — *The preterite tense*

To form the <u>preterite tense of regular verbs</u>, find the <u>stem</u> (see p.83) and then <u>add these endings</u>...

-ar verb endings

I	-é	-amos	we
you (inf., sing.)	-aste	-asteis	you (inf., pl.)
he/she/it/you (form., sing.)	-ó	-aron	they/you (form., pl.)

-er and -ir verb endings

I	-í	-imos	we
you (inf., sing.)	-iste	-isteis	you (inf., pl.)
he/she/it/you (form., sing.)	-ió	-ieron	they/you (form., pl.)

Habló con Marcela.
He spoke to Marcela.

<u>Don't forget the accent</u> — without it, you'd be saying 'I speak to Marcela'.

Nací en Japón.
I was born in Japan.

Bebisteis mucho.
You (inf., pl.) drank a lot.

Irregular verbs in the preterite tense

Here are four important <u>irregular verbs</u> in the <u>preterite tense</u>. 'Ser' and 'ir' are the <u>same</u> in the <u>preterite tense</u>.

ser — *to be*; ir — *to go*

I was / went	fui
you (inf., sing.) were / went	fuiste
he/she/it/you (form., sing.) was (were) / went	fue
we were / went	fuimos
you (inf., pl.) were / went	fuisteis
they/you (form., pl.) were / went	fueron

estar — *to be*

I was	estuve
you (inf., sing.) were	estuviste
he/she/it/you (form., sing.) was (were)	estuvo
we were	estuvimos
you (inf., pl.) were	estuvisteis
they/you (form., pl.) were	estuvieron

hacer — *to do / make*

I did / made	hice
you (inf., sing.) did / made	hiciste
he/she/it/you (form., sing.) did / made	hizo
we did / made	hicimos
you (inf., pl.) did / made	hicisteis
they/you (form., pl.) did / made	hicieron

Verbs ending in '-<u>car</u>' change their '<u>c</u>' to a '<u>qu</u>' in the '<u>I</u>' form of the <u>preterite tense</u> — '<u>tocar</u>' becomes '<u>toqué</u>'.
Verbs ending in '-<u>zar</u>' change their '<u>z</u>' to a '<u>c</u>' in the '<u>I</u>' form of the <u>preterite tense</u> — '<u>cruzar</u>' becomes '<u>crucé</u>'.

Even more irregular verbs

Some verbs <u>change their stem</u> in the <u>preterite tense</u>. If you know what the stem change is, you can predict what the verb is going to be in its other forms.

Infinitive	I	he/she/it
dar (to give)	di	dio
decir (to say)	dije	dijo
poder (to be able to)	pude	pudo
poner (to put)	puse	puso
querer (to want)	quise	quiso
tener (to have)	tuve	tuvo
traer (to bring)	traje	trajo
venir (to come)	vine	vino

 The 'he/she/it/you (form., sing.)' form is sometimes different to what you might expect.

Le dimos un gato. *We gave him a cat.*

Pero dijiste que te gustó. *But you (inf., sing.) said you liked it.*

Tuvisteis una idea. *You (inf., pl.) had an idea.*

Vinieron a mi fiesta. *They came to my party.*

Irregular verbs are a regular pain...

Put these verbs into the preterite tense. The subject is given in brackets.

1. llorar (ellos)	**3.** escribir (vosotros)	**5.** dar (tú)	**7.** hacer (vosotros)	**9.** venir (tú)
2. comer (nosotros)	**4.** cenar (yo)	**6.** poder (yo)	**8.** poner (usted)	**10.** traer (nosotros)

Talking About the Past

The imperfect tense is used to describe things in the past. It helps you say what you 'were doing', what 'was happening' and what you 'used to do'.

I was going / I used to go — *The imperfect tense*

To form the imperfect tense, find the stem (see p.83) and then add these endings. The 'I' form and the 'he/she/it/you (form., sing.)' form look the same, so you'll have to use the context to tell which is which.

-ar verb endings

I	-aba	-ábamos	we
you (inf., sing.)	-abas	-abais	you (inf., pl.)
he/she/it/you (form., sing.)	-aba	-aban	they/you (form., pl.)

Hablábamos por teléfono.
We were talking / used to talk on the phone.

-er and -ir verb endings

I	-ía	-íamos	we
you (inf., sing.)	-ías	-íais	you (inf., pl.)
he/she/it/you (form., sing.)	-ía	-ían	they/you (form., pl.)

Hacía mucho deporte.
I was doing / used to do a lot of sport.

You can also say what you used to do using the imperfect tense of the verb 'soler' ('solía') and then the infinitive.

Solía viajar mucho.   *I used to travel a lot.*

Irregular verbs in the imperfect tense

1) 'Ser', 'ir' and 'ver' are the only three verbs which don't follow the pattern. 'Ser' and 'ir' are irregular...

ser — *to be*

I was	era	éramos	we were
you (inf., sing.) were	eras	erais	you (inf., pl.) were
he/she/it/you (form., sing.) was (were)	era	eran	they/you (form., pl.) were

Mi padre era pintor.
My dad was / used to be a painter.

ir — *to go*

I went	iba	íbamos	we went
you went (inf., sing.)	ibas	ibais	you went (inf., pl.)
he/she/it/you (form., sing.) went	iba	iban	they/you (form., pl.) went

Iba a muchos conciertos.
I went / used to go to lots of concerts.

2) ...but 'ver' is almost regular — just add the '-er' endings onto 've-', e.g. 'veía'.

Veía la tele.   *I watched / used to watch TV.*

Había — *there was / there were*

In the present tense 'hay' means 'there is' or 'there are'. The imperfect form of 'hay' is 'había', which means 'there was' or 'there were' — it stays the same, regardless of whether the noun is singular or plural.

Había un mono en el árbol.   *There was a monkey in the tree.*

Siempre había muchos niños allí.   *There were always lots of children there.*

'Hay' and 'había' come from the verb 'haber'.

Learning the imperfect — a perfect way to spend your time...

Put these verbs into the imperfect tense. The subject is given in brackets.

1. cantar (yo)	**3.** aprender (usted)	**5.** volver (ustedes)	**7.** nadar (tú)
2. ser (nosotros)	**4.** decir (él)	**6.** seguir (vosotros)	**8.** ir (ellos)

| Preterite vs. Imperfect | **Talking About the Past** |

Choosing which past tense to use can be a tricky business — even for people who have been learning Spanish for ages. Here are some guidelines to get you started — read them carefully.

Use the preterite tense to...

① ...talk about a single completed action in the past.

Fui al cine el jueves.   *I went to the cinema on Thursday.*

② ...talk about events that happened during a set period of time.

Ayer hizo calor.   *Yesterday it was hot.*

Remember to use 'hacer' with nouns such as 'calor', 'frío', 'viento' and 'sol' to say 'it's hot / cold / windy / sunny'. See p.41 for more weather vocabulary.

③ ...interrupt a description of movement taking place in the imperfect tense.

Volvía del gimnasio cuando vi a Irene.   *I was coming back from the gym when I saw Irene.*

Use the imperfect tense to...

① ...talk about what you used to do repeatedly in the past.

Iba al cine cada jueves.   *I used to go to the cinema every Thursday.*

② ...describe something, like the weather, in the past.

Hacía calor, pero estaba nublado.   *It was hot, but it was cloudy.*

Camping in the rain was bad enough, but imperfect tents were unforgivable...

③ ...say where you were going when something else happened. You use the imperfect tense to describe the background situation.

Volvía del gimnasio cuando vi a Irene.
I was coming back from the gym when I saw Irene.

④ ...say how long something had been happening for. For this, you also need 'desde hacía', which is the imperfect form of 'desde hace' (see p.83).

Leía desde hacía una hora cuando me llamó.
I had been reading for an hour when he called me.

You only need to be able to recognise this structure — you don't need to be able to use it.

Preterite or imperfect? It's a very tense business...

In each of the following sentences, choose whether you need the preterite or the imperfect tense.
1. Siempre hizo / hacía mucho viento.
2. Ayer volví / volvía de mis vacaciones.
3. ¿Fuiste / Ibas a la piscina ayer?
4. Fui / Iba al colegio cuando tuve / tenía una idea.

Talking About the Past

The perfect and pluperfect tenses allow you to say what you 'have done' or 'had done'. They're pretty easy to learn and are a useful addition to your magic bag of grammatical tricks.

Finding the past participle

1) In the sentence 'I have done', 'done' is a past participle. You need to know how to form past participles before you get started on the perfect and pluperfect tenses.

2) For '-ar' verbs, remove the 'ar' and add '-ado'.

esperar (*to wait*) ⟶ esperado (*waited*)

3) For '-er' and '-ir' verbs, remove the 'er' or 'ir' and add '-ido'.

comer (*to eat*) ⟶ comido (*eaten*)

elegir (*to choose*) ⟶ elegido (*chosen*)

4) There are some irregular participles that you also need to learn...

Infinitive	Past participle	Infinitive	Past participle
abrir	abierto (*opened*)	leer	leído (*read*)
cubrir	cubierto (*covered*)	poner	puesto (*put*)
decir	dicho (*said*)	romper	roto (*broken*)
escribir	escrito (*written*)	ver	visto (*seen*)
hacer	hecho (*done / made*)	volver	vuelto (*returned*)

In these tenses, the participle stays the same — you don't need to make it feminine or plural.

He hecho — *I have done*

'I have done' is the perfect tense.

To say what you 'have done', you need the present tense of the verb 'haber' and the past participle.

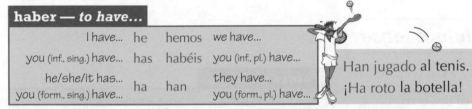

haber — *to have...*

I have...	he	hemos	*we have...*
you (inf., sing.) have...	has	habéis	*you (inf., pl.) have...*
he/she/it has...	ha	han	*they have...*
you (form., sing.) have...			*you (form., pl.) have...*

Han jugado al tenis. *They have played tennis.*
¡Ha roto la botella! *He has broken the bottle!*

Me gustaría ir a Roma porque nunca he estado allí. *I'd like to go to Rome because I've never been there.*

Había hecho — *I had done*

'I had done' is the pluperfect tense.

To say what you 'had done', you need the imperfect tense of the verb 'haber' and the past participle.

haber — *to have...*

Learn more about the imperfect tense on p.87.

I had...	había	habíamos	*we had...*
you (inf., sing.) had...	habías	habíais	*you (inf., pl.) had...*
he/she/it had...	había	habían	*they had...*
you (form., sing.) had...			*you (form., pl.) had...*

Había comprado **un gato**. *He had bought a cat.*
Habían visto **el coche**. *They had seen the car.*

No pude ir porque no había hecho mis deberes. *I couldn't go because I hadn't done my homework.*

If only I had learned my past participles...

Translate these sentences into Spanish using the perfect and pluperfect tenses.

1. They had sung.   **3.** You have (inf., pl.) learned.   **5.** I had drunk.   **7.** She has followed.

2. He has travelled.   **4.** You have (form., sing.) seen.   **6.** We had finished.   **8.** You have (inf., sing.) lived.

Talking About the Future

You'll need to talk about things that are going to happen at some point in the future.
There are two ways you can do it — and the first one's a piece of cake...

I'm going to... — *The immediate future*

ir — to go

I am going	voy
you (inf., sing.) are going	vas
he/she/it is going	va
you (form., sing.) are going	
we are going	vamos
you (inf., pl.) are going	vais
they/you (form., pl.) are going	van

1) The <u>immediate future</u> tense can be used to talk about something that's <u>about to happen</u>, as well as something <u>further</u> on in the future.

2) To form the immediate future, take the <u>present tense</u> of '<u>ir</u>' (*to go*) that goes with the person you're talking about.

3) Then, add '<u>a</u>' and a verb in the <u>infinitive</u>.

voy	+	a	+	comer	=	Voy a comer.
I am going <u>Present tense</u> of 'ir'.				*to eat* Another verb in the <u>infinitive</u>.		*I am going to eat.* A sentence about the <u>future</u>.

Susana va a leer una revista.   *Susana is going to read a magazine.*

El sábado, vamos a ir a Francia.   *On Saturday, we are going to go to France.*

⌇⌇⌇⌇⌇⌇⌇⌇⌇⌇⌇⌇⌇⌇⌇
Put in phrases to say when you're
going to do something (p.2-3).
⌇⌇⌇⌇⌇⌇⌇⌇⌇⌇⌇⌇⌇⌇⌇

Just a little light reading...

I will... — *The proper future tense*

1) Use the proper <u>future tense</u> to say what will happen.

2) To form it, take the '<u>future stem</u>' of the verb — for most verbs, this is the <u>infinitive</u>.

3) Add the <u>ending</u> that matches the person you're talking about (the endings are the <u>same</u> for <u>all verbs</u>).

Future endings

I	-é	-emos	we
you (inf., sing.)	-ás	-éis	you (inf., pl.)
he/she/it/you (form., sing.)	-á	-án	they/you (form., pl.)

hablar	+	é	=	hablaré
infinitive		*future ending*		*I will talk.*

⌇⌇⌇⌇⌇⌇⌇⌇⌇⌇⌇⌇⌇⌇⌇⌇⌇⌇⌇
There are a few verbs that have a
special future stem, so you just have
to learn them off by heart.
These are the most important ones.
⌇⌇⌇⌇⌇⌇⌇⌇⌇⌇⌇⌇⌇⌇⌇⌇⌇⌇⌇

Dormirás.   *You will sleep.*

Jugaré al tenis.   *I will play tennis.*

Cogerá el autobús.   *He will take the bus.*

I will win
this match...

Venderemos el perro.   *We will sell the dog.*

Infinitive	'yo' form
decir (*to say*)	diré
haber (*to have...*)	habré
hacer (*to do / make*)	haré
tener (*to have*)	tendré
poner (*to put*)	pondré
querer (*to want*)	querré
saber (*to know*)	sabré
venir (*to come*)	vendré
salir (*to go out*)	saldré
poder (*to be able to*)	podré

Predicting the future might be difficult, but talking about it isn't...

Put these present tense verbs into the immediate and proper future tenses, keeping the subject the same.

1. como	**3.** baila	**5.** ponen	**7.** puedes	**9.** queremos
2. tenemos	**4.** doy	**6.** jugáis	**8.** canta	**10.** vivís

Would, Could and Should

Now it's time to talk about what could or would happen in the future.

Future stem + imperfect -er / -ir endings — *The conditional*

1) The conditional tense can be used for saying 'would'. It uses the same stems as the proper future tense (see p.90) and adds these endings:

comer	+	comía	=	comería
to eat		*I was eating.*		*I would eat.*
This is the infinitive. Not all verbs use the same future stem though (see p.82).		This is the -er / -ir ending of the imperfect tense.		A sentence in the conditional.

Conditional endings

I	-ía
you (inf., sing.)	-ías
he/she/it/you (form., sing.)	-ía
we	-íamos
you (inf., pl.)	-íais
they/you (form., pl.)	-ían

Podría **ayudarme?**   *Could you (form., sing) help me?*

Debería **hacer mis deberes.**   *I should do my homework.*

Using 'poder' (to be able to) in the conditional lets you say 'could', and 'deber' (to have to) helps you form sentences with 'should'.

2) You can combine the conditional with other tenses to make more complicated sentences:

Bailaría, **pero me duelen los pies.**   *I would dance, but my feet hurt.*

Les gustaría **ir a la playa, sin embargo no pueden ir porque está lloviendo.**
They would like to go to the beach, however they can't go because it's raining.

For more on conjunctions, check out p.82.

3) If you want to seriously wow the examiners, use the conditional tense of 'haber' (*to have...*) with the past participle (see p.89) to mean 'would have...'.

Habría comprado **un libro, pero no tengo dinero.**   *I would have bought a book, but I have no money.*

Quisiera — *I would like*

Two really common verbs sometimes get replaced in the conditional by a different form.

1) The conditional form of 'querer' (*to want*) is often replaced by 'quisiera' — it means *'I would like'*.

Quisiera un coche.   *I would like a car.*   Quisiera una manzana.   *I would like an apple.*

2) You can use 'quisiera' in polite requests.

Quisiera reservar una mesa para tres personas.   *I would like to reserve a table for three.*

3) The conditional of 'haber' (*to have...*) can also be replaced by 'hubiera'.

'Quisiera' and 'hubiera' are in the imperfect subjunctive. See p.97 for more.

Hubiera venido antes.   *I would have come earlier.*

You can move on to the next topic, on one condition...

Write these verbs in the conditional. The subject has been given to you in brackets.

1. ir (tú)   **3.** venir (nosotros)   **5.** partir (yo)   **7.** hablar (usted)
2. cantar (él)   **4.** decir (vosotros)   **6.** salir (ellos)   **8.** tener (nosotros)

Reflexive Verbs	# Reflexive Verbs

Sometimes you'll have to talk about things you do to yourself — like 'washing yourself' or 'getting yourself up' in the morning. It sounds weird in English, but in Spanish they do it all the time.

Me, te, se... — *Reflexive pronouns*

1) '<u>Se</u>' means '<u>oneself</u>'. Here are all the different ways to say 'self':

myself	me	ourselves	nos	
yourself (inf., sing.)	te	yourselves (inf., pl.)	os	
himself/herself/oneself	se	themselves, each other	se	
yourself (form., sing.)		yourselves (form., pl.)		

You can tell which verbs need 'self' by checking in the dictionary. 'To get washed' in the dictionary would be 'lavarse'.

2) Reflexive verbs follow a straightforward pattern, e.g. '<u>lavarse</u>' = to get washed (literally '<u>to wash oneself</u>'). The <u>reflexive pronoun</u> usually just goes in <u>front</u> of the normal <u>verb</u>.

I get washed	me lavo	we get washed	nos lavamos
you (inf., sing.) get washed	te lavas	you (inf., pl.) get washed	os laváis
he/she/it gets washed you (form., sing.) get washed	se lava	they get washed you (form., pl.) get washed	se lavan

I hope that's p.m...

¿Te sientes mal?	*Do you feel ill?*	No me despierto temprano.	*I don't wake up early.*

3) There are lots of these verbs, but here are the ones you really <u>should know</u>:

'acostarse', 'sentirse', 'despertarse' and 'vestirse' are all radical-changing verbs (see p.84).

acostarse	*to go to bed*	sentirse	*to feel*
levantarse	*to get up*	llamarse	*to be called*

despertarse	*to wake up*	vestirse	*to get dressed*
irse	*to go away*	ponerse	*to put on*

Putting reflexive verbs in the perfect tense

When you want to use reflexive verbs in the <u>perfect tense</u>, put the <u>reflexive pronoun</u> (e.g. 'me', 'se') in front of the <u>verb</u> as usual:

Me Stick the reflexive pronoun at the start.	+	he puesto Then put the whole of the perfect tense verb (see p.89).	=	Me he puesto el sombrero. *I've put on my hat.*

Use 'se' to make impersonal phrases

The reflexive pronoun '<u>se</u>' is often used in front of a verb that's not reflexive to make it <u>impersonal</u>. It's like saying '<u>one does something</u>' in English. The verb has to be in the '<u>he / she / it</u>' form.

¿Se puede comer afuera?	*Can one eat outside?*

For more about impersonal verbs, turn to p.95.

Just me, <u>myself</u> and I revising reflexive verbs...

Write these reflexive verbs in the present and perfect tenses. The subject has been given to you in brackets.

1. llamarse (yo)
2. levantarse (ellos)
3. lavarse (él)
4. acostarse (tú)
5. sentirse (nosotros)
6. irse (vosotros)
7. vestirse (usted)
8. despertarse (tú)

Verbs with '-ing' and 'Just Done'

The continuous tenses are great if you want to specify that something is ongoing at a particular moment.

Use the present continuous for something happening right now

1) <u>Most</u> of the time you'd translate phrases such as 'I am doing' and 'I was doing' with <u>normal tenses</u> — those two would be 'hago' (present tense), and 'hacía' (imperfect tense).

2) If you want <u>to stress</u> that something <u>is happening</u> at the moment, use the <u>present continuous</u>.

> Estoy almorzando.   *I'm having lunch.*

3) To form the present continuous, you need the correct part of '<u>estar</u>' (*to be*) in the <u>present</u> tense...

4) ...and the '<u>-ing</u>' part — also called the <u>present participle</u> or <u>gerund</u>.

5) It's made up of the <u>stem</u> of the verb (p.83), plus the correct <u>ending</u>.

a) if it's an -<u>ar</u> verb, add '-<u>ando</u>'.

> estoy + hablar + -ando = estoy hablando
> *present of 'estar' 'hablar' stem -ar ending I am speaking*

b) if it's an -<u>er</u> or -<u>ir</u> verb, add '-<u>iendo</u>'.

> estás + comer + -iendo = estás comiendo
> *present of 'estar' 'comer' stem -er ending you (inf., sing.) are eating*

estar — *to be*

I am	estoy
you (inf., sing.) are	estás
he/she/it is you (form., sing.) are	está
we are	estamos
you (inf. pl.) are	estáis
they / you (form., pl.) are	están

6) There are only a few <u>irregular</u> ones you need to <u>know</u>:

> caer (*to fall*) ⟶ cayendo   servir (*to serve*) ⟶ sirviendo
> leer (*to read*) ⟶ leyendo   pedir (*to ask for*) ⟶ pidiendo
> oír (*to hear*) ⟶ oyendo   morir (*to die*) ⟶ muriendo
> construir (*to build*) ⟶ construyendo   decir (*to say*) ⟶ diciendo

The imperfect continuous is for saying what was happening

1) If you want <u>to stress</u> that something <u>was happening</u> in the past, use the <u>imperfect continuous</u>.

2) The imperfect continuous is <u>similar</u> to the present continuous, except '<u>estar</u>' has to be in the <u>imperfect</u> tense.

> Estaba durmiendo cuando sonó el teléfono.
> *He / She was sleeping when the telephone rang.*

> The <u>preterite</u> tense is used here to show that a <u>sudden</u> action — the telephone ringing — <u>interrupted</u> an <u>ongoing</u> action in the <u>imperfect continuous</u> — i.e. the person sleeping.

'Acabar de'— *to say that something's just happened*

> 'Acabar' is a regular -ar verb.

To say what's <u>just</u> happened, use the present tense of '<u>acabar</u>', followed by '<u>de</u>' and a verb in the <u>infinitive</u>.

> Acabo de ducharme.   *I have just taken a shower.*   Acaba de salir.   *She has just left.*

Learning, learning and more learning...

Put these verbs in the present continuous, the imperfect continuous and the 'acabar de' forms.

1. caer (él)   3. saltar (ella)   5. correr (vosotros)   7. dar (tú)   9. servir (ustedes)
2. abrir (tú)   4. decir (ellos)   6. seguir (nosotros)   8. leer (yo)   10. bailar (nosotros)

Negative Forms

No, I'm not going to write anything here about negatives. Nothing at all... except that they're pretty useful.

'No' in front of the verb means 'not'

1) To change a sentence to mean the <u>opposite</u> in Spanish, you have to put 'no' in front of the <u>action word</u>:

> Soy profesor. *I'm a teacher.* ⟹ No soy profesor. *I'm not a teacher.*

> Hablo español. *I speak Spanish.* ⟹ No hablo español. *I don't speak Spanish.*

2) You can do the <u>same</u> with <u>all of the tenses</u> — look at these examples:

> No vas a leer el libro. *You're not going to read the book.*   No fui al parque. *I didn't go to the park.*

Sometimes you have to say 'no' twice...

1) 'No' in Spanish means both '<u>no</u>' and '<u>not</u>'.

2) This means that if you're answering a <u>question</u>, you may need to say 'no' <u>twice</u>:

> No, no quiero sopa, gracias. *No, I don't want soup, thanks.*

> No, Juan no veía la tele. *No, Juan wasn't watching TV.*

He wasn't remotely interested in any of the programmes.

Even more negatives...

There are more negatives you need to <u>understand</u> — for top marks you should use them too.

ya no	*not any more*
no ... nadie	*not anybody (nobody)*
no ... nunca / jamás	*not ever (never)*
no ... nada	*not anything (nothing)*
no ... ni ... ni	*neither ... nor*
no ... ningún / ninguna	*none / not one / not a single (before noun)*
no .. ninguno / ninguna	*none / not one / not a single one (to replace noun)*

> Ya no voy a York.
> *I don't go to York any more.*

> No hay nadie aquí.
> *There isn't anybody here. / There's nobody here.*

> Julia no va nunca al cine.
> *Julia never goes to the cinema.*

> No hay nada.
> *There isn't anything. / There's nothing.*

> Sam y Clara no van ni a Londres ni a Madrid.
> *Sam and Clara go to neither London nor Madrid.*

> No hay ningún plátano. *There is not a single banana.*

> No hay ninguna pera. *There is not a single pear.*

> Jo no tiene ninguno/a. *Jo doesn't have a single one.*

p.69 has more information on 'ningún'.

On a positive note, that's the negatives finished...

Translate these sentences using negative forms.

1. I didn't go to the cinema.

2. We don't go to the gym any more.

3. You (tú) go to neither Oslo nor Faro.

4. Sally doesn't have a single apple.

5. There's nothing here.

6. There's nobody in the car.

The Passive and Impersonal Verbs

Impersonal verbs and the passive come up occasionally, so it's important that you know a bit about them.

Ser + past participle — *The passive voice*

You don't need to use the passive, but you do need to be able to recognise it.

1) In an <u>active</u> sentence, the <u>subject does</u> something. | Lavé la taza. | *I washed the cup.*

2) In the <u>passive</u> voice, something is <u>done to</u> the <u>subject</u>. | La taza fue lavada. | *The cup was washed.*

3) This means you can say something is <u>happening</u> without always saying <u>who</u> is doing it.

4) The passive is formed using 'ser' (*to be*) and the <u>past participle</u> (see p.89).

fueron	+	limpiado	=	Las mesas fueron limpiadas.
they were		*cleaned*		*The tables were cleaned.*
This is the <u>preterite tense</u> of 'ser' (see p.86). This changes depending on the tense and subject.		<u>past participle</u> of the verb '<u>limpiar</u>'		*A sentence in the <u>passive</u> voice.*

In the passive, the past participle must <u>always</u> match the <u>gender</u> and <u>number</u> of the <u>object</u> that you're talking about. Here 'limpiadas' is used because 'las mesas' are <u>feminine</u> and <u>plural</u>.

5) If you want to add <u>someone</u> or <u>something</u> doing the action, add '<u>por</u>' (*by*) and <u>who / what</u> did it.

| El libro será leído por Jo. | *The book will be read by Jo.* | Fue escrito por Jordi. | *It was written by Jordi.* |

Se + 3rd person — *Impersonal verbs*

1) You can turn <u>any</u> Spanish verb into an <u>impersonal verb</u> (e.g. '<u>one does</u>' rather than '*I do*') by using '<u>se</u>' and the '<u>he / she / it</u>' form of the verb:

| ¿Se necesita un libro? | ¿Se habla francés aquí? |
| *Does one need a book?* | *Does one speak French here?* |

2) If there's a <u>subject</u> in the sentence, use the <u>singular</u> for a single subject, and the <u>plural</u> for plural subjects:

| El arroz se cocina durante quince minutos. | *The rice is cooked for fifteen minutes.* |

| Las puertas se abren a las nueve. | *The doors are opened at nine.* |

Some more important impersonal verbs...

1) '<u>Hay que</u>' is an impersonal way of saying that '*one has to do something*'.

My essay on invisibility.

| Hay que hacer los deberes. | *Homework has to be done.* | ← Literally: *One has to do homework.* |

2) '<u>Parece que</u>' means '*it seems that*': | Parece que todo ha cambiado. | *It seems that everything has changed.* |

3) <u>Weather</u> verbs are <u>always impersonal</u> — they're written in the '<u>he / she / it</u>' form of the verb.

| Llueve. | *It rains.* | Está nevando. | *It's snowing.* | Truena. | *It thunders.* |

Tronar (to thunder) is a radical-changing verb.

One has to learn this — it's nothing personal...

A) *Decide which of these 4 sentences are in the passive voice.*
1. Comimos la sopa.
2. El poema fue escrito.
3. La mesa es puesta.
4. Cierras la puerta.

B) *Complete using the impersonal form.*
1. .... la bufanda. (comprar)
2. .... los postres. (comer)

The Subjunctive

Oh yes, you're in for a treat — it's time to learn about the Spanish subjunctive...

Forming the present subjunctive

1) Sometimes, the <u>present subjunctive</u> is needed <u>instead</u> of the <u>normal present</u> tense.

2) To <u>form</u> the subjunctive, use the same <u>stem</u> as the '<u>I</u>' form of the normal <u>present tense</u>.

3) For -<u>ar</u> verbs, add the -<u>er</u> present tense <u>endings</u>. For -<u>er</u> or -<u>ir</u> verbs, add the -<u>ar</u> endings.

infinitive	hablar	comer	vivir
'yo form'	hablo	como	vivo
I	hable	coma	viva
you (inf., sing.)	hables	comas	vivas
he/she/it/you (form., sing.)	hable	coma	viva
we	hablemos	comamos	vivamos
you (inf., pl.)	habléis	comáis	viváis
they/you (form., pl.)	hablen	coman	vivan

Irregular verbs in the present subjunctive

1) Some verbs are <u>irregular</u> in the 'I' form of the <u>present</u> tense, so the <u>subjunctive</u> has to <u>match</u> this.

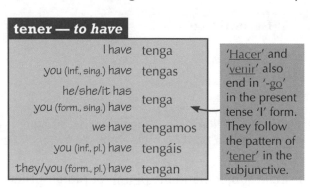

tener — to have

I have	tenga
you (inf., sing.) have	tengas
he/she/it has you (form., sing.) have	tenga
we have	tengamos
you (inf., pl.) have	tengáis
they/you (form., pl.) have	tengan

'Hacer' and 'venir' also end in '-go' in the present tense 'I' form. They follow the pattern of 'tener' in the subjunctive.

poder — to be able to

I can	pueda
you (inf., sing.) can	puedas
he/she/it can you (form., sing.) can	pueda
we can	podamos
you (inf., pl.) can	podáis
they/you (form., pl.) can	puedan

I can... I really really can...

The '<u>we</u>' and '<u>you</u>' (inf., pl.) forms of <u>radical-changing</u> verbs have <u>regular</u> stems.

2) But <u>some verbs</u> are completely <u>irregular</u> in the <u>subjunctive</u>. Here are some of them:

ser — to be

I am	sea	seamos	we are
you (inf., sing.) are	seas	seáis	you (inf., pl.) are
he/she/it is you (form., sing.) are	sea	sean	they are you (form., pl.) are

estar — to be

I am	esté	estemos	we are
you (inf., sing.) are	estés	estéis	you (inf., pl.) are
he/she/it is you (form., sing.) are	esté	estén	they are you (form., pl.) are

ir — to go

I go	vaya	vayamos	we go
you (inf., sing.) go	vayas	vayáis	you (inf., pl.) go
he/she/it goes you (form., sing.) go	vaya	vayan	they go you (form., pl.) go

dar — to give

I give	dé	demos	we give
you (inf., sing.) give	des	deis	you (inf., pl.) give
he/she/it gives you (form., sing.) give	dé	den	they give you (form., pl.) give

I want you to revise the subjunctive...

Write these verbs in the present subjunctive. The subject has been given to you in brackets.

1. saltar (tú)   **3.** limpiar (nosotros)   **5.** venir (él)   **7.** poder (ustedes)

2. escuchar (yo)   **4.** abrir (ellos)   **6.** hacer (nosotros)   **8.** tener (vosotros)

The Subjunctive

Now it's time to find out when you need to use the subjunctive. It's a tricky old page so take your time.

Use the present subjunctive...

① ...to get <u>someone else</u> to do something:

> Ana quiere que lavemos los platos. *Ana wants us to wash the dishes.*

② ...to express a <u>wish</u> or <u>desire</u>:

> Espero que haya fresas en el supermercado. *I hope that there are strawberries in the supermarket.*

③ ...after expressing an <u>emotion</u> or <u>opinion</u>:

> Es importante que estudiéis. *It's important that you (inf., pl.) study.*

④ ...to say that something's <u>unlikely</u> to happen:

> No creo que vaya a venir. *I don't believe he's going to come.*

⑤ ...when there's a <u>requirement</u>:

'sepa' is from the verb 'saber' (to know). It's also irregular in the subjunctive — its stem is 'sep'.

Between cooking and the subjunctive, these guys had a lot on their plates.

> Necesito a alguien que sepa cocinar. *I need someone who knows how to cook.*

⑥ ...after '<u>cuando</u>' ('*when*'), '<u>antes de que</u>' ('*before*') and '<u>aunque</u>' ('*even if*') when talking about the future:

> Vamos al teatro cuando llegue Marta. *We're going to the theatre when Marta arrives.*

⑦ ...after '<u>para que</u>' ('*so that*') to express purpose:

> Van a la tienda para que pueda comprar leche. *They're going to the shop so that he can buy milk.*

If I *were* to go to Spain...

1) The <u>imperfect subjunctive</u> is like the 'were' in '*if I were to go to Spain*'. You <u>don't</u> need to use it, but you'll need to <u>recognise</u> it.

2) '<u>Quisiera</u>' ('*I would like*') is a <u>common example</u> of the imperfect subjunctive. See p.91 for more about using it in <u>polite requests</u>.

	hablar	comer	vivir
I	hablara	comiera	viviera
you (inf., sing.)	hablaras	comieras	vivieras
he/she/it/you (form., sing.)	hablara	comiera	viviera
we	habláramos	comiéramos	viviéramos
you (inf., pl.)	hablarais	comierais	vivierais
they/you (form., pl.)	hablaran	comieran	vivieran

If I were in charge, there would be no exams...

Decide which sentences use the present subjunctive and which use the imperfect subjunctive.

1. Quiere que le des el abrigo.
2. Si tuviera mucho dinero, compraría un coche.
3. Vamos a hacerlo cuando tengamos tiempo.
4. Mi madre pido que mi padre sacara la basura.

Imperative	Giving Orders

Learn what's on this page and you'll be giving out orders in no time...

Informal commands

1) To form a <u>singular informal</u> command, take the '<u>tú</u>' part of the <u>present tense</u> verb and <u>take off</u> the '<u>s</u>'.

> escribe**s** *you write* → ¡Escribe! *Write!*   escucha**s** *you listen* → ¡Escucha! *Listen!*

2) With commands, <u>pronouns</u> (e.g. *me, them, it*) are placed at the <u>end</u> of the word and you need to <u>add</u> an <u>accent</u> to show where the <u>stress</u> is.

> ¡Cómelo!   *Eat it!*

3) To tell <u>two or more people</u> what to do in an <u>informal</u> way, take the <u>infinitive</u> and <u>change</u> the final '<u>r</u>' to a '<u>d</u>'.

> hablar (*to speak*) → ¡Hablad! *Speak!*
>
> leer (*to read*) → ¡Leed! *Read!*
>
> salir (*to go out*) → ¡Salid! *Go out!*

There are a few common irregular imperatives.

Infinitive	Informal Singular
decir (*to say*)	¡Di!
hacer (*to do / make*)	¡Haz!
ir (*to go*)	¡Ve!
poner (*to put*)	¡Pon!
salir (*to go out*)	¡Sal!
ser (*to be*)	¡Sé!
tener (*to have*)	¡Ten!
venir (*to come*)	¡Ven!

Formal commands

1) To <u>politely</u> tell someone what to do, use the <u>formal 'you'</u> form of the <u>present subjunctive</u>.

> ¡Hable!   *Speak!*

For a reminder of the present subjunctive, head back to p.96.

> Siga todo recto.   *Continue straight on.*

Infinitive	Present Subjunctive
dar (*to give*)	dé
haber (*to have...*)	haya
ir (*to go*)	vaya
saber (*to know*)	sepa
ser (*to be*)	sea

2) As always, there are some <u>irregular forms</u> that you just need to <u>learn</u>.

3) When politely telling <u>more than one</u> person what to do, use the <u>formal plural</u> of the <u>subjunctive</u>.

> ¡Entren!   *Enter!*

> Cojan la primera calle a la derecha.   *Take the first street on the right.*

Making commands negative

1) To tell someone <u>not</u> to do something, <u>always</u> use the <u>subjunctive</u>.

> ¡No escuches!   *Don't listen!*

2) Watch out — any <u>pronouns</u> have to go before the verb:

> ¡Tócalo!   *Touch it!* → ¡No lo toques!   *Don't touch it!*

Do these exercises... go on...

Write these verbs as positive and negative commands. The type of command is in brackets.

1. cantar (inf., sing.)
2. bailar (form., pl.)
3. tener (inf., sing.)
4. dar (form., sing.)
5. abrir (inf., pl.)
6. venir (inf., pl.)
7. ser (form., sing.)
8. ir (form., pl.)

The Listening Exam

Ah. Your reward for conquering all that grammar is a section about those pesky exams... Sorry about that. But there is some good news — these pages are crammed full of advice to help you tackle them head on.

There are four exams for GCSE Spanish

1) Your Spanish GCSE is assessed by four separate exams — Listening, Speaking, Reading and Writing.

2) Each exam is worth 25% of your final mark. You'll get a grade between 1 and 9 (with 9 being the highest).

3) You won't sit all of the papers at the same time — you'll probably have your speaking exam a couple of weeks before the rest of your exams.

The Listening Exam has two sections

1) For the listening paper, you'll listen to various recordings of people speaking in Spanish and answer questions on what you've heard.

2) The paper is 45 minutes long (including 5 minutes reading time).

3) You'll get one section where the questions are in English, so you'll write these answers in English too. The questions in the other section will be in Spanish — you may need to answer these in Spanish.

Foundation tier papers will be slightly different, and the exact format of the exams varies between exam boards. Ask your teacher for more details.

Read through the paper carefully at the start of the test

1) Before the recordings begin, you'll be given five minutes to read through the paper.

2) Use this time to read each question carefully. Some are multiple choice, and others require you to write some short answers — make sure you know what each one is asking you to do.

3) In particular, look at the questions which are written in Spanish. Try to work out what the questions mean. There's a list of exam-style Spanish question words and phrases on the inside front cover of this book to help you prepare for this.

Miguel read 'whole model' instead of 'role-model' — it went downhill from there.

4) Reading the question titles, and the questions themselves, will give you a good idea of the topics you'll be asked about. This should help you predict what to listen out for.

5) You can write on the exam paper, so scribble down anything that might be useful.

Make notes while listening to the recordings

1) You'll hear each audio track twice, and then there'll be a pause for you to write down your answer.

2) While you're listening, it's a good idea to jot down a few details — e.g. dates, times, names or key words. But make sure you keep listening while you're writing down any notes.

3) Listen right to the end, even if you think you've got the answer — sometimes the person will change their mind or add an important detail at the end.

4) Don't worry if you can't understand every word that's being said — just listen carefully both times and try to pick out the vocabulary you need to answer the question.

Listen to the speaker's tone, too — this will hint at their mood, e.g. angry or excited.

Don't worry, I'm all ears...

If you've heard a track twice, and you're still not sure of the answer, scribble one down anyway — you never know, it might be the right one. You may as well write something sensible just in case — it's worth a shot.

The Speaking Exam

The Speaking Exam can seem daunting, but remember — no one is trying to catch you out, so try to stay calm.

There are three parts to the Speaking Exam

During your preparation time, you can make notes to take in with you for the first two tasks. You can't keep the notes for the conversation.

1) Your speaking exam will be conducted and recorded by your teacher.

2) The exam is in three parts. Before you start, you'll get 10-12 minutes to prepare for the first two sections:

① Role-play (2 min.)	② Photo Card (3 min.)	③ Conversation (5-7 min.)
You'll get a card with a scenario on it. It'll have five bullet points — most will have notes on what to say, in Spanish. The '!' means you'll be asked an unknown question, and '?' shows you have to ask a question about the words next to it. See p.5 for an example.	Before the exam, you'll receive a photo and some questions relating to it (look at the example on p.46). Your teacher will ask you the questions that are on the photo card, as well as some questions you haven't seen.	You and your teacher will have a conversation based on one or two themes that you've studied. You may get to choose one of the themes, and you may also have to ask your teacher a question during the conversation.

3) The role-play card will tell you if you need to use 'tú', but otherwise, use 'usted' to talk to your teacher.

Try to be imaginative with your answers

You need to find ways to show off the full extent of your Spanish knowledge. You should try to:

1) Use a range of tenses — e.g. for a question on daily routine, think of when something different happens.

> Pero mañana será diferente porque jugaré al tenis después del instituto.   *But tomorrow it will be different because I will play tennis after school.*

If you can't remember a word, just say something suitable that you do know instead, e.g. swap 'tennis' for 'hockey', or 'nephew' for 'sister'.

2) Talk about other people, not just yourself — it's fine to make people up if that helps.

> Me gusta el rugby, pero mi sobrino lo odia.   *I like rugby, but my nephew hates it.*

3) Give loads of opinions and reasons for your opinions.

> En mi opinión, debemos reciclar más porque producimos demasiada basura.   *In my opinion, we must recycle more because we produce too much rubbish.*

If you're really struggling, ask for help in Spanish

1) If you get really stuck trying to think of a word or phrase, you can ask for help — as long as it's in Spanish.

2) For example, if you can't remember how to say 'homework' in Spanish, ask your teacher. You won't get any marks for vocabulary your teacher's given you though.

> ¿Cómo se dice 'homework' en español?   *How do you say 'homework' in Spanish?*

3) If you don't hear something clearly, just ask:

> ¿Puede repetir, por favor?   *Can you repeat, please?*

You could also ask this if you're desperately in need of time to think of an answer.

Don't speak too soon — wait for the teacher to tell you to start...

Given that you're only human, you're bound to have a few slip-ups in the speaking exam. Don't panic — it's completely natural. What's important is how you deal with a mistake — just correct yourself and move on.

The Reading Exam

After all that listening and speaking, the reading exam offers some nice peace and quiet. Apart from the voice inside your head that screams "WHAT ON EARTH DOES THAT WORD MEAN?!" (Or maybe that's just me...)

Read the questions and texts carefully

1) The <u>higher tier</u> reading paper is around <u>1 hour long</u>.

2) You'll be given a <u>variety of Spanish texts</u> and then asked questions about them. The texts could include blog posts, emails, newspaper reports, adverts and literary texts. Some questions will be in <u>English</u> and some will be in <u>Spanish</u>. You need to write your <u>answers</u> in the <u>same language</u> as the question.

3) <u>Scan through the text</u> first to <u>get an idea</u> of what it's about. Then read the <u>questions</u> that go with it carefully, making sure you understand <u>what information</u> you should be looking out for.

4) Next, <u>go back through the text</u>. You're not expected to understand every word, so don't get distracted by trying to work out what everything means — <u>focus</u> on finding the <u>information you need</u>.

The inside front cover of this book has a list of common Spanish question words, phrases and instructions.

5) The <u>last</u> question is a <u>translation</u> question — you'll have to translate a short passage of text from Spanish <u>into English</u>. See p.103 for more tips on tackling translation questions.

Don't give up if you don't understand something

1) Use the <u>context</u> of the text to help you understand what it might be saying. You might be able to find some clues in the <u>title of the text</u> or the <u>type of text</u>.

2) Knowing how to spot <u>different word types</u> (e.g. nouns, verbs) can help you work out what's happening in a sentence. See the <u>grammar section</u> (p.66-98) for more.

Look for words that look like ones you know, e.g. 'la comida basura'. 'La comida' means 'food', and 'basura' means 'rubbish', so you can guess it means 'junk food'.

3) You can <u>guess</u> some Spanish words that look or sound the <u>same as English</u> words, e.g. el problema — *problem*, la música — *music*, el color — *colour*.

4) Be careful though — you might come across some '<u>false friends</u>'. These are Spanish words that look like an English word, but have a <u>completely different meaning</u>:

la nota	*mark*	la carpeta	*folder, file*	la arena	*sand*	la librería	*bookshop*	actual	*present*
el pie	*foot*	la dirección	*address*	el éxito	*success*	sensible	*sensitive*	fatal	*awful*
el campo	*countryside*	el pariente	*relative*	la ropa	*clothes*	largo	*long*	embarazada	*pregnant*

Keep an eye on the time

1) There are quite a few questions to get through in the reading exam, so you need to work at a <u>good speed</u>.

2) If you're having trouble with a particular question, you might want to <u>move on</u> and <u>come back to it later</u>.

Manolo and his colleagues never underestimated the importance of thyme.

3) Don't forget that the <u>last question</u> in the paper is a <u>translation</u> — this is worth <u>more marks</u> than any other question, so you should leave <u>plenty of time</u> to tackle it.

4) Make sure you put an answer down for <u>every question</u> — lots of the questions are multiple choice, so even if you can't work out the answer, it's always worth putting down one of the options.

Exams are important — failing can be fatal...

Don't forget, some of the questions will be in Spanish. Don't panic if you don't understand them — search for any familiar vocabulary and use any answer lines or boxes to help you guess what you have to do.

The Writing Exam

The writing exam is a great way of showing off what you can do — try to use varied vocabulary, include a range of tenses, and pack in any clever expressions that you've learnt over the years.

There'll be three tasks in the Writing Exam

1) The <u>higher tier</u> writing paper is about <u>1 hour and 15 minutes long</u> and has <u>three tasks</u>.

① Structured Task	② Open-ended Task	③ Translation
You'll be asked to write about 90 words in Spanish, based on some bullet points. Make sure you write about each bullet point and give some opinions. There may be a choice of two questions.	There will be a choice of tasks. You'll need to write about 150 words in Spanish, based on some bullet points. This task is more creative — make sure you include some opinions with reasons.	You'll be given an English passage to translate into Spanish. The passage could be on any topic you've studied. There's more advice for doing translations on p.103.

2) Each task is worth a <u>different number of marks</u>, so you should spend more time on the higher-mark tasks.

Read the instructions carefully, and spend some time planning

1) Read the instructions for questions 1 and 2 carefully — you'll need to make sure you cover <u>all of the bullet points</u>. You can often use <u>words from the question</u> in your answer too.

2) Spend a few minutes for each question <u>planning out</u> your answer. Decide <u>how</u> you're going to cover everything that's required and <u>in what order</u> you're going to write things.

Try to use varied vocab and a range of tenses.

3) Write the <u>best answer</u> you can, using the Spanish <u>that you know</u> — it doesn't matter if it's not true.

Check through your work thoroughly

Checking your work is <u>really important</u> — even small mistakes can cost marks. Take a look at this checklist:

- Are all the <u>verbs</u> in the <u>right tense</u>?
  Mañana, trabajé en el jardín. ✘   Mañana, trabajaré en el jardín. ✓

- Are the <u>verb endings</u> correct?
  ¿No te gusta las fresas? ✘   ¿No te gustan las fresas? ✓

- Do your <u>adjectives agree</u> with their nouns?
  La camisa es amarillo. ✘   La camisa es amarilla. ✓

- Are your <u>adjectives</u> in the <u>right place</u>?
  Una blanca falda. ✘   Una falda blanca. ✓

- Do your <u>reflexive verbs</u> and <u>pronouns</u> agree?
  A las siete, me levantamos. ✘   A las siete, me levanto. ✓

- Have you <u>spelt</u> everything correctly, including using the right <u>accents</u>?
  El toca la guitar con su tio. ✘   Él toca la guitarra con su tío. ✓

All of the points on this checklist are covered in the grammar section — see p.66-98.

And lastly, don't forget your pen...

When you're nervous and stressed, it's dead easy to miss out something the question has asked you to do. For tasks one and two, try to write about the bullet points in order, and tick them off as you go along.

The Translation Tasks

When you're studying Spanish, you do little bits of translation in your head all the time. For the translation questions, you just need to apply those skills — one sentence at a time — to a couple of short passages.

In the Reading Exam, you'll translate from Spanish to English

1) The final question of the reading paper will ask you to translate a <u>short Spanish passage</u> (about 50 words) <u>into English</u>. The passage will be on a <u>topic you've studied</u>, so most of the vocabulary should be familiar.

2) Here are some <u>top tips</u> for doing your translation:

- Read the whole text <u>before you start</u>. Make some <u>notes in English</u> to remind you of the main ideas.

- Translate the text <u>one sentence at a time</u>, rather than word by word — this will avoid any of the Spanish word order being carried into the English.

Ella compra la manzana roja.	*She buys the apple red.* ✖	*She buys the red apple.* ✔
Salma lo comió.	*Salma it ate.* ✖	*Salma ate it.* ✔

- Keep an eye out for <u>different tenses</u> — there will definitely be a variety in the passage.

- <u>Read through</u> your translation to make sure it sounds <u>natural</u>. Some words and phrases don't translate literally, so you'll need to make sure that your sentences sound like <u>normal English</u>:

Watch out for adverbs that might suggest a change in tense, e.g. en el futuro — *in the future*, mañana — *tomorrow*, ayer — *yesterday*.

La semana pasada, Irene hizo su maleta.	*The week last, Irene made her suitcase.* ✖	*Last week, Irene packed her suitcase.* ✔

3) Make sure you've translated <u>everything</u> from the original text — you'll lose marks if you miss something.

In the Writing Exam, you'll translate from English to Spanish

1) In the writing paper, you will have to translate <u>a short English passage</u> (about 50 words) <u>into Spanish</u>.

2) Here are <u>some ideas</u> for how you could approach the translation:

- <u>Read</u> through the <u>whole text</u> before you get started so you know exactly what the text is about.

- Tackle the passage <u>one sentence at a time</u> — work slowly and carefully through each one.

- <u>Don't</u> translate things <u>literally</u> — think about what each English sentence means and try to write it in the <u>most Spanish way</u> you know. Don't worry — the translation is likely to include similar sentences to the ones you've learnt.

Don't try to write a perfect translation first time — do it roughly first, and then write it up properly, crossing out any old drafts. Remember to keep an eye on the time.

- Work on the <u>word order</u> — remember that most Spanish adjectives follow the noun. If you need a <u>double negative</u>, remember to include both bits.

3) Once you've got something that you're happy with, go back through and <u>check that you've covered everything</u> that was in the English.

4) Now <u>check</u> your Spanish text thoroughly using the <u>list from p.102</u>.

Thankfully, none of that got lost in translation... Elena's translations got the seal of approval.

Congratulations — you've made it to the end of the book. 103 pages is no mean feat, so give yourself a pat on the back. Make sure you still read this page properly though, and take the translation advice on board.

Vocabulary

Section One — General Stuff

Numbers (p.1)

cero	zero
uno (un) / una	one
dos	two
tres	three
cuatro	four
cinco	five
seis	six
siete	seven
ocho	eight
nueve	nine
diez	ten
once	eleven
doce	twelve
trece	thirteen
catorce	fourteen
quince	fifteen
dieciséis	sixteen
diecisiete	seventeen
dieciocho	eighteen
diecinueve	nineteen
veinte	twenty
veintiuno	twenty-one
veintidós	twenty-two
treinta	thirty
treinta y uno	thirty-one
cuarenta	forty
cincuenta	fifty
sesenta	sixty
setenta	seventy
ochenta	eighty
noventa	ninety
ciento (cien)	hundred
ciento setenta y siete	one hundred and seventy-seven
doscientos/as	two hundred
quinientos veintiocho	five hundred and twenty-eight
novecientos noventa y tres	nine hundred and ninety-three
mil	thousand
mil cuatrocientos cincuenta y tres	one thousand four hundred and fifty-three
millón	million
primero / primera	first
segundo/a	second
tercero/a	third
cuarto/a	fourth
quinto/a	fifth
sexto/a	sixth
séptimo/a	seventh
octavo/a	eighth
noveno/a	ninth
décimo/a	tenth
una docena	dozen
el número	number

un par	pair / couple
unos (diez)	about (10)

Times and Dates (p.2-3)

el lunes	Monday
el martes	Tuesday
el miércoles	Wednesday
el jueves	Thursday
el viernes	Friday
el sábado	Saturday
el domingo	Sunday
enero	January
febrero	February
marzo	March
abril	April
mayo	May
junio	June
julio	July
agosto	August
septiembre	September
octubre	October
noviembre	November
diciembre	December
la estación	season
el invierno	winter
el otoño	autumn
la primavera	spring
el verano	summer
a diario	daily / everyday
a eso de ...	at about ...
a fines de ...	at / to the end of ...
a mediados de ...	around the middle of ...
a menudo	often
a partir de	from
a veces	sometimes
ahora	now / nowadays
al mismo tiempo	at the same time
algunas veces	sometimes
anoche	last night
el año	year
anteayer	the day before yesterday
antes (de)	before
ayer	yesterday
breve	brief / short
cada (...) días / horas	every (...) days / hours
casi	nearly
de momento	at the moment / right now
de nuevo	again
de repente	suddenly
de vez en cuando	now and then / from time to time
dentro de (...) días / horas	within (...) days / hours
desde	since

desde hace	since
despacio	slowly
después (de)	after / afterwards
el día	day
durante	during / for
durar	to last
en seguida / enseguida	straightaway
esta noche	tonight
la fecha	date
el fin de semana	weekend
hace (un mes) que	it's been a month since
hace (un mes)	a month ago
hoy	today
lento	slow
los lunes etc.	(on) Mondays etc.
luego	then / afterwards
mañana	tomorrow
la mañana	morning
el mes	month
mientras tanto	meanwhile
mucho tiempo	a long time
la noche	night
otra vez	again
el pasado	past
pasado (adj)	past / last
pasado mañana	the day after tomorrow
pocas veces	seldom / a few times
por año	per year
por fin	at last
por lo general	generally
el porvenir	future
al principio	at the beginning
pronto	soon
próximo	next
que viene (el mes etc.)	next (month etc.)
quince días	fortnight
el rato	while / short time
la semana	week
siempre	always
el siglo	century
siguiente	next / following
sobre	on / around
solo (sólo)	only
tardar	to take time
tarde	late
la tarde	afternoon / evening
la temporada	period / spell / season
temprano	early
tener prisa	to be in a hurry
el tiempo	time
todas (las semanas)	every (week)
todavía	still / yet

todos (los días / meses)	every (day / month)	hasta mañana	see you tomorrow	divertirse	to have a good time
último	last	hasta pronto	see you soon	dudar	to doubt
una vez	once	¡Hola!	Hello!	duro	hard
dos veces	twice	Le presento a...	May I introduce...?	emocionante	exciting / thrilling / moving

Questions (p.4-5)

¿(a)dónde?	where (to)?	lo siento	I'm sorry	encantador	charming
¿a qué hora?	at what time?	mucho gusto	pleased to meet you	encantar	to delight
¿cómo?	how?	(muy) bien	(very) well	entretenido	entertaining / amusing
¿cuál(es)?	which?	no muy bien	not very well	esperar	to hope
¿cuándo?	when?	¡Ojo!	Watch out! Careful!	espléndido	fantastic / terrific
¿cuánto?	how much?	perdón	sorry / excuse me	estar a favor de	to be in favour of
¿cuánto cuesta(n)?	how much does it / do they cost?	perdone	sorry / excuse me	estar de acuerdo	to agree
¿cuánto es?	how much is it?	por favor	please	estar en contra de	to be against
¿cuánto vale(n)?	how much does it / do they cost?	¿Puedo...?	May I...?	estar harto de	to be fed up of
¿cuántos...?	how many?	¡Qué (+ adjective)!	How ...!	estupendo	fantastic
¿cuántos años tiene(s)?	how old are you?	¡Qué (+ noun)!	What a ...!	fabuloso	fabulous
¿de dónde?	where from?	¿Qué hay?	What's happening? What's the matter?	fácil	easy
¿de qué color (es)?	what colour (is it)?	¡Que lo pase(s) bien!	Have a good time!	fastidiar	to annoy / to bother
¿de quién?	whose?	¿Qué pasa?	What's happening? What's the matter?	fatal	awful / fatal
¿es...?	is it...?	¿Qué tal?	How are you? How's ...?	fenomenal	great / fantastic
¿por cuánto tiempo?	for how long?	¡Qué va!	Come on! Rubbish! Nonsense!	feo	ugly
¿por dónde?	through where?	Quisiera...	I would like...	genial	brilliant / great
¿por qué?	why?	saludar	to greet / say hello	guay	cool
¿qué?	what?	saludos	regards / greetings	hermoso	beautiful
¿qué día?	what day?	¡Socorro!	Help!	horroroso	horrible
¿qué fecha?	what date?	vale	ok	impresionante	impressive / striking
¿qué hora es?	what time is it?			increíble	incredible
¿quién?	who?			inseguro	unsafe / uncertain

Opinions (p.8-10)

		aburrido	boring / bored	interesante	interesting
		aburrirse	to get bored	interesar(se)	to interest / to be interested in

Being Polite (p.6-7)

¡Adiós!	Goodbye!	adorar	to adore / to love	inútil	useless
así así	so-so	afortunado	lucky	malo	bad
¡Basta ya!	That's enough!	agradable	pleasant	maravilloso	marvellous
¡Bienvenido/a!	Welcome!	alegrar	to cheer up	nuevo	new
¡Buen viaje!	Have a good trip!	alegrarse (de)	to be happy (about)	odiar	to hate
¡Buena suerte!	Good luck!	amable	nice / kind / friendly	opinar	to think / to give an opinion
¡Buenas noches!	Good night!	antiguo	old	parecer	to seem
¡Buenas tardes!	Good afternoon! / Good evening!	apreciar	to appreciate	pasarlo bien	to have a good time
¡Buenos días!	Good morning! / Good day!	apropiado	correct / appropriate	pensar	to think
¡Claro!	Of course!	aprovechar	to make the most of	perfecto	perfect
¿Cómo está(s)?	How are you?	aprovecharse (de)	to take advantage (of)	ponerse de acuerdo	to agree
con permiso	excuse me	barato	cheap	porque	because
¡Cuidado!	Careful! Watch out!	bonito	pretty	precioso	precious / beautiful
de nada	you're welcome / don't mention it	bueno	good	preferir	to prefer
¿De veras?	Really?	la calidad	quality	profundo	deep / profound
encantado/a	pleased to meet you	caro	expensive	quedar en	to agree
¡Enhorabuena!	Congratulations!	creer	to believe	querer decir	to mean
Este/a es...	This is...	dar igual	to be all the same / to make no difference	raro	strange / rare
fatal	terrible	decepcionante	disappointing	la razón	reason
¡Felices vacaciones!	Have a good holiday!	decir	to say	reconocer	to recognise
¡Felicidades!	Best wishes! Congratulations!	desagradable	unpleasant	ridículo	ridiculous
¡Felicitaciones!	Congratulations!	desear	to wish	seguro	safe / certain
hasta el (lunes)	till / see you (Monday)	la desventaja	disadvantage	sencillo	simple / plain / straightforward
hasta luego	see you later	disfrutar	to enjoy	sentir(se)	to feel
		distinto	different	sorprendido	surprised
		divertido	amusing / entertaining / fun	tener ganas de hacer algo	to feel like doing something
				tener razón	to be right
				tonto	silly

Vocabulary

tranquilo	*peaceful / quiet*		
único	*unique / only / single*		
útil	*useful*		
valer la pena	*to be worth the trouble*		
la ventaja	*advantage*		
viejo	*old*		

Access

abierto	*open*
abrir	*to open*
cerrado	*closed*
cerrar	*to close*
gratis / gratuito	*free (of charge)*
libre	*free / unoccupied*
ocupado	*engaged / occupied*
permitir	*to allow*
prohibido	*forbidden*

Colours and Shapes

amarillo	*yellow*
azul	*blue*
blanco	*white*
claro	*light*
cuadrado	*square*
el color	*colour*
la forma	*shape*
gris	*grey*
marrón	*brown*
morado	*purple*
naranja	*orange*
negro	*black*
oscuro	*dark*
pálido	*pale*
redondo	*round*
rojo	*red*
rosa / rosado	*pink*
verde	*green*
vivo	*vivid / bright*

Common Abbreviations

Sr (señor)	*Mr*
Sra (señora)	*Mrs*
Srta (señorita)	*Miss*
Sta (santa)	*Saint*
c/ (calle)	*street*
1° / primero (2°, 3° etc.)	*1st (2nd, 3rd etc.)*
1ª / primera (2ª, 3ª etc.)	*1st (2nd, 3rd etc.)*
Dr (doctor)	*Dr*
Dra (doctora)	*Dr*
el AVE	*high-speed train*
Renfe / RENFE	*Spanish railways*
IVA	*VAT*
Avda (avenida)	*avenue*
EEUU (Estados Unidos)	*USA*

Connectives

además	*moreover / besides*
aparte de	*apart from*
claro que	*of course*
dado que	*given that*

es decir	*in other words / that is to say*
por un lado / por otro lado	*on the one hand / on the other hand*
por una parte / por otra parte	*on the one hand / on the other hand*
sin duda	*obviously / certainly*

Correctness

cierto	*certain / sure / true*
corregir	*to correct*
equivocado	*wrong*
la falta	*error*
mal	*badly*
mentir	*to lie*
la mentira	*lie / untruth*
mentiroso	*liar*
tener razón	*to be right*
la verdad	*truth*
verdadero	*true*

Materials

el algodón	*cotton*
la cerámica	*pottery*
el cristal	*glass / crystal*
el cuero	*leather*
la lana	*wool*
la madera	*wood*
el oro	*gold*
el papel	*paper*
la piel	*leather / skin*
la plata	*silver*
la seda	*silk*
la tela	*fabric / material*
el vidrio	*glass*

Comparisons (p.73-74)

bastante	*sufficient / enough / quite*
comparar	*to compare*
demasiado	*too, too much*
igual que	*same as*
más (que)	*more (than)*
mayor	*main / larger / bigger / greater / older*
la mayoría	*most / majority*
mejor	*better / best*
menor	*smaller / less / least / younger*
menos (que)	*less (than)*
mismo	*same*
muy	*very*
parecido a	*like / similar to*
peor	*worse / worst*
poco (e.g. poco ruidoso)	*not very*
tan ... como	*as ... as*
tanto ... como	*as much ... as*

Prepositions (p.80)

a	*to / at*
de	*from / of*
en	*in / at*
hacia	*towards*
hasta	*until*

para	*for*
por	*through / by / in / for / per*
según	*according to*
sin	*without*

Conjunctions (p.82)

a pesar de	*in spite of / despite*
así que	*so / therefore*
aun (si)	*even (if)*
aunque	*although / (even) though*
como	*as / since*
cuando	*when*
de manera que	*in such a way that*
entonces	*then*
incluso	*even*
mientras (que)	*while, meanwhile*
o / u	*or*
pero	*but*
por eso	*for that reason / therefore*
por lo tanto	*therefore*
porque	*because*
pues	*then / since*
si	*if*
sin embargo	*however*
tal vez	*maybe / perhaps*
también	*also*
y / e	*and*
ya (que)	*as / since*

Negative Forms (p.94)

jamás	*never*
ni ... ni	*neither ... nor*
nada	*nothing*
nadie	*nobody*
ninguno	*none / no-one*
nunca	*never*
sino	*but (rather) / except*
tampoco	*neither / not ... either ...*
ya no	*not any more*

Important Verbs

acabar de + infinitive	*to have just (done something)*
comenzar	*to begin*
continuar	*to continue*
dar	*to give*
darse cuenta (de)	*to realise*
deber	*must / have to*
decidir	*to decide*
dejar de (hacer algo)	*to stop (doing something)*
echar	*to throw*
empezar	*to begin*
estar	*to be*
hace(n) falta	*to need / to be necessary*
hacer	*to do / to make*
hacerse	*to become*
hay	*there is / there are*

hay que	one must / one has to	poder	to be able / can	ser	to be
ir	to go	poner	to put	soler	to usually do something
ir a (hacer algo)	to be going to (do something)	ponerse a (hacer algo)	to start (doing something)	tener	to have / to own
irse	to go away / to leave	querer	to want / to love	tener lugar	to take place
necesitar	to need	quisiera...	I'd like...	tener que	to have to do something
ocurrir	to happen	saber	to know (a fact / how to do something)	volver a hacer algo	to do something again
pasar	to happen / to spend (time)	seguir	to continue / to follow	volverse	to become

Section Two — Me, My Family and Friends

You and Your Family (p.11-12)

el/la abuelo/a	grandfather / grandmother
el apellido	last name
el apodo	nickname
el bebé	baby
cuidar	to look after
el cumpleaños	birthday
cumplir años	to have a birthday
la edad	age
el/la gemelo/a	twin
la gente	people
el/la hermanastro/a	stepbrother/sister
el/la hijo/a (único/a)	(only) child
los hijos	children
el hogar	home
llamarse	to be called
la madrastra	stepmother
la madre	mother
el miembro	member
nacer	to be born
el nacimiento	birth
la nacionalidad	nationality
el/la nieto/a	grandchild
el/la niño/a	child
el nombre	name
el padrastro	stepfather
el padre, los padres	father, parents
los parientes	relatives
el/la primo/a	cousin
el recuerdo	memory
la reunión	get-together
el/la sobrino/a	nephew / niece
tener ... años	to be ... years old
el/la tío/a	uncle / aunt
el/la vecino/a	neighbour

Describing People (p.13-14)

el/la adolescente	teenager
alegre	happy
alto	tall
(de) altura mediana	(of) medium height
amistoso	friendly
anciano	elderly
el/la anciano/a	old person
animado	lively

antipático	unpleasant
el aspecto	appearance / looks
atrevido	daring / cheeky
bajo	short (height)
la barba	beard
el bigote	moustache
callado	quiet / reserved
calvo	bald
la cara	face
cariñoso	affectionate / tender
castaño	chestnut / brown
celoso	jealous
cobarde	coward
comprensivo	understanding
cortés	polite
corto	short (length)
delgado	slim
deportivo	sporty
educado	polite
egoísta	selfish
feliz	happy
fuerte	strong
las gafas	glasses
gordo	fat
gracioso	funny
guapo	good-looking
hablador	chatty / talkative
honrado	honest
joven	young
el/la joven	young person
jubilado	retired
el/la jubilado	OAP / pensioner
la juventud	youth / young people
largo	long
liso	straight (hair)
maduro	mature
maleducado	rude
moreno	dark (-haired / -skined)
el ojo	eye
la oreja	ear
orgulloso	proud
parecerse a	to look like
las pecas	freckles
pelirrojo	red-haired
el pelo	hair

perezoso	lazy / idle
rico	wealthy / rich
rizado	curly
rubio	blonde
sensible	sensitive
serio	serious / responsible
simpático	kind / nice / pleasant
torpe	clumsy
travieso	naughty / mischievous
triste	sad
valiente	brave / bold
viejo	old
el/la viudo/a	widow(er)

Pets (p.15)

el animal doméstico	pet
el cobayo / el conejillo de Indias	guinea pig
el conejo	rabbit
fiel	loyal
el gato	cat
el hámster	hamster
mandón	bossy / demanding
la mascota	pet
el olor	smell
el perro	dog
el pez de colores	goldfish
el pez tropical	tropical fish
la serpiente	snake
la tortuga	tortoise

Style and Fashion (p.16)

el abrigo	coat
afeitarse	to shave
ajustado	tight
el anillo	ring
anticuado	old-fashioned
la barra de labios	lipstick
el bolso	handbag
las botas	boots
la bufanda	scarf
los calcetines	socks
la camisa	shirt
la chaqueta	jacket
la chaqueta de punto	cardigan (knitted)
el cinturón	belt

el collar	necklace	el tatuaje	tattoo	la disputa	argument
cortarse el pelo	to have your hair cut	tatuarse	to get a tattoo	divorciarse	to get divorced
de estilo retro	vintage style	teñido	dyed	echar de menos	to miss (someone)
de lunares	spotty	el traje	suit	enamorado	in love
de rayas / rayado	striped	el traje de baño	swimming costume	enamorarse	to fall in love
elegante	smart / elegant		/ trunks	el/la esposo/a	husband / wife
estar de moda	to be in fashion	los vaqueros	jeans	el estado civil	marital status
	(thing)	vestido de	dressed in	fastidiar	to annoy / to bother
estar en la onda	to be fashionable	la zapatería	shoe shop	hacer amigos	to make friends
	(person)	las zapatillas	slippers	el hombre	man
el estilo	style	las zapatillas de	trainers	juntos	together
la falda	skirt	deporte		llevarse bien / mal	to get on well / badly
el/la famoso/a	celebrity			con	with someone

Relationships (p.17-19)

la gorra	cap	acordar	to agree on	el marido	husband
los guantes	gloves	aguantar	to bear / to put up	el matrimonio	marriage / married
holgado	loose / baggy		with		couple
ir vestido a la moda	to dress fashionably	la amistad	friendship	mimado	spoilt
el jérsey	jumper	el amor	love	el modelo de	role model
las joyas	jewellery	el anillo	ring	conducta	
el maquillaje	make-up	la barrera	generation gap	molestar	to bother
maquillarse	to put make-up on	generacional		la mujer	wife / woman
la marca	brand	la boda	wedding	el/la novio/a	boyfriend / girlfriend
el/la modelo	model	besar	to kiss	optimista	optimistic
el paraguas	umbrella	casado	married	la pandilla	gang
pasado de moda	out of fashion	casarse	to get married	la pareja	couple / partner
los pendientes	earrings	el/la compañero/a	classmate /	pelear(se)	to fight
el piercing	body piercing		colleague	perdonar	to forgive
pintarse	to put make-up on	comprometerse	to get engaged	reírse	to laugh
el polo	poloshirt	el compromiso	engagement	relacionarse con	to be in contact with
la pulsera	bracelet	confiar en	to trust	romper	to break
la rebeca	cardigan	conocer	to know / be familiar	roto	broken
el reloj	watch		with / get to know	salir	to go out
la ropa de deporte	sports kit	el/la conocido	acquaintance	el sentimiento	feeling
el sombrero de paja	straw hat	de buen humor	in a good mood	solo	alone
la sudadera	sweatshirt	disculpar(se)	to apologise	soltero	single (not married)
suelto	loose	discutir	to discuss / argue	sonreír	to smile

Section Three — Technology in Everyday Life

Technology (p.20-23)

acceder	to access	el disco duro	hard drive	el portátil	laptop
adjuntar	to attach	enviar	to send	publicar	to publish
el archivo	file	funcionar	to work / function	punto	dot / full stop
arroba	@	grabar	to burn (a disk)	puntocom	.com
el blog	blog	guardar	to save	el ratón	mouse
borrar	to erase / delete	el guión	hyphen	recibir	to receive
el buscador	search engine	el guión bajo	underscore	la red	network / Internet
el buzón	inbox / mailbox	hablar	to speak / talk	la red social	social network
cargar	load	la herramienta	tool	el riesgo	risk
charlar	to chat	inalámbrico	wireless	la sala de chat	chat room
colgar	to post (photos on	el/la internauta	Internet user	el sitio web	website
	social media, etc.)	mandar	to send	el servidor de	firewall
la contraseña	password	el mensaje	(text) message	seguridad	
el correo basura	spam	(de texto)		el teclado	keyboard
el correo	email	el móvil	mobile phone	usar	to use
electrónico		el muro	wall	el/la usuario/a	user
la cuenta	account	el navegador	browser	utilizar	to use
crear	to create	navegar	to surf	el videojuego	video game
desactivar	to deactivate / block	el ordenador	computer		
descargar	to download	la pantalla	screen		
		la portada	home page		

Section Four — Free-Time Activities

Books and Reading (p.24)

el lector de libros electrónicos	e-reader
la lectura	reading
leer	to read
el libro	book
el libro electrónico	e-book
la novela	novel
la novela de suspense	thriller
el periódico	newspaper
la prensa	the press
la revista	magazine
el tebeo	comic strip

Music, Cinema and TV (p.25-27)

el/la artista	artist
el actor	actor
la actriz	actress
la actuación	performance
el anuncio (publicitario)	advert
la banda sonora	soundtrack
la batería	drums
la cadena	channel
la canción	song
el/la cantante	singer
cantar	to sing
la ciencia ficción	science fiction
el concurso	game show / contest
los dibujos animados	cartoons
divertir(se)	to have a good time
el documental	documentary
en directo	live
la entrada	ticket
el espectáculo	show
la estrella	star
el género	genre
la grabación	recording
el grupo	band
hacer cola	to queue
la historia	story
la letra	song lyrics
el/la músico/a	musician
la música pop	pop music
la música rap	rap music
la música rock	rock music
la música clásica	classical music
las noticias	news
el papel	role
la película	film
la película de acción	action film
la película de aventuras	adventure film
la película romántica	romantic film
la película de terror	horror film

policíaco	detective (adj.)
el programa	programme
el reality show	reality show
el reparto	cast
ser aficionado a	to be very keen on / fond of (activity)
la taquilla	box office
la telenovela	soap opera
tocar	to play (an instrument)
la trama	plot

Food and Eating Out (p.28-29)

a la plancha	grilled
el aceite	oil
el agua mineral (con / sin gas) (f)	(fizzy / still) mineral water
el ajo	garlic
la alimentación	food / nutrition
el alimento	type of food
almorzar	to have lunch
el almuerzo	lunch
apetecer	to fancy / to feel like
el arroz	rice
asado	roast(ed)
el atún	tuna
el azúcar	sugar
el bacalao	cod
la barra (de pan)	loaf (of bread)
beber	to drink
la bebida	drink
el bistec	steak
el bocadillo	sandwich
los calamares	squid
el caramelo	boiled sweet
la carne	meat
de cerdo	pork
de cordero	lamb
de ternera	veal
de vaca	beef
la carta	menu
la cebolla	onion
la cena	dinner
cenar	to have the evening meal
la cerveza	beer
los champiñones	mushrooms
el chorizo	Spanish sausage
la chuleta	chop
los churros	fritters
la cocina	cuisine / cooking
cocinar	to cook
la col	cabbage
comer	to eat
la comida (basura / rápida)	junk / fast food
la comida	meal / lunch
la copa	wine glass
la cuchara	spoon
el cuchillo	knife

la cuenta	bill
desayunar	to have breakfast
el desayuno	breakfast
dulce	sweet
elegir	to choose
escoger	to choose
el filete	steak
la fresa	strawberry
frito	fried
la galleta	biscuit
las gambas	prawns
el gazpacho	cold soup
la grasa	fat
los guisantes	peas
la heladería	ice cream parlour
el helado	ice cream
hervido	boiled
el hielo	ice
el huevo	egg
incluido	included
el jamón	ham
las judías verdes	string beans
la leche	milk
la lechuga	lettuce
las legumbres	vegetables / pulses
la mantequilla	butter
la manzana	apple
los mariscos	seafood
el melocotón	peach
merendar	to have an afternoon snack / picnic
la merienda	afternoon snack / picnic
la mermelada	jam
nada más	nothing else
la naranja	orange
la nata	cream
el pastel	cake / pie
la patata	potato
pedir	to order / ask for
la pera	pear
el pescado	fish
picante	spicy
la pimienta	pepper (seasoning)
el pimiento	pepper (vegetable)
la piña	pineapple
el plátano	banana
el plato (combinado)	(set) dish
el pollo	chicken
el postre	dessert
el primer plato	starter
probar	to taste / to try
la propina	tip
el queso	cheese
rico	tasty
sabroso	tasty
la sal	salt
salado	salty
la salchicha	sausage
la salsa	sauce

Vocabulary

el segundo plato	main meal / course	andar	to walk	jugar	to play
los servicios	toilets	bailar	to dance	marcar (un gol)	to score (a goal)
la sopa	soup	el baile	dancing	el monopatín	skateboard
las tapas	nibbles / bar snacks	el baloncesto	basketball	montar	to ride
el té	tea	la bicicleta / bici	bicycle / bike	(a caballo / en bici)	(horse / bike)
el tenedor	fork	el campeón	champion	nadar	to swim
tener hambre	to be hungry	la campeona		la natación	swimming
tener sed	to be thirsty	el campeonato	championship	el partido	match
tomar	to have / to take	la carrera	race	el patinaje	skating
la tortilla	omelette	el concurso	contest / competition	patinar	to skate
la tostada	toast	la copa	cup / trophy	la pelota	ball
traer	to bring	correr	to run	perder	to lose
las uvas	grapes	el deporte	sport	la pesca	fishing
el vaso	glass	los deportes de	adventure sports	pescar	to fish
las verduras	vegetables	riesgo		el piragüismo	canoeing
el vino (blanco /	(white / rosé / red)	el/la deportista	sportsperson	la pista	track / court / run /
rosado / tinto)	wine	el equipo	team / equipment		slope / rink
la zanahoria	carrot	la equitación	horse riding	la pista de hielo	ice rink
el zumo (de fruta)	(fruit) juice	el estadio	stadium	el premio	prize
		ganar	to win	el/la socio/a	member
Sport (p.30-31)		el gol	goal	el torneo	tournament
al aire libre	outdoors	el juego	game	la vela	sail / sailing
el alpinismo	mountain climbing	el/la jugador/a	player		

Section Five — Customs and Festivals

Customs and Festivals		disfrazarse de	to dress up as	Nochevieja	31 December
(p.32-34)		el Eid al-Fitr	Eid al-Fitr	Papá Noel	Father Christmas
el Año Nuevo	New Year	la fecha patria	national day to	la Pascua	Easter
la bandera	flag		commemorate	el paso	statue paraded at
la broma	joke / trick		historic event		Easter
las castañuelas	castanets	¡Feliz Año Nuevo!	Happy New Year!	la plaza de toros	bullring
celebrar	to celebrate	¡Feliz cumpleaños!	Happy Birthday!	la procesión	procession
la corrida	bullfight	¡Feliz Navidad!	Merry Christmas!	los Reyes Magos	the Three Kings
la costumbre	custom / way	la feria	fair	el santo	saint's day
cristiano	Christian	festejar	to celebrate	la Semana Santa	Easter week
el Día de los	28 December	la fiesta	festival / party	la tradición	tradition
Inocentes	(equivalent of April	el Hannukah	Hannukah	la Tomatina	tomato-throwing
	Fools' Day)	judío	Jewish		festival
el Día de los	All Souls' Day	el juguete	toy	tener suerte	to be lucky
Muertos		el mariachi	Mexican musician	el/la torero/a	bullfighter
el Día de Reyes	Epiphany /	el/la muerto/a	dead (person)	el toro	bull
	6 January	musulmán	Muslim	el turrón	Spanish nougat
el día festivo	public holiday	Navidad	Christmas	el villancico	Christmas carol
el disfraz	fancy dress	Nochebuena	Christmas Eve		

Section Six — Where You Live

Where You Live (p.35-36)		el baño	bathroom / bath	la casa (adosada)	(semi-detached)
las afueras	outskirts	el barrio	neighbourhood		house
la aldea	village	la biblioteca	library	el centro	town centre
la alfombra	rug	la bolera	bowling alley	el centro comercial	shopping centre
alquilar	to rent / to hire	el bosque	forest / woods	el chalet / chalé	bungalow / house
el alquiler	rent	la butaca	armchair	el cine	cinema
el aparcamiento	parking	la calefacción	heating	la ciudad	city
el árbol	tree	la calle	street	el club (de jóvenes)	(youth) club
el armario	wardrobe / cupboard	la cama	bed	la cocina	cooker / kitchen
el ascensor	lift	el campo	countryside /	el comedor	dining room
el aseo	toilet		grounds	la comisaría	police station
el ayuntamiento	town hall	la cancha (de tenis)	(tennis) court	cómodo	comfortable /
bajar	to go down	la carnicería	butcher's		convenient / handy

compartir	to share
la comunidad	community
concurrido	busy / crowded
construir	to build
Correos	Post Office
la cortina	curtain
el cuarto de baño	bathroom
dar a	to look onto
de lujo	luxury
la dirección	address
el domicilio	address / home
el dormitorio	bedroom
la ducha	shower
el edificio	building
la entrada	entrance
entrar	to go in / enter
los electrodomésticos	electrical appliances
la escalera	stairs
el espacio	space
el espejo	mirror
la esquina	corner
el estanco	tobacconist's
el estante	shelf
la estantería	shelves
la fábrica	factory
el fregadero	kitchen sink
los grandes almacenes	department store
la granja	farm
la habitación	room
el/la habitante	inhabitant
el horno	oven
la iglesia	church
la joyería	jeweller's
la juguetería	toy shop
el lavabo	washbasin
la lavadora	washing machine
el lavaplatos	dishwasher
la librería	bookcase / bookshop
la llave	key
la luz	light
la máquina	machine
el mercado	market
la mesa	table
la mezquita	mosque
el microondas	microwave oven
mudarse (de casa)	to move (house)
los muebles	furniture
el museo	museum
el negocio	business
la nevera	fridge
el paisaje	landscape / scenery
la panadería	bakery
la papelera	wastepaper basket
la papelería	stationery shop
la pared	wall
el parque	park
el parque infantil	playground
el pasillo	corridor
la pastelería	pastry shop
la peluquería	hairdresser's

las persianas	blinds, shutters
la pescadería	fishmonger's
el piso	flat / floor (of room)
la planta baja	ground floor
la planta	floor / plant
la población	population
el polideportivo	sports centre
propio	own
el pueblo	town / village / people / nation
el puente	bridge
la puerta	door
el puerto	port / harbour
el río	river
el ruido	noise
ruidoso	noisy
el salón	lounge
la segunda planta	second floor
el semáforo	traffic lights
la sierra	mountain range
la silla	chair
el sillón	armchair
el sótano	basement / cellar
subir	to go up
el suelo	floor
el teatro	theatre
la terraza	terrace
la tienda de comestibles	grocery shop
la tienda de ropa	clothes shop
la ventana	window
el vestíbulo	entrance hall / lobby / foyer
la vivienda	dwelling / housing / accommodation
la zona peatonal	pedestrian zone

What You Do at Home (p.37)

acostarse	to go to bed
arreglar	to tidy / to fix
ayudar	to help
cortar el césped	to mow the lawn
despertarse	to wake up
dormirse	to go to sleep
ducharse	to have a shower
hacer la cama	to make the bed
hacer las compras	to do the shopping
lavar los platos	to do the washing-up
lavarse la cara	to wash your face
levantarse	to get up
limpiar	to clean
limpio	clean
la paga	pocket money
pasar la aspiradora	to do the vacuuming
pasear al perro	to walk the dog
poner la mesa	to lay the table
quitar la mesa	to clear the table
sacar la basura	to take out the rubbish
sentarse	to sit down
la tarea doméstica	chore
vestirse	to get dressed

Shopping (p.38-39)

a mitad de precio	half-price
el agujero	hole
Aquí lo tienes.	Here you are.
bastante	enough
la bolsa	paper / plastic bag
la caja	box / till
cambiar	to change
la cantidad	quantity
el cartón	carton
el centro comercial	shopping centre
el chándal	tracksuit
el/la cliente	customer
la corbata	tie
el/la dependiente/a	sales assistant
el descuento	discount
devolver	to return
el dinero	money
en efectivo	(in) cash
el escaparate	shop window
exactamente	exactly
el gramo	gram
los grandes almacenes	department store
el hipermercado	hypermarket
el kilo	kilogram
la lata	tin
el litro	litre
lleno	full
el número (de zapato)	shoe size
pagar	to pay
el paquete	packet
el pedazo	piece
pesar	to weigh
los probadores	changing rooms
quejarse	to complain
la ración	portion
rasgado	ripped
las rebajas	the sales
la rebanada	slice
el recibo	receipt
reembolsar	to refund
reemplazar	to replace
roto	broken
el servicio de reparto a domicilio	home delivery service
suficiente	enough
la talla	size (clothes)
la tarjeta de crédito	credit card
el tarro	jar
el tercio	third
la tienda de comestibles	grocery shop
el trozo	slice, piece
vacío	empty
varios/as	several

Directions (p.40)

a un paso (de)	a few steps away (from)
abajo (de)	under / below
afuera (de)	outside
ahí	(just) there
aislado	isolated
al final (de)	at the end (of)
allá	(over) there
allí	(over) there
alrededor (de)	around
aquí	here
arriba (de)	above / on top (of)
atrás	behind
cerca (de)	near
cercano	nearby
contra	against
cruzar	to cross
debajo (de)	under
delante (de)	in front of
dentro (de)	inside
a la derecha	on / to the right
(todo) derecho	straight ahead
detrás (de)	behind
en / por todas partes	everywhere
en la esquina	on the corner
en las afueras	in the outskirts
encima (de)	above / on top / overhead

encontrarse	to be situated
enfrente (de)	opposite
entre	between
estar situado	to be situated
el este	east
en el / al fondo	at the back / at the bottom
fuera (de)	outside
a la izquierda	on / to the left
al lado (de)	next to
lejano	far away / distant / remote
lejos (de)	far (from)
el lugar	place
en (el) medio (de)	in the middle of
el norte	north
el oeste	west
seguir	to follow / continue
el sitio	place
el sur	south
todo recto	straight ahead
tomar	to take (a road)

Weather (p.41)

buen / mal tiempo	good / bad weather
caliente	hot
caluroso	hot / warm
el chubasco	shower
el cielo	sky
el clima	climate

despejado	clear (skies)
estable	stable / unchanged
fresco	fresh
el grado	degree
hacer (frío / calor etc.)	to be (cold / hot etc.)
helar	to freeze
el hielo	ice
húmedo	humid
llover	to rain
la lluvia	rain
mojar(se)	to get wet
nevar	to snow
la niebla	fog
la nieve	snow
la nube	cloud
nublado / nuboso	cloudy
el pronóstico	forecast
el relámpago	lightning
seco	dry
el sol	sun
la sombra	shade / shadow
templado	mild / temperate
tener (frío / calor)	to feel (cold / hot)
el tiempo	weather
la tormenta	storm
tormentoso	stormy
el trueno	thunder
el viento	wind

Section Seven — Social and Global Issues

Environmental Problems (p.42-43)

agotar	to exhaust / use up
el agujero	hole
amenazar	to threaten
apagar	to turn off (lights etc.)
arruinar	to ruin / destroy
el atasco	traffic jam
aumentar	to increase
beneficiar	to benefit
el beneficio	benefit
el calentamiento global	global warming
el cambio climático	climate change
la capa de ozono	ozone layer
el cartón	cardboard
el combustible	fuel
el consumo	consumption
contaminar	to pollute
el contenedor	container
cultivar	to grow / cultivate
el cultivo	crop
dañar	to harm / damage
el daño	harm / damage
desaparecer	to disappear
el desperdicio	waste / rubbish / squandering
ducharse	to have a shower

el efecto invernadero	greenhouse effect
encender	to turn on (lights etc.)
ensuciar	to make dirty / soil / make a mess
el envase	wrapping / packaging / container
la escasez	shortage / lack
escaso	scarce / meagre
estropear	to ruin / spoil
la falta	lack
faltar	to be missing
el fuego	fire
los gases de escape	exhaust fumes
el huracán	hurricane
el incendio	fire
la inundación	flood
la lluvia ácida	acid rain
malgastar	to waste / misuse / squander
la marea negra	oil spill
el medio ambiente	environment
medioambiental	environmental
mundial	global / worldwide
el mundo	world
la naturaleza	nature
nocivo	harmful

el pájaro	bird
el petróleo	oil
la pila	battery
la preocupación	worry
preocupado	worried / anxious
preocupante	worrying
los productos químicos	chemicals
proteger	to protect
químico (adj)	chemical
recargable	rechargeable
el recurso	resource
la selva	jungle / tropical forest
la sequía	drought
solucionar	to solve / resolve
sucio	dirty
la Tierra	Earth
tirar	to throw (away)
utilizar	to use
la ventaja	advantage
el vertedero	rubbish dump / tip

Problems in Society (p.44-45)

la belleza	beauty
combatir	to fight / combat
cometer	to commit
la culpa	fault / blame / guilt
el desarrollo	development
el desempleo	unemployment

los derechos	rights	la pobreza	poverty	la residencia (para ancianos)	(old people's) home
la desigualdad	inequality	el prejuicio	prejudice	los residuos	refuse / waste / rubbish
la discriminación	discrimination	el/la refugiado/a	refugee		
echar la culpa	to blame	robar	to steal	reutilizar	to reuse
estar en paro	to be unemployed	el robo	theft / burglary	salvar	to save
el/la extranjero/a	foreigner	los "sin techo"	homeless people	la tienda con fines benéficos	charity shop
el/la gamberro/a	hooligan / lout / troublemaker	el/la testigo	witness	la tienda solidaria	charity shop
		la violencia	violence	voluntario	voluntary
el gobierno	government			el/la voluntario/a	volunteer
grave	serious				

Contributing to Society (p.46)

la basura	rubbish / garbage
los desechos	rubbish / waste
la encuesta	poll / survey
la obra benéfica	charity
la ONG	NGO (non-governmental organisation)
la organización benéfica	charitable organisation
organizar	to organise
la participación	participation
el reciclaje	recycling
reciclar	to recycle
recoger	to collect / gather / pick up
renovable	renewable

la guerra	war
la igualdad	equality
injusto	unjust / unfair
inquietante	worrying / disturbing
inquietar(se)	to worry
justo	just / fair
el ladrón / la ladrona	thief
la ley	law
la libertad	liberty / freedom
luchar	to fight / struggle
matar	to kill
la multa	fine
los necesitados	needy people
el peligro	danger
peligroso	dangerous
pobre	poor

Global Events (p.47)

a beneficio de	in aid of
asistir a	to attend
la campaña	campaign
estar en desventaja	to be disadvantaged
el evento	event
el festival (de música)	(music) festival
los Juegos Olímpicos	Olympic Games
llamar la atención	to attract attention
el Mundial	World Cup (football)
la organización caritativa	charitable organisation
recaudar dinero	to raise money

Section Eight — Lifestyle

Health (p.48-49)

activo	active
advertir	to warn
el asco	disgust
asqueroso	disgusting
el aviso	warning / notice
el azúcar	sugar
borracho	drunk
el botellón	drinking party in the street
caer(se)	to fall down
cansado	tired / tiring
cansar(se)	to get tired
el cigarrillo	cigarette
contribuir	to contribute
el cuerpo	body
dedicar(se)	to do / to go in for / to devote oneself
la dieta	diet
dormir	to sleep
la droga (blanda / dura)	(soft / hard) drug
drogarse	to take drugs
el ejercicio (físico)	(physical) exercise
emborracharse	to get drunk
el entrenamiento	training
entrenar(se)	to train
equilibrado	balanced
el esfuerzo	effort
estar en forma	to be fit
evitar	to avoid
formar parte (de)	to be part (of)

el/la fumador/a (pasivo/a)	(passive) smoker
fumar	to smoke
hacer daño	to injure / harm
el humo	smoke
malsano	unhealthy
mantenerse en forma	to keep fit / in shape
morir	to die
muerto	dead
la necesidad	need
oler	to smell
el olor	smell
el porro	joint
la posibilidad	possibility
el propósito	aim / purpose / objective
provocar	to cause / provoke
respirar	to breathe
respiratorio	respiratory
la salud	health
saludable	healthy
sano	healthy / wholesome
el síndrome de abstinencia	withdrawal symptoms
el sobrepeso	overweight / obesity
el tabaquismo	addiction to tobacco
tener sueño	to feel sleepy
la tentación	temptation
la vida	life
vivo	alive

Illnesses (p.50)

el ataque cardíaco	heart attack
el brazo	arm
la cabeza	head
el cerebro	brain
el corazón	heart
el dedo	finger
doler	to hurt
el dolor	pain / ache
el dolor de oídos	earache
encontrarse bien / mal	to feel well / ill
la enfermedad	illness
enfermo	ill
la espalda	back
estar bien / mal	to be well / ill
el estómago	stomach
el estrés	stress
la garganta	throat
el hígado	liver
el/la médico/a	doctor
mejorar(se)	to get better
el pie	foot
la pierna	leg
los primeros auxilios	first aid
los pulmones	lungs
la receta	prescription
sentirse	to feel
seropositivo	HIV-positive
el sida	AIDS
tener dolor (de)...	to have a pain (in)...

Section Nine — Travel and Tourism

Where to Go (p.51)

alemán	German
Alemania	Germany
Argentina	Argentina
Australia	Australia
Brasil	Brazil
británico	British
las Islas Canarias	Canary Islands
Canadá	Canada
castellano	Castilian, Spanish spoken in Spain
Chile	Chile
Colombia	Colombia
Cuba	Cuba
escocés	Scottish
Escocia	Scotland
España	Spain
español	Spanish
los Estados Unidos	United States
Europa	Europe
europeo	European
francés	French
Francia	France
Gales	Wales
galés	Welsh
Gran Bretaña	Great Britain
Grecia	Greece
griego	Greek
la India	India
Inglaterra	England
inglés	English
Irlanda	Ireland
irlandés	Irish
Irlanda del Norte	Northern Ireland
la isla	island
Italia	Italy
italiano	Italian
latinoamericano	Latin American
Londres	London
el mar	sea
el mar Mediterráneo	Mediterranean Sea
México	Mexico
la montaña	mountain
el mundo	world
norirlandés	Northern Irish
norteamericano	North American
el país	country
Perú	Peru
Portugal	Portugal
portugués	Portuguese
la playa	beach
Rusia	Russia
sudamericano	South American

Preparation (p.52-53)

la agencia (de viajes)	(travel) agent's
el aire acondicionado	air conditioning

el albergue juvenil	youth hostel
el alojamiento	accommodation
alojarse	to lodge / stay
el ambiente	atmosphere
buscar	to look for
la cama de matrimonio	double bed
cambiar	to change
el camping	campsite
la caravana	caravan
el carnet de conducir	driving licence
el carnet de identidad	identity card
el cheque (de viaje)	traveller's cheque
la crema solar	sun cream
la dirección	management
disponible	available
DNI	ID card
el equipaje	luggage
el formulario	registration form
la ficha	registration form
el folleto	leaflet / pamphlet
(no) fumador	(non) smoking
el/la guía	guide
la guía	guidebook
la habitación (doble / individual)	(double / single) room
informarse	to find out
irse de camping	to go camping
las instalaciones	facilities
libre	available
llevar	to take
el lugar	place
la maleta	suitcase
la máquina (de fotos)	camera
media pensión	half board
el papel higiénico	toilet paper
el parador	state-owned hotel (in Spain)
el pasaporte	passport
pensión completa	full board
la pensión	boarding house / B&B
perder	to lose
el permiso de conducir	driving licence
quedarse	to stay
la queja	complaint
quejarse	to complain
la recepción	reception
recordar	to remember
la reserva	reservation
reservar	to book / reserve
el sitio	space / room / place / site
la tienda	tent
las vacaciones	holidays
la vista	view

How to Get There (p.54)

a mano derecha / izquierda	on the right- / left-hand side
a pie	on foot / walking
el aeropuerto	airport
el andén	platform
aparcar	to park
el autocar	coach
la autopista	motorway
el avión	aeroplane
el barco	boat
el billete (de ida / de ida y vuelta)	(single / return) ticket
la carretera	highway
el casco	helmet
el cinturón de seguridad	seat belt
el coche	car
coger	to take / catch
conducir	to drive / lead
el/la conductor/a	driver
la consigna	left luggage office
el cruce	crossroads / intersection
el crucero	cruise
cruzar	to cross
detener(se)	to stop
doblar	to turn
esperar	to wait
la estación (de autobuses / autocares / trenes)	(bus / coach / train) station
la estación de servicio	service station
el ferrocarril	railway system
la gasolina (sin plomo)	(unleaded) petrol
hacer transbordo	to change / transfer
la llegada	arrival
llegar	to arrive
el metro	underground
la parada	stop
parar	to stop
el/la pasajero/a	passenger
pasar (por)	to go (through) / pass
el paso subterráneo	underpass / subway
perder (vuelo etc.)	to miss (flight etc.)
perderse	to get lost
regresar	to go back
el retraso	delay
la rueda	wheel
la sala de espera	waiting room
la salida	exit
la señal	sign / signal
tardar	to take (time)
torcer	to turn
el tranvía	tram
venir	to come

la vía	track / lane
viajar	to travel
el viaje	trip / journey
el/la viajero/a	traveller
volver	to return
el vuelo	flight

What To Do (p.55)

el abanico	fan
bañarse	to bathe / swim
broncearse	to get a tan
caminar	to walk
el camino	path / route / road
los deportes acuáticos	water sports
descansar	to rest
el descanso	rest / pause
el esquí	skiing
esquiar	to ski
estar de vacaciones	to be on holiday

la excursión	trip / excursion
el lago	lake
la montaña	mountain
el museo	museum
la naturaleza	nature
el parque de atracciones	fairground
el parque temático	theme park
pasar (tiempo)	to spend (time)
la playa	beach
la postal	postcard
el recuerdo	souvenir
relajarse	to relax
el río	river
sacar fotos	to take photos
la tarjeta (postal)	card / (post)card
tomar el sol	to sunbathe

Practical Stuff (p.56)

asegurar	to insure
la avería	breakdown

el cajero automático	ATM / cashpoint
el camión	lorry
la cartera	wallet
chocar	to crash
la colisión	crash
la comisaría	police station
confirmar un billete	to validate a ticket
la consigna automática	left luggage locker
el desvío	diversion
la factura	bill (invoice)
el garaje	garage
la gasolina	petrol
el monedero	purse
perder	to lose
el/la revisor/a	ticket inspector
robar	to steal / rob

Section Ten — Current and Future Study and Employment

School Subjects (p.57)

el alemán	German
el arte dramático	drama
la asignatura	school subject
la biología	biology
las ciencias económicas	economics
las ciencias	science
la cocina	food technology
el comercio	business studies
el curso	school year
el dibujo	art
la educación física	PE
enseñar	to teach
el español	Spanish
la física	physics
el francés	French
la geografía	geography
la gimnasia	gymnastics
la historia	history
el idioma	language
la informática	IT
el inglés	English
la lengua	language / tongue
las matemáticas	maths
la música	music
optar	to choose / opt for
optativo	optional
la química	chemistry
la religión	RE
riguroso	severe / harsh
sencillo	simple / easy
los trabajos manuales	handicrafts

School Life (p.58-60)

el acoso (escolar)	(school) bullying

la agenda	diary
el/la alumno/a	pupil / student
apoyar	to support / help
el apoyo	support / help
aprender	to learn
aprobar	to approve / pass (an exam)
los apuntes	notes
el aula (f)	classroom
ausente	absent
la ayuda	help
el bolígrafo	pen
callar(se)	to shut up
el campo de deportes	sports field
la cantina	canteen
la carpeta	folder / file
castigar	to punish
el castigo	punishment
la clase	lesson
el colegio mixto	mixed school
el colegio privado	private school
el colegio público	state school
el colegio religioso	religious school
el comportamiento	behaviour
comportarse	to behave
la conducta	behaviour / conduct
contestar	to answer
charlar	to chat
el chicle	chewing gum
el cuaderno	exercise book
los deberes	homework
el despacho	office
dibujar	to draw
el/la director/a	head teacher
diseñar	to design
educativo	educational

la enseñanza	teaching / education
entender	to understand
entregar	to hand in
escribir	to write
la escuela (primaria)	(primary) school
esforzarse	to make an effort
estresante	stressful
el estuche	pencil case
la evaluación	assessment
el examen	exam
el éxito	success
la explicación	explanation
explicar	to explain
la falta	mistake / absence
faltar	to be absent
fracasar	to fail
el gimnasio	gymnasium
la hora de comer	lunchtime
el horario	timetable
el instituto	secondary school / institute
el intercambio	exchange
la intimidación	bullying
los lápices de colores	colour pencils
la lección	lesson
la letra	letter of the alphabet
levantar la mano	to put your hand up
el libro	book
mirar	to look
la mochila	rucksack / school bag
molestar	to annoy / bother
el nivel	level
la nota	mark
obligatorio	compulsory

oír	to listen / hear
olvidar	to forget
la página	page
la palabra	word
pasar (la) lista	to call the register
pedir prestado	to borrow
el permiso	permission
la pizarra interactiva	smart board
la pregunta	question
preguntar	to ask a question
la presión	pressure
privado	private
prometer	to promise / show promise
la prueba	test / proof
el recreo	break
la regla	rule / ruler
repartir	to hand out
repasar	to revise
la respuesta	answer
la rutina	routine
sacar buenas / malas notas	to get good / bad marks
la sala de profesores	staffroom
el salón de actos	hall / assembly room
sobresaliente	outstanding
suspender	to fail (exam / subject)
el taller	workshop
la tarea	task / piece of homework
el tema	topic / theme
tener miedo	to be afraid
terminar	to finish
las tijeras	scissors
trabajador	hard-working
el trabajo	work
el trimestre	(school) term
el uniforme	uniform

School Events (p.61)

el/la amigo/a por correspondencia	penfriend
el autobús escolar	school bus
el día de disfraces	fancy dress day
la entrega de premios	prize-giving
la excursión (del colegio)	school trip
(al) extranjero	abroad
el grupo escolar	school group
el intercambio	exchange
participar en	to participate in
el rendimiento	achievement / performance
la reunión de padres	parents' evening
la venta de pasteles	cake sale
la visita guiada	guided tour

la vuelta al colegio	first day back at school

Education Post-16 (p.62)

la academia	academy / school post-16 (for certain careers)
el/la aprendiz/a	apprentice
el aprendizaje	apprenticeship / training / learning
el bachillerato	school leaving exam (e.g. A-levels)
calificado	competent / skilled
la carrera	career / profession
el comienzo	beginning / start
los conocimientos	knowledge
conseguir	to get / achieve
Derecho	law (at university)
esperar	to hope / expect
la experiencia laboral	work experience
la formación (profesional)	vocational training
lograr	to achieve
las perspectivas laborales	employment prospects
la práctica	work placement
tomarse un año libre / sabático	to take a gap year
la universidad	university
útil	useful

Career Choices (p.63)

a tiempo completo	full time
a tiempo parcial	part time
el/la abogado/a	lawyer / solicitor
el arquitecto/a	architect
el/la bombero/a	firefighter
el/la cajero/a	bank-teller / cashier
el/la carnicero/a	butcher
el/la cocinero/a	cook
el/la constructor/a	builder
el/la contable	accountant
desafiante	challenging
el/la electricista	electrician
el/la empleado/a	employee / worker
el empleo	job / employment
la empresa	company
encontrar	to find
el/la enfermero/a	nurse
el/la escritor/a	writer
estar en paro	to be unemployed
estimulante	stimulating
el/la fontanero/a	plumber
el/la funcionario/a	civil servant
ganar	to earn
el/la gerente	manager
el/la granjero/a	farmer
gratificante	rewarding
el hombre / la mujer de negocios	businessman/ woman
el/la ingeniero/a	engineer
el/la jefe	boss

laboral	working
llegar a ser	to become
el/la mecánico/a	mechanic
el objetivo	aim / objective
obtener	to get / obtain
el/la oficial de policía	police officer
el/la orientador/a	careers adviser
parado	unemployed
el paro	unemployment
el/la peluquero/a	hairdresser
el periodismo	journalism
el/la periodista	journalist
probar	to have a go / try
el sueldo	salary
trabajar	to work
el trabajo	work / job
el/la traductor/a	translator
triunfar	to triumph / succeed
variado	varied
el/la veterinario/a	veterinary surgeon

Languages for the Future (p.64)

el/la auxiliar de lengua	language assistant
el/la azafato/a	flight attendant
comunicarse	to communicate
expresarse	to express yourself
el idioma	language
internacional	international
el laboratorio de idiomas	language lab
la lengua	language
multicultural	multicultural
pronunciar	to pronounce
traducir	to translate
viajar por el mundo	to travel the world

Applying for Jobs (p.65)

adjuntar	to attach
el anuncio de trabajo	job advertisement
bien pagado	well-paid
la carta de solicitud	application letter
la cita	appointment
con experiencia	experienced
las condiciones de empleo	terms of employment
despedir	to dismiss
el/la director/a	boss
la entrevista	interview
la habilidad	skill
por hora	per hour
las posibilidades de promoción	promotion prospects
rellenar	to fill in
solicitar un puesto de trabajo	to apply for a job
la solicitud	appliciation form
el sueldo	salary
la vacante	vacancy

Answers

The answers to the translation questions are sample answers only, just to give you an idea of one way to translate them. There may be different ways to translate these passages that are also correct.

Section 1 — General Stuff

Page 1: Numbers

1) Tiene diecisiete años.
2) Tiene ochenta y ocho años.
3) Vive en la segunda calle a la derecha.

Page 3: Times and Dates

1) the day before yesterday　　2) London　　3) Friday

Page 9: Opinions

1) Luis prefers watching films at home.
2) No, he doesn't. He thinks they're boring.
3) Elena thinks sometimes they're ridiculous.

Page 10: Putting it All Together

1) F　　2) T　　3) F　　4) T　　5) F

Section 2 — Me, My Family and Friends

Page 12: My Family

I live with my mother, my older sister and my two younger sisters. They are twins. For me, it's important to have brothers and sisters because you always have someone to go out with. At the weekend, I visit my father, his wife and my stepbrother. He was born last year and he is only six months old. I would like to spend more time there with them because it's great fun / entertaining.

Page 13: Describing People

Descripción 1 = foto b　　Descripción 3 = foto a
Descripción 2 = foto d　　Descripción 4 = foto c

Page 15: Pets

I have a bird as a pet. He has always been very chatty — he repeats what you say and it's very funny when he says rude things. The good thing about birds is that they eat fruit, vegetables and cereals, so their food doesn't cost much. However, next weekend I have to take him to the vet and I think it will cost a lot of money.

Page 16: Style and Fashion

1) A　　　2) C

Page 19: Partnership

1 a) False　　b) True　　c) False
2) Jerez

Section 3 — Technology in Everyday Life

Page 21: Technology

No podría vivir sin la tecnología porque es muy útil. Me gusta jugar a los videojuegos en la red con mi hermano. Hablamos con internautas en otros países. Ayer, jugué con un chico en Chile, pero para proteger mi identidad, no uso nunca mi nombre. Lo mejor de los móviles es que no tienes que estar en casa para usar la red. En el futuro, pienso que los niños tendrán móviles cuando tengan dos o tres años.

Page 22: Social Media

1) V　　2) V　　3) F　　4) F

Section 4 — Free-Time Activities

Page 25: Music

1) the saxophone
2) It's very quick to get songs.
   It's cheaper than going to a shop and buying a CD.
3) Live music is always very exciting.

Page 26: Cinema

Me encantan las películas. En mi opinión, las películas policíacas son las mejores. Son las películas más divertidas porque tienes que pensar en la trama. La semana pasada, vi una película muy divertida. Me gusta ver películas con mis amigos los fines de semana. En el futuro, me encantaría ser actriz.

Page 27: TV

1) False　　2) False　　3) True　　4) True

Page 28: Food

The correct sentences are 2 and 3.

Section 5 — Customs and Festivals

Page 32: Customs and Festivals

1) F　　2) F　　3) T　　4) T　　5) T

Page 34: Customs and Festivals

1) A　　2) C　　3) C　　4) B

Section 6 — Where You Live

Page 36: The Home

1) False　　2) False　　3) True　　4) False　　5) True

Page 37: What You Do at Home

I believe it's important to help at home, but I don't think it's fair if I do a lot and my younger brother does very little. I love walking the dog. My dad gives me money if I mow the lawn, so I will do it next Sunday. Last week I had to clean the bathroom. How disgusting!

Page 39: Shopping

1) half a kilo
2) salt
3) he's just sold the last bottle
4) €6.50

Page 40: Giving and Asking for Directions

1) F   2) F   3) V   4) F

Page 41: Weather

1) the south
2) in the west (near Portugal)
3) It'll be good weather.
4) The temperatures will drop.
5) There might be storms.

Section 7 — Social and Global Issues

Page 43: Environmental Problems

El cambio climático me preocupa mucho. Las fábricas y los coches contribuyen al efecto invernadero. Para mí, lo peor es que la gente en algunos países pobres sufre debido a las inundaciones y las sequías. No es justo. Creo que deberíamos trabajar juntos para reducir los efectos del cambio climático, pero será muy difícil.

Page 45: Problems in Society

1) economic problems
2) very difficult
3) prejudice
4) lazy
5) work together

Page 47: Global Events

Este año, hemos trabajado con una organización caritativa que ayuda a niños en desventaja en Asia. Organizamos un concierto y escribimos a unos cantantes para preguntarles si nos apoyarían. Tres de ellos vinieron y todo el mundo lo pasó bien. En el futuro, me encantaría ir al Mundial. Creo que sería muy divertido.

Section 8 — Lifestyle

Page 50: Illnesses

I feel very ill. Last week, I went to the countryside, but unfortunately it was raining and I hadn't brought my umbrella. My throat hurts a lot and I can hardly speak. I have had to drink lots of liquids for a few days and I don't feel like eating. I will have to go to the doctor if I don't get better soon. The worst thing is that if I'm still ill on Saturday, I won't be able to go to my friend's party.

Section 9 — Travel and Tourism

Page 51: Where to Go

1) Está en la costa del océano Atlántico en el norte de España.
2) Es famosa por su catedral y sus peregrinaciones.
3) Se puede nadar en uno de los ríos.

Page 52: Accommodation

1) A   2) 3   3) modern, elegant   4) B

Page 54: How to Get There

My city has many types of transport. The underground, which opened in 1924, is very clean and fast. Moreover, there is a tram network by which you can visit the majority of the neighbourhoods of the city. From the airport, it is possible to fly to all the important cities in Europe and it's not very far from the centre. Soon, they're going to improve the bus network, which will be great.

Section 10 — Current and Future Study and Employment

Page 58: School Routine

1) el comercio
2) el dibujo
3) la música

Page 59: School Life

Statements 2, 5 and 6 are true.

Page 62: Education Post-16

Cuando era joven, pensaba que me gustaría ser profesor/a. Mis padres son profesores y aunque encuentran el empleo interesante, mi padre dice que es bastante estresante. Ahora he decidido que voy a ir a una academia para estudiar fotografía. ¡Me encantaría sacar fotos de bodas!

Page 63: Career Choices and Ambitions

"When I was fifteen, it was difficult to get a job," said my mother. "Yes, but a lot has changed in recent years," I replied. "I want to be a lawyer. They earn a good salary and I would like to help people. The work would be so varied!"

Page 64: Languages for the Future

1) know at least three languages
2) start going to German evening classes
3) it will have language labs
4) the pronunciation

Section 11 — Grammar

Page 66: Words for People and Objects

1) el; los sombreros
2) el; los problemas
3) la; las tradiciones
4) el; los viernes
5) el; los porcentajes
6) el; los franceses
7) la; las tensiones
8) la; las dificultades
9) la; las ciudades
10) el; los mapas

Page 67: 'The', 'A', 'Some' and Other Little Words

1) Me gusta el chocolate.
2) No tengo agua.
3) Es profesora.
4) Quiere unas patatas.
5) Quiero hablar con la señora López.
6) Cada persona tiene dos perros.

Answers

Page 68: Words to Describe Things

1) el perro feliz
2) siete faldas rojas
3) los coches azules
4) dos mujeres bajas
5) cinco gatos pequeños
6) nueve sillas violeta
7) cuatro libros beis
8) una persona triste

Page 69: Words to Describe Things

1) Hay muchos gatos.
2) el primer día
3) el mismo perro
4) los otros alumnos
5) Algunas personas creen que... / Alguna gente cree que...
6) Es un gran profesor.

Page 70: Words to Describe Things

1) Sus libros son nuevos. / Los libros suyos son nuevos.
2) Quiero esa manzana.
3) Aquel león está comiendo.
4) Estas peras son buenas.
5) Ese hombre, cuya mujer es española, es alto.
6) Lucas es el chico cuyos padres son simpáticos.

Page 71: Words to Describe Actions

1) Lloran ruidosamente.
2) Vive saludablemente.
3) Habla claramente.
4) Hablamos inteligentemente.
5) El bebé duerme bien.
6) Corro rápidamente / deprisa.
7) Bailas / Bailáis mal.
8) Leo lentamente / despacio.

Page 72: Words to Describe Actions

1) Mis zapatos están aquí.
2) Quiero hacerlo de nuevo. / Lo quiero hacer de nuevo.
3) Lo hice con paciencia.
4) Vivimos lejos.
5) Lo hizo en seguida.
6) Bailó con entusiasmo.

Page 73: Words to Compare Things

1) Mi gato es el más gordo.
2) Soy tan alto/a como mi padre.
3) Juan es mayor que Marta.
4) Fue el peor día de la semana.
5) La película es mejor que el libro.
6) Nuestra revista es la más interesante.

Page 74: Words to Compare Actions

1) Carmen come más rápidamente.
2) Luis canta tan bien como Adela.
3) Selina es la que mejor conduce.
4) Estudio mejor que mis amigos.
5) Andamos / caminamos más lentamente / más despacio que Rob.
6) Ed es el que peor corre.

Page 75: Words to Say How Much

1) Hay demasiados gatos aquí.
2) Es bastante interesante.
3) Tengo muchos amigos.
4) Hablan demasiado lentamente / despacio.
5) Hay tantas playas en España.
6) El libro es buenísimo.

Page 76: I, You, We

1) ellos
2) ella
3) nosotros
4) vosotros
5) él
6) ustedes
7) ellas
8) ellos

Page 77: Me, You, Them

1) La rompe.
2) La bebo.
3) Le compró una falda.
4) Le envío / mando un correo electrónico.
5) Quiero hacerlo. / Lo quiero hacer.
6) Nos lo dijo.

Page 78: More Pronouns

1) Mi hermana, que tiene siete años, es baja.
2) Fui a Madrid, que es la capital de España.
3) ¿Cuál es tu dirección?
4) ¿Con quién vives?
5) ¿De quién es este perro?
6) ¿Cuál prefieres?

Page 79: More Pronouns

1) Son los míos.
2) ¿Qué es aquello?
3) Esta cama es más grande que aquélla.
4) Este libro es más interesante que ése.
5) ¿Es el vuestro?
6) Alguien está hablando tranquilamente.

Page 80: Prepositions

1) La casa está enfrente del banco.
2) El tren va hasta Italia.
3) Lo escuché en la radio.
4) Entro en el supermercado.
5) Soy de Hull, pero vivo en Crewe.
6) A partir de septiembre, tendré un trabajo.

Page 81: 'Por', 'Para' and the Personal 'a'

1) para
2) a
3) Por
4) por
5) por
6) para

Page 82: Conjunctions

1) La geografía es divertida, pero es difícil.
2) Me gusta la historia porque es fácil.
3) Como estoy enfermo/a, me quedo en casa.
4) Voy al parque cuando hace calor.
5) Hablo francés e italiano.
6) ¿Prefieres azul o amarillo?

Answers

Page 83: Verbs in the Present Tense

1) bailo   4) corre   7) escribes
2) bebemos   5) aprende   8) Vive aquí desde hace un año.
3) nadáis   6) visitan

Page 84: Irregular Verbs in the Present Tense

1) Comienza   3) Queremos   5) Puedes
2) Vais   4) Doy   6) Sé

Page 85: 'Ser' and 'Estar' in the Present Tense

1) Está   3) Somos   5) es
2) Es   4) Estoy   6) es

Page 86: Talking About the Past

1) lloraron   6) pude
2) comimos   7) hicisteis
3) escribisteis   8) puso
4) cené   9) viniste
5) diste   10) trajimos

Page 87: Talking About the Past

1) cantaba   3) aprendía   5) volvían   7) nadabas
2) éramos   4) decía   6) seguíais   8) iban

Page 88: Talking About the Past

1) hacía   2) volví   3) Fuiste   4) Iba; tuve

Page 89: Talking About the Past

1) Habían cantado.   5) Había bebido.
2) Ha viajado.   6) Habíamos terminado.
3) Habéis aprendido.   7) Ha seguido.
4) Ha visto.   8) Has vivido.

Page 90: Talking About the Future

1) voy a comer; comeré
2) vamos a tener; tendremos
3) va a bailar; bailará
4) voy a dar; daré
5) van a poner; pondrán
6) vais a jugar; jugaréis
7) vas a poder; podrás
8) va a cantar; cantará
9) vamos a querer; querremos
10) vais a vivir; viviréis

Page 91: Would, Could and Should

1) irías   5) partiría
2) cantaría   6) saldrían
3) vendríamos   7) hablaría
4) diríais   8) tendríamos

Page 92: Reflexive Verbs

1) me llamo; me he llamado
2) se levantan; se han levantado
3) se lava; se ha lavado
4) te acuestas; te has acostado
5) nos sentimos; nos hemos sentido
6) os vais; os habéis ido
7) se viste; se ha vestido
8) te despiertas; te has despertado

Page 93: Verbs with '-ing' and 'Just Done'

1) está cayendo; estaba cayendo; acaba de caer
2) estás abriendo; estabas abriendo; acabas de abrir
3) está saltando; estaba saltando; acaba de saltar
4) están diciendo; estaban diciendo; acaban de decir
5) estáis corriendo; estabais corriendo; acabáis de correr
6) estamos siguiendo; estábamos siguiendo; acabamos de seguir
7) estás dando; estabas dando; acabas de dar
8) estoy leyendo; estaba leyendo; acabo de leer
9) están sirviendo; estaban sirviendo; acaban de servir
10) estamos bailando; estábamos bailando; acabamos de bailar

Page 94: Negative Forms

1) No fui al cine.
2) Ya no vamos al gimnasio.
3) No vas ni a Oslo ni a Faro.
4) Sally no tiene ninguna manzana.
5) No hay nada aquí.
6) No hay nadie en el coche.

Page 95: The Passive and Impersonal Verbs

A) Sentences 2 and 3 are written in the passive voice.
B) 1) Se compra   2) Se comen

Page 96: The Subjunctive

1) saltes   5) venga
2) escuche   6) hagamos
3) limpiemos   7) puedan
4) abran   8) tengáis

Page 97: The Subjunctive

1) present subjunctive   3) present subjunctive
2) imperfect subjunctive   4) imperfect subjunctive

Page 98: Giving Orders

1) ¡Canta!; ¡No cantes!   5) ¡Abrid!; ¡No abráis!
2) ¡Bailen!; ¡No bailen!   6) ¡Venid!; ¡No vengáis!
3) ¡Ten!; ¡No tengas!   7) ¡Sea!; ¡No sea!
4) ¡Dé!; ¡No dé!   8) ¡Vayan!; ¡No vayan!

Answers

Transcript

Section 1 — General Stuff

Track 1 — p.3

E.g. **M1:** ¡Hola! Soy Carlos. Voy al gimnasio todos los días y los jueves juego al fútbol.

1) **F1:** ¡Buenos días! Me llamo Anabel. Celebré mi cumpleaños anteayer y fui a un restaurante con mi familia y mis amigos.

2) **F1:** Ayer, fuimos de compras a Londres, pero mañana por la mañana, iremos a Oxford. Me encantan las cafeterías en Oxford.

3) **F2:** ¡Hola! Me llamo Julia. Mañana voy a ir al cine con mis amigas, y el viernes vamos a ir al teatro.

Track 2 — p.10

E.g. **M1:** ¿Qué te gusta hacer los fines de semana, Carolina?
F1: Me encanta ir a la piscina.

1) **F1:** Y tú Antonio, ¿qué te gusta hacer los fines de semana?
M1: A mí me gusta ir de compras, pero no me gusta escuchar música.

2) **F1:** ¿Por qué te gusta ir de compras?
M1: Me gusta ir de compras porque es muy divertido y las tiendas en mi ciudad son estupendas. Alguna gente cree que ir de compras es para chicas, pero eso no es verdad.

3) **F1:** Ah, muy bien. Pero, ¿por qué no te gusta escuchar música?
M1: Mucha gente adora la música, pero a mí nunca me ha interesado. Prefiero leer. Acabo de terminar una novela fenomenal. Las novelas y los periódicos sí que son interesantes porque se puede aprender mucho. ¿Estás de acuerdo?

4) **F1:** Sí, estoy de acuerdo. Me encanta leer porque es relajante, pero me gusta escuchar música también.

5) **F1:** Prefiero los grupos de música pop porque la música pop me parece guay.

Section 2 — Me, My Family and Friends

Track 3 — p.13

1) **F2:** Esta persona parece bastante baja. Tiene el pelo liso y castaño, pero no lo tiene especialmente largo. Lleva unas gafas bastante grandes. Es una persona joven.

2) **M1:** Tiene el pelo negro, pero no es ni liso ni rizado. Creo que tiene los ojos marrones y que es una persona bastante alta. No lleva gafas.

3) **F2:** Esta persona no tiene ni barba ni bigote. Tiene el pelo largo y moreno, y creo que es bastante delgada. Lleva maquillaje y no tiene pecas.

4) **M1:** No es totalmente calvo, pero no tiene mucho pelo. Tiene el pelo gris, y tiene barba. No sé el color de sus ojos. No es joven — la verdad, parece bastante viejo.

Section 4 — Free-Time Activities

Track 4 — p.25

E.g. **M1:** ¡Hola Marisol! ¿Cuál es el género de música más importante para ti?
F2: Diría que mi género preferido es la música rap porque creo que es la música más original y distinta. Me encanta la música clásica también porque es relajante. Sin embargo, según mi hermana menor, la música más importante para nuestra generación sería la música pop.

1) **M1:** ¿Tocas algún instrumento?
F2: Cuando era más joven, tocaba el piano, pero en este momento, no tengo suficiente tiempo para practicar. Me encantaría aprender a tocar el saxofón porque es un instrumento fenomenal y porque el jazz es un tipo de música que siempre me ha fascinado.

2) **M1:** ¿Cómo escuchas música, Marisol?
F2: Me gusta escuchar música por Internet, porque es muy rápido descargar canciones y cuesta menos que ir a una tienda para comprar un CD.

3) **F2:** Me encanta ir a conciertos también, porque la música en directo es siempre muy emocionante.

Track 5 — p.28

E.g. **M1:** ¡Hola! Soy Joaquín. Cuando era pequeño, me gustaba comer muchos caramelos y helados y odiaba las verduras. ¡No me importaba para nada la salud!

1) **M1:** Ahora como de todo — mariscos, legumbres y carne. Odio la comida basura porque no solo engorda, sino que suele llevar cantidades enormes de sal y azúcar. ¿Qué te gusta comer, Alejandra?

2) **F1:** Creo que comes mejor que yo, Joaquín. Si pudiera comer caramelos todos los días, lo haría. Sería mejor si comiera más fruta, pero no me gusta mucho. Mis padres me dicen que bebo demasiado café, así que ahora estoy intentando beber más agua.

3) **F2:** Me llamo Raquel. No como ni pescado ni carne — soy vegetariana. Normalmente es bastante fácil evitar la carne porque me gustan las legumbres. Sin embargo, cuando voy a restaurantes con mis amigos, es más difícil porque hay pocos platos sin carne. Por otro lado, los platos vegetarianos suelen ser más baratos que los que contienen carne o pescado.

Section 5 — Customs and Festivals

Track 6 — p.34

1) **M1:** El premio es trece millones de euros y el número ganador es… ochenta mil seiscientos setenta y tres. ¡Felicitaciones a todos!

2) **F1:** ¡Hola! Soy Ana. Estoy contentísima porque gané 2.000.000 de euros en El Gordo. Voy a comprar un apartamento de lujo, y luego iré al Mediterráneo con mi novio tres semanas.

3) **F1:** Carla, ¿qué hiciste esta Navidad?
F2: En Navidad, me lo pasé fenomenal porque mis abuelos vinieron a quedarse con nosotros. Viven muy lejos de aquí, así que casi nunca los veo. En Nochebuena, mi madre preparó una cena deliciosa. Había mariscos, carne y varios postres, pero lo que más me gustó fue el turrón de chocolate.

4) **F2:** ¿Recibiste regalos, Diego?
M1: Sí, se me cayó el móvil el mes pasado, y por lo tanto, mis padres me dieron un móvil nuevo. Mi hermano había pedido unos juguetes pero le regalaron una bicicleta azul. Cuando la vio, estaba tan emocionado que ¡empezó a bailar por el salón!

Transcript

Section 6 — Where You Live

Track 7 — p.39

E.g. **F2:** ¡Hola! Quiero hacer una tortilla española para una fiesta de cumpleaños y necesito unos ingredientes. ¿Me puede ayudar?
M1: Sí, claro. ¿Qué le hace falta?

1) **F2:** Pues primero, necesito un kilo de patatas. Y póngame también medio kilo de cebollas.
M1: Claro. ¿Algo más?

2) **F2:** Sí, deme seis huevos, pero no necesito sal, porque ya la tengo en casa.
M1: Aquí tiene.

3) **F2:** ¡Ay, casi se me ha olvidado! Necesito también una botella de aceite de oliva.
M1: Desafortunadamente, no tengo aceite de oliva. Acabo de vender la última botella.

4) **F2:** ¡Qué pena! Tendré que ir a otra tienda. ¿Cuánto cuesta todo?
M1: Cuesta seis euros cincuenta.
F2: Vale, gracias. Aquí tiene. ¡Adiós!
M1: Gracias. ¡Adiós!

Track 8 — p.40

E.g. **M1:** ¡Hola! Te voy a hablar de mi barrio. Es un barrio histórico, así que hay un castillo, un ayuntamiento y un teatro.

1) **M1:** El teatro está en la parte este del barrio donde también hay muchos restaurantes. Está al lado de un museo muy impresionante.

2) **M1:** En la plaza hay un bar que es muy popular tanto con los jóvenes como con los jubilados. Había tres supermercados hace un par de años, pero ahora solo hay uno.

3) **M1:** Se puede encontrar el supermercado al fondo de la calle San Felipe, enfrente de la comisaría.

4) **M1:** Luego, si sigues esa calle y tomas la segunda calle a la derecha, encontrarás la iglesia.

Section 7 — Social and Global Issues

Track 9 — p.45

E.g. **F2:** Desafortunadamente, hay miles de personas sin techo en España.

1) **F2:** Debido a los problemas económicos que tenemos, muchas personas han perdido su trabajo y no tienen suficiente dinero para pagar el alquiler.

2) **F2:** Algunos pueden pedir ayuda a sus padres o amigos, pero otros acaban en la calle. Lo que todos tienen en común es que tienen una vida dificilísima.

3) **F2:** Sin embargo, lo peor es que frecuentemente son víctimas del prejuicio, lo que les puede dificultar la vida bastante.

4) **F2:** Este prejuicio existe porque mucha gente cree que los sin techo no pueden pagar su alquiler porque son perezosos.

5) **F2:** Si queremos cambiar la situación de estas personas, tenemos que trabajar juntos — es la única manera de hacerlo.

Section 9 — Travel and Tourism

Track 10 — p.52

1) **M1:** Los hoteles son regulares en general, contándose dos buenos.

2) **M1:** Los tres mejores que hay dentro de la ciudad son el de Pfaroux, el de las cuatro Naciones, y el de Europa. Fuera de la ciudad, y en el camino de Botafogo, hay dos ingleses y uno francés: el mejor de todos, tanto de los de la ciudad, como de los de fuera, es el Hotel de los Extranjeros en la plaza de Catette.

3) **M1:** Es una gran casa, de moderna y elegante construcción, sólida, con anchas y magníficas habitaciones: un gran jardín al pie del mar, vistas admirables, comodidades muchas.

4) **M1:** El hotel todo está alumbrado por el gas: tiene baños, billares y grande capacidad: en el Hotel de los Extranjeros, viven la mayor parte de los individuos del Cuerpo Diplomático extranjero.

Section 10 — Current and Future Study and Employment

Track 11 — p.58

1) **M1:** ¡Ay, Marta! Odio los lunes.
F1: ¿Por qué?
M1: ¿No es obvio? Tenemos matemáticas, comercio y después del recreo, inglés. Es horrible.

2) **F1:** Pero los martes son mejores, ¿no? Me gustan las ciencias y el dibujo.
M1: ¿Y el francés?
F1: No me emociona mucho. Prefiero las asignaturas más prácticas.

3) **M1:** Estoy de acuerdo. Yo prefiero los miércoles. Es una oportunidad para ser creativo. Por ejemplo, empezamos con los trabajos manuales. Después hay el español y a las diez y media, tenemos música. Es mi día preferido.

Index

Index

SPHR44